MW00560333

Reductionism and the Development of Knowledge

The Jean Piaget Symposium Series
Available from LEA

OVERTON, W. F. (Ed.) • The Relationship Between Social and Cognitive Development

LIBEN, L. S. (Ed.) • Piaget and the Foundations of Knowledge

SCHOLNICK, E. K. (Ed.) • New Trends in Conceptual Representation: Challenges to Piaget's Theory?

NIEMARK, E. D., DeLISI, R., & NEWMAN, J. L. (Eds.) • Moderators on Competence

BEARISON, D. J. & ZIMILES, H. (Eds.) • Thought and Emotion: Developmental Perspectives

LIBEN, L. S. (Ed.) • Development and Learning: Conflict or Congruence?

FORMAN, G. & PUFALL, P. B. (Eds.) • Constructivism in the Computer Age

OVERTON, W. F. (Ed.) • Reasoning, Necessity, and Logic: Developmental Perspectives

KEATING, D. P. & ROSEN, H. (Eds.) • Constructivist Perspectives on Developmental Psychopathology and Atypical Development

CAREY, S. & GELMAN, R. (Eds.) • The Epigenesis of Mind: Essays on Biology

BEILIN, H. & PUFALL, P. (Eds.) • Piaget's Theory: Prospects and Possibilities

WOZNIAK, R. H. & FISCHER, K. W. (Eds.) • Development in Context: Acting and Thinking in Specific Environments

OVERTON, W. F. & PALERMO, D. S. (Eds.) • The Nature and Ontogenesis of Meaning

NOAM, G. G. & FISCHER, K. W. (Eds.) • Development and Vulnerability in Close Relationships

REED, E. S., TURIEL, E., & BROWN, T. (Eds.) • Values and Knowledge

AMSEL, E. & RENNINGER, K. A. (Eds.) • Change and Development: Issues of Theory, Method, and Application

LANGER, J. & KILLEN, M. (Eds.) • Piaget, Evolution, and Development

SCHOLNICK, E., NELSON, K., GELMAN, S. A., & MILLER, P. H. (Eds.) • Conceptual Development: Piaget's Legacy

NUCCI, L. P., SAXE, G. B., & TURIEL, E. (Eds.) • Culture, Thought, and Development

AMSEL, E. & BYRNES, J. P. (Eds.) • Language, Literacy, and Cognitive Development: The Development and Consequences of Symbolic Communication

BROWN, T. & SMITH, L. (Eds.) • Reductionism and the Development of Knowledge

Reductionism and the Development of Knowledge

Edited by

Terrance Brown
Chicago, IL

Leslie Smith
Lancaster University

LEA LAWRENCE ERLBAUM ASSOCIATES, PUBLISHERS
2003   Mahwah, New Jersey   London

Lawrence Erlbaum Associates, Inc., Publishers
10 Industrial Avenue
Mahwah, NJ 07430

Cover design by Kathryn Houghtaling Lacey

Library of Congress Cataloging-in-Publication Data

Reduction and the development of knowledge / edited by Terrance Brown, Leslie Smith.
    p. cm. (The Jean Piaget Symposium series)
Papers originally presented at the 29th Annual Symposium of the Jean Piaget Society.
    Includes bibliographical references and index.
ISBN 0-8058-4069-9 (cloth : alk. paper)
1. Cognition—Congresses. 2. Knowledge, Theory of—Congresses. 3. Reductionism—Congresses. I. Brown, Terrance. II. Smith, Leslie, 1943– . III. Jean Piaget Society, Symposium (29th). IV. Series.
BF311 .R356   2002
146—dc21   2001058365
                                                   CIP

Printed in the United States of America
10 9 8 7 6 5 4 3 2 1

Contents

PART III LOOKING TOWARD THE FUTURE

Preface

Among the many conceits of modern thought is the idea that philosophy, tainted as it is by subjective evaluation, is a shaky guide for human affairs. People, it is argued, are better off if they base their conduct either on know-how, with its pragmatic criterion of truth (i.e., possibility), or on science, with its universal criterion of rational necessity. The simple fact is, however, that human intelligence is fundamentally philosophical (Piaget, 1965/ 1971). Subjective values were the selective principle that made the first forms of intelligence possible and, in almost every way that counts, they remain the most powerful form of intellectual selection. The problem comes when philosophical and scientific solutions are conflated, when ideas that owe their existence to subjective evaluation are put forward as scientific truths. A dramatic current example may be drawn from the incestuous dealings of a motley group: neuroscience, neuropsychology, neurophysiology, psychology, neurology, psychiatry, the pharmaceutical industry, government, and the popular press. In the mythology that has arisen and, unfortunately, in the practices stemming from that mythology, it is often assumed that mind can be discovered by studying brain. Pondering this strange and dangerous development leads ineluctably to the question of reductionism in science, a topic on which Piaget shed much light with his conception of the "circle of the sciences" (Piaget, 1967).

Since Helmholtz (Boring, 1950), really, but even more so in the 20th century, there has been increasing concern in the life sciences about the role of reductionism in the construction of knowledge. Is a psychophysics really possible, as Helmholtz dreamed? Are biological phenomena just the deducible results of chemical phenomena? Moreover, if life can be reduced to molecular mechanisms only, where do these miraculous molecules come from and how do they work? On the psychological level, people wonder whether psychological phenomena result simply from genetically hardwired structures in the brain or whether, even if not genetically determined, they can be identified with the biochemical processes of that organ. In sociology, identical questions arise. Are social behaviors genetically determined? Can they be biochemically or biophysiologically explained? Finally, if physical or chemical reduction is not practicable, should we think in terms of other forms of reduction, say, the reduction of psychological to sociological phenomena or in terms of what Piaget has called the "reduction of the lower to the higher," that is, teleology? All in all, then, reductionism in both naive and sophisticated forms permeates all of human thought and may, at least in certain cases, be necessary to it. If so, what exactly are those cases?

The answer to that question depends on how the different forms of knowledge are constructed and on how they relate to one another. The first of these issues leads to the idea of intratheoretic reduction, the second to the idea of intertheoretic reduction. In the previous paragraph, several types of intratheoretic reduction are noted, for example, the notion that psychological or sociological knowledge can be reduced to the accumulated products of the functioning of biologically given mental programs or modules. Here, theories in one science are supposedly reduced to theories in the same science. Perhaps because this is a bad example, even these contentions are heatedly contested. The idea of intratheoretic reduction is better documented (but still not completely accepted) in the inorganic sciences. Turning to the conceit, concept, phenomenon—what should we call it?—of intertheoretic reduction, the most widely accepted view of the relation of the sciences to one another holds to what has been termed the "wedding cake" depiction. On this view, the bottom and largest layer of the cake is physics and chemistry, the next tier—smaller than the one on which it stands—is biology, and, constantly decreasing in size, come the layers of psychology and sociology (Hull, 1978). The belief was or is that each of the upper layers can be reduced to the layer below until, finally, one has a complete physical description of the world. This idea meets with even more vigorous objection. Not only have convincing examples never been exhibited, but, insist its detractors, physics can be reduced to mathematics, which reduces to logic, which reduces to psychology, making the whole affair more of a bundt cake than a wedding cake, and so the battle rages.

The chapters collected in this volume are all derived from the 29th Annual Symposium of the Jean Piaget Society. The meeting was held in Mexico City in June 1999. The intent of the volume is to examine the issue of reductionism on the theoretical level in several sciences, including biology, psychology, and sociology. A complementary intent is to examine it from the point of view of the practical effects of reductionistic doctrine on daily life. With regard to the first, evolutionary biologists have a much harder time finding grant money than molecular biologists, even though the DNA story is a very incomplete account of transmission genetics (Mayr, 1982). With regard to the second, it is well documented that biological reductionism in medicine, psychology, and psychiatry is driven by economic factors (Valenstein, 1998). Despite a national campaign to "Say No to Drugs," psychiatrists, internists, and general practitioners place more and more persons in the United States on psychoactive medications, despite the lack of strong evidence for their efficacy in many cases.

Like all edited books of restricted length, this volume cannot deal with every issue of the problematics just identified. It can only provide a number of stimulating and provocative chapters dealing with the role reductionism plays in constructing knowledge and in the ways we live our lives.

—*Terrance Brown*
—*Leslie Smith*

REFERENCES

Boring, E. G. (1950). *A history of experimental psychology* (2nd ed.). Englewood Cliffs, NJ: Prentice-Hall.

Hull, D. L. (1978). Génétique et réductionisme [Genetics and reductionism]. *La Recherche, 87,* 220–227.

Mayr, E. (1982). *The growth of biological thought.* Cambridge, MA: Harvard University Press.

Piaget, J. (1965/1971). *Insights and illusions of philosophy.* (W. Mays, Trans.). New York: World.

Piaget, J. (1967). Le système et la classification des sciences [System and classification of the sciences]. In J. Piaget (Ed.), *Logique et connaissance scientifique* [Logic and scientific knowledge] (pp. 1151–1224). Paris: Gallimard.

Valenstein, E. S. (1998). *Blaming the brain.* New York: The Free Press.

INTRODUCTION

1

Reductionism and the Circle of the Sciences

Terrance Brown
Chicago, IL

INTRODUCTION

Reductionism is often viewed as an arcane subject. When, however, I proposed it as a possible theme for the Annual Meeting of The Jean Piaget Society, I did so for completely practical reasons. Over the now many years that I have practiced psychiatry, it has become more and more the case that patients come to me after having seen a variety of therapists, usually including several psychiatrists, and after having been treated with a variety of psychotropic medications. In general, they are disaffected with mental health professionals, discouraged about undertaking further therapy, and fairly desperate about how their lives are going. Complicating matters, their insurance companies are increasingly unwilling to pay for therapy extending beyond infrequent 15-minute visits and a bottle of pills.[1] Having heard that my fees are such that they can pay from their own pockets and that I am generous with my time, they call me as a last resort.

Beyond the concerns raised by my experience with patients, I have also become alarmed by a number of generalized trends reported in both the technical and popular presses. There are too many of these to list them all, so permit me only to illustrate my anxieties with some questions. Why, for

---

[1]There may, however, be some room for hope. The Accreditation Council for Graduate Medical Education recently decreed that, for a psychiatric residency program to be accredited, it will have to teach psychotherapy (Sherman, 2001). At present, about two thirds of the training programs have dropped psychotherapy training.

instance, is the prevalence of Attention-Deficit Hyperactivity Disorder (ADHD) estimated at 6% in the United States and why are 2.5 million American children on psychostimulant medications (Grinfeld, 2000; Valenstein, 1998, p. 180), whereas the prevalence of the same disorder is estimated to be much lower in other countries? For example, ADHD is estimated at about 2% in Great Britain (Popper, 1988, p. 653), where many fewer children are given drugs. Why also have two states filed class action suits against the American Psychiatric Association and Novartis Pharmaceuticals, alleging that they invented the diagnoses of Attention-Deficit Disorder (ADD) and ADHD in order to sell drugs and make money (Fulton, 2000)? More alarming still, why, in 1996 when the drug was not approved for use in children, were over 203,000 prescriptions for Prozac written for children between 6 and 12 years of age? Furthermore, why did this represent a 298% increase over the number of such prescriptions written in 1995 (Valenstein, 1998, p. 175)? Is it any wonder that a speaker whom I recently heard recommended that all schools in the United States have a psychopharmacologist on staff? But let me continue with my questions. Why do psychiatrists keep telling people that they have chemical imbalances in their brains when there is no compelling evidence that this is so? No deficit in either norepinephrine or serotonin has been demonstrated in depressed persons,[2] no excess of dopamine has been demonstrated in schizophrenics, and no deficit of gamma-aminobutyric acid has been demonstrated in anxious people. Could the answer to this question have anything to do with facts such as: (a) the pharmaceutical industry spends upwards of $12.3 billion yearly to advertise drugs in the United States and $5,000 on every physician in the country in order to influence prescribing patterns (Valenstein, 1998, p. 197); (b) in 1997, U.S. sales of psychotropic drugs were estimated to exceed $8 billion (Valenstein, 1998, p. 166); (c) in 1994, the pharmaceutical industry gave $1.5 billion to universities and their affiliates for biomedical research (Valenstein, 1998, p. 187); (d) pharmaceutical companies pay for most of the clinical trials required for FDA approval of new drugs (Valenstein, 1998, p. 230); (e) Pfizer, Inc., a large pharmaceutical company, ranks among the top 10 legislative lobbying spenders in the United States (*Chicago Tribune*, 1999); (f) the pharmaceutical industry gives around $4.75 million to the American Psychiatric Association (APA) each year for advertisements in their publications, educational activities and exhibit spaces at APA meetings, and a variety of other activities used to promote the idea that psychiatric illness should be treated pharmacologically (Valenstein, 1998, p. 186)? That such massive

---

[2]Despite this fact, five antidepressant medications acting to increase levels of these neurotransmitters in the intersynaptic space were among the top 10 drugs prescribed by psychiatrists from July 1999 to June 2000. Just under 25 million prescriptions for these drugs were written, about 23% of all prescriptions written by psychiatrists (Clinical Psychiatry News, December, 2000).

promotional efforts succeed is amply evidenced by a recent article entitled "Understanding Depression: A Long-Term, Recurring Disorder" (Montgomery et al., 2001), which reported on talks presented at a symposium. It consists of six short pieces, none of which mentions psychotherapeutic treatments known for some time to be as effective as or more effective than pharmacological treatments for many forms depression (Elkin et al., 1989; Ginsberg, 2001, p. 3; Valenstein, 1998, pp. 212–217).

I could continue, but I think these few facts suffice to establish the practical basis of my concerns about the economically driven institutionalization of a doctrine based on *ex juvantibus* reasoning and reductionistic thought. The doctrine I refer to is the belief that psychiatric illnesses can be understood biologically and that biological abnormalities require biological treatments. By *ex juvantibus* reasoning, I mean reasoning about the cause of an illness based on the effectiveness of a treatment. By reductionistic thought, I mean thinking that understanding the mind is in some way equivalent to understanding the brain.

I shall not dwell on the doctrinal issue. It is so evident that life experience plays a large role in personality development and emotional vicissitudes that no argument is required. It is also admitted, even by the worst reductionists (as will be documented later), that we have no idea about the biological mechanisms that accomplish these psychological functions and malfunctions. As for the idea that somatic aberrations can only be treated somatically, it is patently false. The treatment of phenylketonuria is to restrict certain foods—a behavioral intervention. The same is in part true for diabetes (where biological measures are also helpful). My point is that behavioral interventions are the backbone of therapy in somatic conditions varying from alcohol-induced cirrhosis of the liver to the various forms of spondylitis and that contentions to the contrary are not worth considering. I turn then to *ex juvantibus* reasoning and reductionistic thought.

EX JUVANTIBUS REASONING AND REDUCTIONISTIC THOUGHT

Ex juvantibus reasoning so permeates contemporary psychiatric thought that systematic documentation would require volumes. I shall therefore offer only what I consider a central example, taken from a special issue of *Scientific American* entitled "Mind and Brain":

> Insight into the way antidepressant agents act began with the study of reserpine ... one of the first effective medications for high blood pressure. Physicians noted ... that the drug sometimes brought on severe depression in patients.... Biochemists discovered that reserpine depletes certain neurotransmitters ... among them norepinephrine, dopamine and serotonin. All antidepressant drugs known in the mid-1960's effectively concentrated these

monoamines in the synapse.... This pattern led Joseph J. Schildkraut ... to propose ... that depression was associated with reduction in synaptic availability of catecholamines ... and mania with an increase of catecholamines. (Gershon & Rieder, 1992, p. 131)

The authors go on to explain how contradictions to the catecholamine theory arose because drugs were found that had antidepressant effects without having effects on catecholamine kinetics or metabolism. Arguments were then constructed to get around this and other factual inconveniences and to keep the catecholamine hypothesis of mood disorders alive. Without going into the details, let me simply say that the development of modern theories of the cause or causes of depression[3] have continued to follow Schildkraut's *ex juvantibus* form of reasoning. As Valenstein (1998, pp. 133) points out, however, such reasoning has many pitfalls. For example, diuretic drugs have been found to be useful in treating congestive heart failure even though their effect is on the kidneys, which are normal: Their therapeutic efficacy is due to their ability to increase the output of water and electrolytes, thereby decreasing the functional burden on the weakened heart. A similar story concerning antidepressant medications (the efficacy of which is in any case overestimated—Valenstein, 1998, p. 266, fn51)[4] may eventually be told. That said, I turn now to the more perplexing problem of reductionistic thought.

There are two levels to be examined here. The first is limited to reductionism in psychiatry, a bedfellow to its *ex juvantibus* reasoning. The second has to do with reductionism in biology, neurology, neuropsychology, and neuroscience in general and the assumption of those disciplines about how the sciences relate to one another.

Reductionism in Psychiatry

To introduce this subject, I shall revisit a passage written by Joseph Coyle, the well-known psychiatrist currently at Harvard.[5] In 1988, Coyle provided

---

[3]I do not mention mania because *ex juvantibus* reasoning has been less successful here, although it is still very much alive. The action of lithium, the first successful antimanic drug, is still unknown and the actions of the now frequently used anti-epileptic medications vary.

[4]If the reader needs further evidence of just how distorted reports of efficacy are, consider the following statement from Ginsberg (2001, p. 2): In a comparison of venlafaxine with SSRI antidepressants (most frequently fluoxetine, paroxetine, and fluvoamine), "the results showed that about 45% of subjects on venlafaxine showed a remission compared to 35% of subjects treated with SSRIs and 25% of those on placebo." What this means is that venlafaxine is about 20% better than sugar pills and that SSRIs are about 10% better than sugar pills at producing remission of depression. It does not mean that venlafaxine produces remission in 45% of depressed patients, as its manufacturer would like (pay?) you to believe.

[5]The argument presented here follows in part a more extensive and somewhat different critique of psychiatric thought in Brown (1991).

the opening chapter of the *Textbook of Psychiatry* published by the American Psychiatric Press, an organ of the APA. The title of the chapter was "Neuroscience and Psychiatry." His bold opening statement read as follows:

> Advances in research on the brain have occurred with a rapidly increasing pace over the last 15 years and have reached the point that neuroscience can justifiably be considered the biomedical foundation for psychiatry. Logarithmic growth in our understanding of the organization and function of the brain has made it feasible to begin to analyze behavior at the molecular level. (p. 3)

Coyle continued:

> Fears that these advances, which are based on increasingly reductionistic approaches, will undermine the humanistic tradition of psychiatry and negate the important relationship between physician and patient seem unfounded. First, even when gene-based diagnostic techniques become feasible . . . , the clinical method for developing provisional diagnosis that is used at present will still be necessary to determine which individuals warrant testing. . . . (p. 30)

We see here the tell-tale signs of reductionistic thought, blatantly admitted by Coyle (1988). Behavior is to become a matter of molecules, diagnoses are to be based on genes, psychological examination will only serve as triage for deciding what sort of biological analysis is appropriate, and so on. Apparently, there is no possibility that emotional experience, learning, development, or other psychological processes will play a role in the etiologies of psychiatric illnesses. Mind becomes simply a matter of brain.

The problem with all of this is that, despite his rhetoric, Coyle (1988) did little to support his thesis that we are in a position to analyze behavior molecularly and made no attempt at all to support his thesis that the "increasingly reductive" approaches he defends will not "negate the important relationship between physician and patient" (p.). In the introduction, I have already provided personal testimony concerning how devastating reductionistic thought has been to the psychiatrist–patient relationship. Here, I shall simply indicate what I consider to be the four major objections to Coyle's assertion that we are in a position to analyze behavior molecularly and then hurry on to consider the problems of reductionistic thought in general. The four major objections are: (a) Much of Coyle's argument rests on *ex juvantibus* reasoning; (b) psychotropic medications produce their chemical effects within hours but their therapeutic effects take weeks (Montgomery et al., 2001, p. 380; Valenstein, 1998, p. 114), so we must consider what is really going on; (c) although our knowledge of neurotransmitters and brain physiology has advanced exponentially, our biological theories of the etiology of mental illness and the logic of the treatments we use have not kept pace (Valenstein, 1998, pp. 109–110); and (d) correlating drug actions and psychological symptoms in no way establishes causal understanding and does not constitute the reduction of mind to brain.

In sum, although there appears to be little reason to challenge the claim that neuroscience has established at least some of the actions of psychotropic drugs and has identified the pathways in which they are involved, there seems every reason to question whether such discoveries link specific psychological phenomena to neurochemical mechanisms or whether they establish causation of any kind. Let me move on, then, to the potentially more important (given that it is less economically driven and more profoundly relative to theories of knowledge) claim that psychology, *ex juvantibus* claims apart, can be reduced to neurophysiology.

Eliminative Reductionism[6]

In the preface to his authoritative tome *The Cognitive Neurosciences*, Gazzaniga (1995) writes:

> At some point in the future, cognitive neuroscience will be able to describe the algorithms that drive structural neural elements into the physiological activity that results in perception, cognition, and perhaps even consciousness. ... Simple descriptions of clinical disorders are a beginning, as is understanding basic mechanisms of neural action. The future of the field, however, is in working toward a science that truly relates brain and cognition in a mechanistic way. (p. xiii)

Although the statement contains many subtle problems, we could probably live with it translated into some non-jargonistic language, such as English. I would rephrase the statement as follows:

> At some point in the future, cognitive neuroscience will be able to say exactly what the brain does to produce consciousness, either perceptual or representative, and action or thought. ... Right now, all we can do is to begin to classify a few mental illnesses, to say something about the biochemical actions of drugs that sometimes alleviate them, and to understand a few of the basic mechanisms of neural action. The future of the field, however, is in working toward a science that relates neurophysiology and psychology in a comprehensible way. (paraphrase)

---

[6]Aspects of the discussion in this section were first presented in Brown (1998). Subsequently they were incorporated in abbreviated form into Brown and Kozak (1998, pp. 137–140).

Unfortunately, however, Gazzaniga's (1995) jargon hides a much more virulent idea, and it is that idea, eliminative reduction, that I now address. Phyllis Churchland (1986) exposits the doctrine in the following way: Although it is obvious that no truly psychological phenomenon has yet been reduced to neurophysiology, there is no principled reason why "neuroscience will never reduce psychology in such a way that subjective experience can be identified with states of the brain" (p. 327).[7]

This peculiar statement is based on a thorough study of intertheoretic reduction in the history of science. That study led Churchland (1986) to replace the logical empiricist theory of reduction with a recently developed account. From the new perspective, theories interactively co-evolve such that, when all is said and done, the reduced theory can be derived from the reducing theory. In the process, both theories undergo change; concepts of either theory may be revised or eliminated altogether. Reasonable though it sounds, the way in which Churchland applies her account of intertheoretic reduction to mind and brain is cause for alarm.

---

[7]Note already Churchland's (1986) conflation of the ideas of reduction and identification, a somewhat ubiquitous phenomenon. To *identify* one thing with another, is to say that it is the same as something of the same kind. For example, it is to say that two plus two is the same as four, all things involved being natural numbers. In contrast, to *reduce* one thing to another is to claim that it is the same as something of a different kind. For example, it is to claim that clouds are water vapor, or in other words that a meteorological thing is really just a particular form of a chemical thing. Such reductions work up to a point if one does not worry about the origin of the cloud or its particular form. When, however, one begins to consider not only the chemical constituents of a cloud but also its form, reduction to water vapor becomes impossible. A cloud is much more than water vapor. It is also meteorological history, something that is inexpressible in water vapor terms.

When this line of reasoning is applied to phenomena involving much more complicated constituents and histories, it becomes immediately apparent how poorly the idea of reduction has been conceived. In Churchland's case, when she says that there is no principled reason why neuroscience will never reduce psychology what she really means is that there is no principled reason why neurophysiological phenomena will never be correlated or coordinated with psychological phenomena. But such coordination or correlation hardly constitutes identity or reduction. What is really at issue is the function-mechanism relation. The whole history of science demonstrates that neither an understanding of function nor an understanding of mechanism is satisfying in itself. Without functional understanding, mechanisms have no meaning. For example, nearly all of the mechanisms of the circulation of the blood were known long before Harvey gave his functional account, at which point people felt they understood. Conversely, without understanding the mechanisms by which functions are achieved, functional explanations have no "reality." For example, Darwin gave an account of transmission genetics 100 years before its mechanisms were discovered and his ideas fully accepted. Neither function nor mechanism alone constitutes a satisfactory explanation. It is only by discovering what is accomplished and how it is accomplished that we feel we understand (cf. Cellérier, 1983; Overton, chap. 2, this volume).

Despite all of her talk about theoretical co-evolution, Churchland (1986) called her book *Neurophilosophy*, not *Psychoneurophilosophy*. Despite her recognition that intertheoretic reduction can be smooth and that cross-theoretical mapping of concepts can be straightforward, her contentious rhetoric makes clear that she really believes that the reduction of the higher mental processes to neuroscience will involve "outright elimination with no cross-theoretic identifications at all" (p. 284). In this respect, it is significant (and somewhat characteristic of the neuroscience literature) that Churchland's book contains five chapters on neuroscience, five chapters on recent philosophy of science, a lengthy chapter on theories of brain function, but not a single chapter on psychology.[8] It is equally significant that almost all of the examples of reduction that Churchland uses are drawn from physics. Her one biological example is genetics, about which she says: "As things stand, molecular genetics has not completely reduced transmission genetics, but its development toward a richer theory that can effect the reduction is guided in part by results and hypotheses in transmission genetics, whose research is in turn inspired in part by questions arising from molecular genetics" (p. 285).[9] She provides no psychological examples. All that she can come up with relative to that discipline is a list of five phenomena whose reduction to neurophysiology she does not believe to be contentious (p. 296). All relate to low-level, unintentional perceptual, conditioning, or discriminatory responses. Contended reductionist propositions, for Churchland, fall into two main categories. The first has to do with what she disdains as folk-psychology concepts that many hold to be indispensable to a theory of psychology and that, they insist, will prove irreducible to neurophysiology. Examples include subjective experience, consciousness, and reasoning (p. 315). The second has to do with functionalist concepts that include certain of the folk-psychology concepts just mentioned as well as intentional states and logical processes "essential to the psychological level of description [that] will not reduce to categories at the neurobiological level of description" (p. 350).

Laying aside the conflation of description and explanation, let me simply remark that Churchland (1986) provides extensive, although not particu-

---

[8]This example could be multiplied almost infinitely. See, for example, Brown's (1986, p. 911) analysis of the 1984 content of *Archives of General Psychiatry*, Brown's (1991, pp. 333–334) analysis of the content of *Textbook of Psychiatry*, Brown and Kozak's (1998, p. 145) remarks about Panksepp's (1994) discussion, *CNS Spectrums: The International Journal of Neuropyschiatric Medicine*'s October 2000 issue entitled "Neurosurgical Approaches and Deep Brain Implants in Neuropsychiatric Illness," or the cover of *Psychiatric Annals, 31*(2) (2001), showing a man's head, brain exposed with various areas represented as parts of a jigsaw puzzle labeled *judgmental, subjective, intuitive, analytical, intellectual,* and so on. Who dares to claim that mainstream attempts to reduce mind to brain are not underway or that Gall's phrenology (Boring, 1950) is dead?

[9]See also footnote 20.

larly convincing, rationales as to why she believes that these objections to reduction do not hold. Space permitting, I would enter that discussion. As it is, it seems more important to address what I think are the essential problems with Churchland's framing of the issues.

As I have said before (Brown & Kozak, 1998):

> It is clear that Churchland [(1986)], like everyone else, wants to know what the mind is for and how mental functions are realized physically. What is wrong with Churchland's manner of going about things is that she believes that the way to get at the problem is through reduction and erroneously assumes a linear explanatory relation among the sciences. Put bluntly, Churchland believes that psychology [and sociology?] reduce to biology, that biology reduces to chemistry, and that chemistry reduces to physics, thereby providing knowledge in its most satisfying form. (pp. 138–139)

Although Churchland appears to have some inkling that reduction does not stop there, she seems to envision reduction within physics as nothing more than creating theories that are more and more all-embracing. She cannot see that physics itself reduces to another discipline. Had she bothered to analyze the relation between empirical and mathematical physics or to read Piaget (unlisted in her bibliography), she would have realized that physics itself admits of what she would consider reductive explanation. Using Churchland's language, this might be expressed in the following way: Physics reduces to mathematics and mathematic reduces (through logic) to psychology and sociology.[10] That being the case, an epistemological circle, undreamt of in Churchland's philosophy, is closed. Oblivious to this possibility and confused about the differences between intra- and intertheoretic reduction, Churchland (along with psychiatry, psychology, neuropsychology, cognitive neuroscience, etc.) is free to fantasize that concepts associated with the higher mental functions will be replaced by as-yet unspecified neurophysiological concepts much in the same way that Aristotle's principle of antiperistasis was replaced by Newton's principle of inertia.

I see at least two problems with this flight of fancy. To begin with, in Churchland's (1986) examples of eliminatory reduction, some concept or some part of a theory in a given discipline is replaced by some concept or some part of another theory in the same discipline, for example, one principle of motion is replaced by another principle of motion. Yet she attempts to argue from intradisciplinary eliminatory reduction to interdisciplinary eliminatory reduction without exhibiting convincing cases. Were Church-

---

[10]Churchland (1986) acknowledges this in indirect fashion when she says, "My account of intertheoretic reduction ideally should be supplemented by a theory of rationality [but] we shall have to make do with an inchoate theory of rationality, which is all we have, until neuroscience and psychology yield a more complete theory of mind-brain function" (p. 283).

land to follow her own logic, theories of mind would not be replaced by theories of brain—they would be replaced by other theories of mind.

More importantly, Churchland's (1986) misguided framing of the relation between mind and brain as a problem of intertheoretic reduction leads her to conflate explanations and causes, concepts of different logical levels (Cellérier, 1983). Explanation is a concept of higher logical order than cause. It has to do with how causes have come together—with how they happen to have been combined in whatever combination they do occur. As far as inorganic phenomena are concerned, the causal mechanisms involved have come to interact by chance (aleatoric morphogenesis). In organic phenomena (phylogenesis excepted), the causal mechanisms involved have come to interact under teleonomic control—either biological, psychological, or social (teleonomic morphogenesis).[11] Explanation rests, therefore, on the morphogenesis of causal systems, not on the causal mechanisms themselves.

To provide a concrete illustration of what is wrong with Churchland's (1986) reasoning, consider the story of David and Goliath (I Samuel 17:51): The cause of Goliath's untimely death may have been an injury to his brain, but that only explains how he died; it says nothing about why he died. A forceful blow to his head caused a cerebral hemorrhage, increased intracranial pressure, uncal herniation, and, following physical law, interrupted the functioning of his respiratory center. Again, that is Newton's how Goliath died; it is not Kepler's why he died. Why Goliath died does not admit of causal explanation. Rather, it is necessary to say how the causal events involved were set in motion. Was Goliath hit on the head by a falling rock? Did a horse kick him? Or did David sling a rock with deadly force?[12] Without the morphogenetic story being known, the case of the dead Philistine goes unsolved. It is nothing more than a headline or the first sentence of a coroner's report: "Local giant found dead of head wound." Only when it is discovered that Goliath died as a result of David's ethnically and politically motivated hatred (not to mention his ambition) that Goliath's death is understood. Repeating myself for emphasis: Biological analysis, however detailed, of just how the rock from David's slingshot fatally disrupted Goliath's neurons is essentially irrelevant to the explanation of Goliath's death as murder and, as I shall eventually argue despite Churchland's claim to the contrary, no physiological explanation of David's motivation is possible in principle.

---

[11]Here I follow Cellérier's (1983) argument and use his vocabulary. In a section to follow, the aleatoric versus teleonomic distinction is mapped onto Mayr's (1988) discussion of unidirectional processes distinguishing *teleomatic*, *teleologic*, and *teleonomic* morphogenesis. This refines but does not change the point under discussion.

[12]I have abbreviated the story for expository reasons. Actually David's stone only stunned Goliath. David then killed the giant with his sword and cut off his head (I Samuel 17:51).

WHAT PSYCHOLOGY IS NOT

Up to this point I have been discussing reductionistic thinking and how it has gained a powerful hold over clinical and theoretical psychology, psychiatry, governmental policy, medical insurance practices, and the popular imagination. What I want to do now is to refocus the discussion on the pivotal position that psychology occupies in the system of the sciences and to examine the function, if any, that reductionism performs in constructing knowledge in general and psychological knowledge in particular. In order to do that, I must say a few things about what psychology is. I shall enter through the back door.

Psychology Is Not the Study of Behavior

It is a sad but unavoidable fact that the academic pageantry of mainstream psychology in the Anglo-Saxon world is, for all intents and purposes, presided over either by unrepentant or by retreaded behaviorists. It is also a sad but unavoidable fact that mainstream academic psychology is largely irrelevant either to practice (child rearing, education, economics, psychotherapy, etc.) or to individual lives. The questions it asks, the methods it uses, and the mandates under which it labors (scientism, statistical significance, publish or perish, etc.) interact to ensure its practical sterility. Its current orientation, inherent in Helmholtz's (Boring, 1950) desire to create a psychophysics, arose in the modern era with behaviorism and, even in its current cognitivist incarnation, depends on measuring observables. Watson, weighed down by the simplicities of empiricist epistemology, believed that limiting the datum of psychology to behavior would make it scientific, whence the term, concepts, and practices of behaviorism. Despite the cognitive revolution and advances in our understanding of how knowledge is constructed, the idea that psychology is the study of behavior lives on today in departments of behavioral science, behavioral therapy, behavioral medicine, and in such things as a circular I received a few days ago announcing a course on "Neurology of Behavior" to be held November 5 to 8, 2001, sponsored jointly by Harvard Medical School and the Division of Behavioral Neurology of Beth Israel Deaconess Medical Center. What Watson and two generations of followers—not to mention a considerable gaggle of contemporary hangers-on—failed to appreciate was that all observables, even in physics, begin in internal experience, require interpretation, and are objectified through a complex system of objective evaluation (Brown, 1996; Overton, chap. 2, this volume)—there are no pure facts. This means that meaning—the stuff of which psychology is made—may be interpreted from behavior but is not itself observable. Complicating matters is the fact that, in the social sciences, "the facts" must, more often than not, be interpreted from a teleonomic rather than a teleomatic[13] point of view. This opens a particularly writhing can of semantic worms. Before attending to those unhappy creatures, there is a myth to be exploded.

Psychology Is Not the Study of Cognition

The cognitive revolution re-admitted the idea of mind into psychology. I suspect, however, that it did so in a way that would not have been acceptable to Rosa Parks. Succinctly, it relegated affect, context, culture, and history to the back of the bus (Gardner, 1985, p. 41). So let me say a few things about cognition.

Cognition and Phrenology. It is a simple fact that the reigning paradigm in academic psychology during the first half of the 20th century was behaviorism. It is also a simple fact that behaviorism was overthrown during the so-called Cognitive Revolution around 1955 and that cognitive psychology became and remains the major paradigm in academic psychology today (Gardner, 1985). As is commonly known, Piaget himself (Piaget, 1981a)—although he would not by any stretch of the imagination have considered himself to be part of the Anglo-Saxon mainstream—was much taken with the idea of a purely cognitive psychology (B. Inhelder, personal communication, August 30, 1995). But what does the term *cognitive psychology* really mean?

Recall in this regard that the term *cognition* comes from faculty psychology's tripartite division of mental activity into cognition, affection, and conation. Although attempts have been made to trace the roots of this division to Augustine or even to Aristotle, there is no believable evidence of continuity. In fact, the modern notion of cognitive, affective, and conative faculties of the mind originated in the era between Leibniz and Kant (Hilgard, 1980). In the 1730s, Christian Wolfe, under the influence of Leibniz, revived the term *psychology* and identified a *facultas cognoscitova* and a *facultas appetiva*. Although Wolfe rejected most of Leibniz's ideas, his faculties retain the flavor of Leibniz's windowless monads. In the 1750s, Gottlieb Baumgarten, reflecting on aesthetics, introduced the notion of *affection* or *feeling*. And finally, in 1755, Moses Mendelssohn gave an explicit exposition naming three fundamental faculties of the soul: understanding, feeling, and will. In our time, these have come to be synonymous with the terms *cognition, affection*, and *conation*.[14]

---

[13]The term comes from Mayr (1988, p. 44). It corresponds roughly to Cellérier's (1983) concept of *aleatoric morphogenesis* used earlier.

[14]The account of faculty psychology in the paragraphs that follow is derived from Boring (1950, pp. 203–207). The original references may be found there.

From these beginnings in the German philosophical psychology of the 18th century, the tripartite division of the mind moved across the channel and the Atlantic Ocean to take up 19th century residence in the writings of Scottish, English, and American associationists. From there, it found its way into the 20th century through the offices of William McDougall.

The thrust of faculty psychology, as it comes down to us today, was to solve a problem that vexed Hume no end and that Quine (1969) ponders in his sad tale of the demise of positivist epistemology. The problem at issue is the problem of how the mind changes sensations that are meaningless into perceptions that are meaningful. For example, visual sensations are two dimensional but give rise to visual perceptions that are three dimensional. How, then, are we to know the world? Do we believe in our sensations or do we believe in our perceptions? Faculty psychology provides a ready if somewhat vacuous answer: We have "mental faculties" that can perform this transformation without distorting a fixed reality.

Thomas Reid (in Boring, 1950), attempting to escape Hume's dilemma, brought faculty psychology into British associationist psychology. According to Reid, there were 24 active powers of the mind that included such things as faculties for self-preservation, hunger, imitation, power-hunger, self-esteem, and so on, and there were six intellectual powers including such things as perception, judgment, memory, conception, and so on. Gall (in Boring, 1950), the phrenologist, drew his 27 powers of the mind from Reid and Reid's student, Stewart, and tried to localize them in specific regions of the brain identified by various topological features of the skull.

Cognition and Modularity. Lest the reader think that I exaggerate the phrenologist leanings of contemporary cognitivism, I invite consideration of the idea of mental modules, a notion strongly embraced by many cognitivists. In *Modularity of Mind*, Fodor (1983), struggling under the awful realization that concepts cannot be learned and unschooled in developmental theory, posits an essentially facultative theory based on Chomsky's notion of an innate *language acquisition device* (Piatelli-Palmarini, 1979). In doing so, he simply displaces the problem of how such modules are acquired onto biology.[15] Fodor's idea of biologically given modules occasioned a good deal of research attempting to establish and locate modules, processors, or innate acquisition devices for many concepts or mental functions.[16] It constitutes, therefore, Gall's (in Boring, 1950) phrenology moved to the neuro-

---

[15]Recall in this respect Piaget's (1979) riposte to Fodor: "I am completely in agreement [with Fodor] on the impossibility of explaining development by a learning theory in the current meaning of that term; but the way in which he reduces my ideas to a learning theory appears a bit excessive. I do not recognize myself in his interpretation" (p. 226, author's translation).

[16]Again (see fn4) I refer the reader to the cover of *Psychiatric Annals, 31*(2) (2001). More substantial support for the claims made here may be found in Tooby and Cosmides (1995).

anatomical level, a feat that Kozak and I (Brown & Kozak, 1998) have elsewhere referred to as *microphrenology*.

To say, then, that psychology is cognitive is, at best, to say that it is facultative and, at worst, to endorse phrenology. For reasons of space, energy, and patience, I shall not go into the fact that cognitive versions of psychology also fail to distinguish epistemic from pragmatic structures or that they exclude important psychological categories like development, feelings, emotions, values, motivations, and intention—all concepts important to teleonomic control—from a science that is precisely about those concepts. In the interest of being scientific, psychology has opted out of being psychology. But let all of this pass. There are greater issues to worry about in the space remaining.

Teleology, Teleomatics, and Teleomony

So what did I mean when I said before that, in the social sciences, the facts must, more often than not, be interpreted from a teleonomic rather than from a teleomatic point of view? I briefly exposit this theme in the present section.

Although explanation in terms of final causes no doubt predates anything that has been written down,[17] Aristotle and his doctrine of final causes is the starting point for the discussion here. Aristotle believed that understanding any phenomenon required explanation in terms of material, efficient, formal, and final causes. Final explanations depended on an "end" or "goal," and, over the centuries, final explanations have kept company with the concepts of finality, unidirectionality, teleology, function, goal direction, goal correction, intention, teleomatics, and teleonomy. These are not disjoint categories. I shall not, however, attempt to untangle the definitional snarls involved. All that I shall say is that I do not believe that anyone any longer disputes the idea that unidirectional processes exist. At the subatomic level, the neutral K-meson may decay in only one direction; at the atomic level, the whole of non-equilibrial thermodynamics concerns directional movement toward increasingly stable states far from thermodynamic equilibrium; at the molecular level, there are myriad examples of movement toward organization including, finally, self-replicating molecules; at the biological level, one arrives not only at complex self-maintaining and self replicating molecular systems, but also at directional creation of regulatory systems that control in some degree the construction of organisms; and at psychological and social levels there is directional development of

---

[17]Children universally explain phenomena in terms of final causes at a certain point in development (Piaget, 1972a) and many adults continue to do so in various forms of superstitious thought.

increasingly complex sensorimotor and semiotic-operational (representational) schemes of action that lead to growing understanding and intentional use of physical and social "reality." So why has the concept of unidirectional processes had so tumultuous a history?

The problem seems to reside in the concept of *teleology*. On the surface, the concept is innocent enough: "the doctrine or study of the ends of final causes, especially as related to the evidences of design or purpose in nature" (Onions, 1956, p. 2142). The rejection of teleology came about—insofar as it has come about—because people who wished to understand things in terms of natural causes had difficulty with the idea that natural phenomena and, in particular, the various forms of life had arisen purposefully. "By whose purposes?" was the question. The answer was, of course (and still is in many people's minds): "God's purposes." That, however, is a supernatural, not a natural, cause. It requires a leap of faith that naturalists cannot take—and the tale continues with Buffon, Lamarck, Darwin, and others.[18]

An overreaction occurred, however. The fact that biological evolution turned out to be unidirectional but not finalized or purposeful was overgeneralized to mean, at least for a while, that no unidirectional process was finalized (Brown, 1997, p. 299; Cellérier, 1983; Piaget, 1967a, pp. 188–189; Piaget, 1936/1968). This involved a conflation of unidirectionality and finality—the very definition of teleology as it is understood today. With the rise of cybernetics, scientists began to accept that finalized unidirectional processes do occur in nature, that they require explanation, and that they only emanate from regulatory apparatuses belonging to highly organized systems, such as the genomic system or intelligence.[19] Thus the appeal of a psychology linked to cybernetics and willing to study finalized processes is not hard to understand.

When previously examining Churchland's (1986) ideas about intertheoretic reduction, I invoked Cellérier's (1976/1983) distinction of aleatoric and teleonomic morphogenesis and suggested that these concepts map, in general, onto Mayr's (1988, pp. 42–53) concepts of teleomatic and teleonomic processes. I shall use Mayr's terminology here for the simple reason that, although Cellérier's thought on this subject is richer and more nuanced, it is less well known, more complicated, and would require lengthier exposition.

---

[18]For want of space, I avoid discussion of the teleological argument claiming to prove God's existence. No doubt this also played into people's abhorrence of teleology as part of the struggle to break away from superstitious thought.

[19]I shall not attempt to deal here with the oxymoronic concept of artificial intelligence. No doubt the persons who create these programs are highly intelligent, but there is no possibility that the machine's activity has meaning to the machine or that the machine is, itself, intelligent (Brown, 1994).

For Mayr (1988), too, teleology arises from the conflation of unidirectional and finalized processes. He points out that unidirectional processes do not, in fact, imply goal direction or finality. Many unidirectional processes are simply the result of natural law; specifically, they are automatic results of physical law acting on uncontrolled objects. If a thing is dropped, it falls and comes to rest, but it does not do so because it had prior knowledge of where it would land and sought that place out. Rather, it just blindly and automatically reached kinetic equilibrium following natural law. For that reason, Mayr terms such processes *teleomatic*: the *telos*, or goal, is automatic, not programmed or thought out. He considers all physical and chemical processes as well as phylogenetic evolution to be teleomatic processes.[20] In contradistinction, Mayr holds that there are many phenomena that are finalized or goal directed, but that these occur only within systems governed by regulatory subsystems (programs, in his parlance) that control functioning. These systems and the phenomena they produce, such as phenotypic development and intelligent conduct, are designated as teleonomic. As far as teleology goes, Mayr grants it marginal credence: "If *teleological* means anything, it means *goal-directed*" (p. 43). To his mind, it is certainly no proof of God's existence or of the goal directedness of organic evolution.

What Then Is Psychology?

Proceeding by the methods of proclamation, definition by exclusion, historico-critical analysis, and a smattering of cybernetic theory, I have suggested that psychology is not the empirical study of behavior, that it cannot be limited to the muddled concept of cognition, that it has to do with the teleonomic control of behavior, and that meaning and interpretation are central to its definition. I have not, however, said in any straightforward way what psychology actually is. I shall attempt to do so now.

Psychology is the study, both synchronic and diachronic, of the organization of conduct, of human action. Its data, though always behavioral (including speech acts and other manifestations of subjectivity), must be interpreted in light of how such organization has come about, whether biologically (reflexive behavior), through habit formation, through sensorimotor intention, or through representations. Moreover, psychological explanations always have both individual and social aspects. One might even say that individual psychology is to sociology as individual genetics is to population genetics. Individuals do not evolve biologically or psychologically on

---

[20]On this point, Mayr (1988) and Piaget (1967a, 1970) would probably have disagreed. Piaget did not believe that a completely teleomatic theory of phylogenesis was believable; Mayr thinks it is. Interestingly, in an obscure and forgotten paper, Cellérier (1973)—undoubtedly Piaget's most brilliant student—sides with Mayr.

their own. On either level, recombination is the most important source of variation. Only the intercourse of genes and the intercourse of minds in relation to an environment make biological and social evolution possible. As for selection in psychosocial evolution, I have argued elsewhere (Brown, 1990, 1993, 1996; Brown & Kozak, 1998; Brown & Weiss, 1987) that psychological selection enjoys the advantage of subjective affective heuristics, something unknown in the biological domain. The affective intelligence, based on subjective values, came before and remains more powerful than the logical intelligence where objective values are the selection criteria. This "make-do" intelligence was and remains the main reason that psychological evolution is infinitely faster than genomic evolution. It was and remains the main reason that the concept of cognitive psychology, cut off from affection and will, is incoherent.

THE CIRCLE OF THE SCIENCES

Having arrived by this circuitous route at a concept of psychology, I would like, now, to return to the project of exploring the pivotal position that psychology occupies in the system of the sciences and to examine the function, if any, that reductionism performs in constructing knowledge. I shall begin with Piaget's ideas about why psychology should be interested in neurophysiology. In *Main Trends in Psychology* (1970/1973), he wrote:

> There is no mental life without organic life, while the opposite is not necessarily true; and there is no behavior without functioning of the nervous system (starting from Coelenterata).... Everything that is organic is subject to definite verification and presents more observable and measurable manifestations than conduct and consciousness. These are all reasons for directing psychological explanations towards the relating of mental processes and behavior to physiological processes.... But it should be made clear from the start that [doing so] assumes two distinct forms.... There is the reductionist trend, the aim of which is pure and simple identification of the mental process, conceived as a simple phenomenological expression, with its direct explanation. There is also a trend that can be called relational or dialectic and which involves distinguishing between many scales of phenomena, both in the organism or nervous system and in behavior or conduct, and discerning the interaction or feedback between processes of different scales, so that there is no longer any reduction from the higher to the lower, but closer and closer solidarity.... The current general tendency is to recognize an isomorphism and not an interaction between the forms of consciousness and those of its [neurophysiological] concomitants.... But to deny any interaction between consciousness as such and its nervous concomitants is in no way to dispute the interaction between conduct (which includes consciousness but goes beyond it) and physiological processes. (p. 19)

Thus, although Piaget agreed that coordinating psychological and neuro-physiological phenomena is important, he did not believe that Church-land's (1986) kind of eliminative reduction was either desirable or possible. Turn next to a chapter entitled "Le Système et la Classification des Sci-ences" [The System and Classification of the Sciences] that Piaget (1967b) wrote for *Logique et Connaissance Scientifique* [Logic and Scientific Knowl-edge]. After examining various ways in which other thinkers have classified the sciences, all of which are linear (with the possible exception of Kedroff [Piaget, 1967b], who saw dialectic philosophy, if not science, as cyclic), Piaget wrote: "For thirty years, I have proposed that the system of the sci-ences necessarily presents an essentially cyclic order irreducible to any lin-ear form" (p. 1172, author's translation).[21] The circle that Piaget envisioned is shown in Fig. 1.1. He went on to explore different possible meanings that this circular relation might have, distinguishing especially the different types of dependence, reduction, or affiliation that are possible between one science and another. His first maneuver was to differentiate two domains of science: the material domain and the conceptual domain. The *material do-main* is defined as the set of objects on which a science bears; the *concep-tual domain* is defined as the set of theories or systematized concepts that a science creates in order to explain its material domain. It is clear that, from the point of view of the material domain, the sciences are cyclically related for the simple reason that there is nowhere to look for an explanation of logico-mathematical phenomena other than in psychological and social ac-

---

[21]Hull (1978) made much the same point in his critique of reductionism in genetics. He re-cently reiterated his argument during a symposium entitled "Reductionism in Science" (Hull, 2000). Hull's thesis was and remains that reductionist theory "ends in a hierarchical organiza-tion of scientific theories" (1978, p. 222). In the 1978 paper, he provides a (delicious-looking) wed-ding-cake image of the structure he believes reductionistic thinking leads to. Physics and chem-istry constitute the bottom and largest layer, biology the next, psychology sets atop biology, and sociology is at the summit (except for a cherub, which effectively indicates the mythical character of this conception). As I suggested in the discussion, logic, mathematics, and there-fore the human subject have no place in such a conception. Theories of the upper layers are, in a sense, derived from the lower levels and they are at the same time reduced to the level from which they are derived. The image is silent about where formal knowledge fits in. In the original (1978) paper, Hull points out that "the only example that the reductionists have given of this kind of 'inter-level' reduction up to now is that of the reduction of Mendelian genetics to molecu-lar biology" (p. 222, author's translation). Mayr (1982) would not even go that far:

The claim that genetics has been reduced to chemistry after the discovery of the struc-ture of DNA, RNA, and certain enzymes cannot be justified. To be sure, the chemical na-ture of a number of black boxes in the classical genetic theory was filled in . . . this does not in the least reduce genetics to chemistry. The essential concepts of genetics, like gene, genotype, mutation, diploidy, heterozygosity, segregation, recombination, and so on, are not chemical concepts at all and one would look for them in vain in a textbook on chemistry. (p. 62)

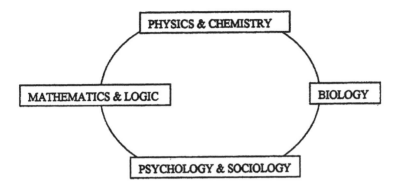

FIG. 1.1. Piaget's "Circle of the Sciences."

tivity. It is, after all, people who create logic and mathematics. By the same token, from the point of view of concepts, it can appear that the sciences follow a linear order for the simple reason that psychologists often appeal to biology, biologists often appeal to chemistry and physics, and physicists often appeal to mathematics to explain phenomena in their respective fields, but it is considered an abomination for logicians and mathematicians to appeal to psychology and sociology. They define their starting points, their axioms, and work from there. That, however, is not the end of the story.

Within any science there occur crises in which the discipline at issue is forced to examine its foundations in order to move past some obstacle. A case in point might be special relativity and a general consideration of what it means to measure time or space. Piaget considered this to be the epistemological domain internal to each scientific discipline. Even from this point of view, however, the sciences continue to enjoy a linear relation. It is only when epistemological reflection must be extended over all scientific disciplines, all knowledge (what Piaget called the *derived epistemological domain*), that we are again forced to deal with the knowing subject in relation to the object of knowledge. At this level, the circle once more closes.

The great significance of recognizing these circular relations among the sciences in the material and derived epistemological domains is that it indicates that the sciences do not all proceed in the same fashion and that there is no linear or hierarchical relation among the sciences. As Piaget (1976b) noted:

While biology and psychosociology explain the knowing subject starting from the laws of the physical universe or starting from actions upon that universe, physics and mathematics explain the universe starting from the operatory structures or the deductive instruments constructed by the subject in function of the coordinations of his actions. (p. 1180)

When scientists attempt to integrate one causal system into another (usually in their search for mechanisms), it makes sense to speak about reduction. When they attempt to make causal systems correspond to systems of implications either by mathematizing reality (mathematical physics, mathematical modeling of neural nets, etc.), by creating isomorphisms between implicative and causal systems (neuroscience, the machine languages used in programming), or by reducing or integrating one implicative system to another through reflective abstraction (mathematics, logic), the concept of reduction has no bearing.

Space permitting, I would spell out the six levels of dependence that Piaget (1967b) envisioned among the sciences, but I need to move on to a final feature of Piaget's concept of psychology that bears directly on reduction. To do this, there are some lexical coordinations to be made.

The reader may recall that, in my critique of Churchland (1986), I pointed out that, although her ostensive program is the coordination of mental activity with neural activity, she attacks many of psychology's central concepts and speaks about eliminative intertheoretic reduction, which she admits has never occurred in neuroscience and which Popper (1974) asserts has never been completely accomplished in science at all. In fact, most of Churchland's examples are examples of theory change (from the theory of caloric to the theory of molecular kinetic energy, from the theory of phlogiston to the theory of oxygen); they are not examples of reduction. In any case, Churchland's notion of intertheoretic reduction corresponds to what Piaget called *interlevel* or *interdisciplinary* reduction. The argument against interdisciplinary reductions is that the phenomena that define the various fields of science are specific to them and, although consistent with, are not contained within the laws and theories of the disciplines on either side. For example, suppose that Galileo had dropped cats or children from the leaning tower in his studies of gravitation. The fact that such objects are biological when singled out for study does not make Galileo's experiment a biological experiment, nor does it reduce living phenomena to the law of gravitation. Only if Galileo had studied those properties that set cats and children apart from inorganic physical objects could one make biological claims.

The difficulty is to find some principle that makes it possible to move between disciplines, that is, to understand the relation between our actions on numbers and our actions on electrons. About this, Piaget (1950) had the following to say:

> Psychology has its roots in biology and has as one of its goals to explain the subject's operations. It therefore forms a bridge between the objective and the subjective. It is not, however, a science of states of consciousness but rather a science of conduct. Defined in that way, psychologists find them-

selves in the presence of two series of facts: the organism's movements (biologically observable) and its states of consciousness. The problem is to figure out the relation between the two. This problem is symmetrical with the problem of the relations between experiment and deduction in mathematical physics. Recall, in this respect, that organic facts constitute causal series just as much as physical facts do, whereas both in psychology and physics, states of consciousness consist in systems of implications without causality, properly speaking. As a result, the question of parallelism in psychology appears to be only a particular case of the general problem posed by all encounters of deductive systems linked to consciousness with the material facts of experiment. With specific reference to psychology, what neurophysiology cannot explain is the phenomenon of logicomathematical necessity. All and everywhere, consciousness is to physiology as implication is to causality. One is, therefore, forced to conclude that physiological explanation and psychological analysis are parallel and irreducible.

By means of the principle of psychophysiological parallelism, the notion of equilibrium gets around this ineluctable division between the causality inherent in the organic aspect of conduct and the implication inherent in conscious operations because it applies to both domains without assuming interaction between the two. Operatory psychology, then, is essentially a theory of the forms of equilibrium and of transitions from one form of equilibrium to another that cuts across causal and implicative domains. (pp. 131–186, fragments excerpted, re-ordered, and translated by the author)

What I take from all of this and the reason that I include it is that I believe that, in the 50 or so years since Piaget wrote his treatise and, despite spectacular advances in neuroscience, much of mainstream psychology—the kind that pays off academically—remains mired in empiricist superstitions and reductionist fantasy. It still believes that the sciences are linearly or hierarchically related; it has no idea that an explanation—not an acquisitional description—of formal knowledge is central to any theory of knowledge,[22] and in very large degree it lends unthinking credence to a greedy and unscientifically supported industry of legalized drug peddling. It is my hope that this chapter and this book will contribute to change.

AUTHOR NOTE

Terrance Brown, 3530 North Lake Shore Drive, 12-A, Chicago, IL 60657.

---

[22]Piaget, of course, had an elaborate theory of what formal knowledge is, where it comes from, and how it is constructed (Beth & Piaget, 1961; Piaget, 1950/1973, 1965, 1972b, 1977a, 1977b, 1981b, 1983; Piaget & García, 1991; Piaget, Grize, Szeminska, & Bang, 1968; Piaget, Sinclair, & Bang, 1968). Sadly, his works on these subjects are little known or understood.

REFERENCES

Beth, E. W., & Piaget, J. (1961). *Épistémologie mathématique et psychologie* [Mathematical episte-mology and psychology]. Paris: Presses Universitaires de France.

Boring, E. G. (1950). *A history of experimental psychology.* Englewood Cliffs, NJ: Prentice-Hall.

Brown, T. (1986). Holzman's fences: Chauvinism or confusion. *Archives of General Psychiatry, 43,* 910–912.

Brown, T. (1990). The biological significance of affectivity. In N. L. Stein, D. L. Leventhal, & T. Trabasso (Eds.), *Biological and psychological approaches to emotion* (pp. 405–434). Hillsdale, NJ: Lawrence Erlbaum Associates.

Brown, T. (1991). Psychiatry's unholy marriage: Psychoanalysis and neuroscience. In D. Offer & M. Sabshin (Eds.), *The diversity of normal behavior* (pp. 305–355). New York: Basic Books.

Brown, T. (1993). Affective dimensions of meaning. In W. F. Overton & D. Palermo (Eds.), *The nature and ontogenesis of meaning* (pp. 167–190). Hillsdale, NJ: Lawrence Erlbaum Associates.

Brown, T. (1994). Man is not a machine, but neither are machines organisms. *Psychological Inquiry, 5,* 241–244.

Brown, T. (1996). Values, knowledge, and Piaget. In E. S. Reed, E. Turiel & T. Brown (Eds.), *Values and knowledge* (pp. 137–170). Mahwah, NJ: Lawrence Erlbaum Associates.

Brown, T. (1997). *¿Es la teleonomía una categoría del entendimiento?* [Is teleonomy a category of understanding?]. In R. García (Ed.), *La epistemología genética y la ciencia contemporánea* [Genetic epistemology and contemporary science] (pp. 297–314). Barcelona: Gedisa.

Brown, T. (1998, May). *Temptations of reductionism.* Paper presented at El Centro de Investigacíon y de Estudios Avanzados, Mexico City, Mexico.

Brown, T., & Kozak, A. (1998). Emotion and the possibility of psychologists entering into heaven. In M. Mascolo & S. Griffin (Eds.), *What develops in emotional development?* (pp. 135–155). New York: Plenum.

Brown, T., & Weiss, L. (1987). Structures, procedures, heuristics, and affectivity. *Archives de Psychologie (Geneva), 55,* 59–94.

Center for Response Politics. (1999, January 31). *The Chicago Tribune,* p. 5-1.

Cellérier, G. (1973). *L' explication en biologie* [Explanation in biology]. In L. Apostel, G. Cellérier, J. T. Desanti, R. García, G. G. Granger, F. Halbwachs, G. V. Henriques, J. Ladrière, J. Piaget, I. Sachs, & H. Sinclair-de Zwaart (Eds.), *L' explication dans les sciences* [Explanation in the sciences] (pp. 120–131). Paris: Flammarion.

Cellérier, G. (1983). The historical genesis of cybernetics: Is teleonomy a category of understanding? (T. Brown, Trans.). *Nature and System, 5,* 211–225. (Original work published 1976)

Churchland, P. S. (1986). *Neurophilosophy: Toward a unified science of the mind/brain.* Cambridge, MA: MIT Press.

Clinical Psychiatric News. (December, 2000). p. 1.

Coyle, J. T. (1988). Neuroscience and psychiatry. In J. A. Talbott, R. E. Hales & S. C. Yudofsky (Eds.), *Textbook of psychiatry* (pp. 3–32). Washington, DC: American Psychiatric Press.

Elkin, I., Shea, T., Watkins, J. T., Imber, S. D., Sotsky, S. M., Collins, J. F., Glass, D. R., Pilkonis, P. A., Leber, W. R., Docherty, J. P., Fiester, S. J., & Parloff, M. B. (1989). National Institute of Mental Health treatment of depression collaborative research program: General effectiveness of treatments. *Archives of General Psychiatry, 46,* 971–982.

Fodor, J. A. (1983). *The modularity of mind.* Cambridge, MA: MIT Press.

Fulton, D. (2000). Class action suits over Ritalin filed against APA. *Clinical Psychiatry News, 28*(10), 1 & 5.

Gardner, H. (1985). *The mind's new science: A history of the cognitive revolution.* New York: Basic Books.

Gazzaniga, M. S. (1995). Preface. In M. S. Gazzaniga (Ed.), *The cognitive neurosciences* (pp. xiii–xiv). Cambridge, MA: The MIT Press.

Gershon, E. S., & Rieder, R. O. (1992). Major disorders of mind and brain. *Scientific American*, September, 126–133.

Ginsberg, D. L. (Ed.). (2001). Remission-oriented treatment of Depression. *CNS Spectrums (Teaching Monograph)*, 6, 1–8.

Grinfeld, M. J. (2000). More kids on drugs: Is the research worth the furor? *Psychiatric Times*, 17(5), 1, 7–8.

Hilgard, E. R. (1980). The trilogy of mind: Cognition, affection, and conation. *Journal of the History of the Behavioral Sciences*, 26, 107–117.

Hull, D. L. (1978). Génétique et réductionisme [Genetics and reductionism]. *La Recherche*, 87, 220–227.

Hull, D. L. (2000, May). *Varieties of reductionism: Derivation and gene selection*. Paper presented at the Reductionism in Science Symposium, Conférences Philippe Laudat, Abbaye du Royaumont, France.

Mayr, E. (1982). *The growth of biological thought*. Cambridge, MA: Harvard University Press.

Mayr, E. (1988). *Toward a new philosophy of biology*. Cambridge, MA: Harvard University Press.

Montgomery, S. A., Racagni, G., Nutt, D. J., Schatzberg, A. F., Kasper, S., & Thase, M. E. (2001). Understanding depression: A long-term, recurring disorder (The role of neurotransmitters in depression). *The Journal of Clinical Psychiatry*, 5, 380–382.

Onions, C. T. (Ed.). (1956). *Shorter Oxford English dictionary* (3rd ed.). London: Oxford University Press.

Panksepp, J. (1994). The basics of basic emotion. In P. Ekman & R. J. Davidson (Eds.), *The nature of emotion: Fundamental questions* (pp. 20–24). New York: Oxford University Press.

Piaget, J. (1950). *Introduction à l'épistémologie génétique: III. La pensée biologique, la pensée psychologique, et la pensée sociologique* [Introduction to genetic epistemology: III. Biological thought, psychological thought, and sociological thought]. Paris: Presses Universitaires de France.

Piaget, J. (1950/1973). *Introduction à l'épistémologie génétique: I. La pensée mathématique* [Introduction to genetic epistemology: I. Mathematical thought]. Paris: Presses Universitaires de France.

Piaget, J. (1965). *The child's conception of number* (Trans. unknown). New York: W. W. Norton & Co. (Original work published 1941)

Piaget, J. (1967a). *Biologie et connaissance* [Biology and knowledge]. Paris: Gallimard.

Piaget, J. (1967b). Le système et la classification des sciences [The system and classification of the sciences]. In J. Piaget (Ed.), *Logique et connaissance scientifique* [Logic and scientific knowledge] (pp. 1151–1224). Paris: Gallimard.

Piaget, J. (1936/1968). *La naissance de l'intelligence chez l'enfant* [The origins of intelligence in children]. Neuchâtel, Switzerland: Delachaux & Niestlé.

Piaget, J. (1927/1972a). *The child's conception of physical causality* (M. Gabain, Trans.). Totowa, NJ: Littlefield, Adams, & Co. (Original work published 1927)

Piaget, J. (1972b). *Essai de logique opératoire* [Attempt at an operatory logic] (2nd ed.). Paris: Dunod.

Piaget, J. (1970/1973). *Main trends in psychology*. New York: Harper and Row.

Piaget, J. (1977a). *Recherches sur l'abstraction réfléchissante: I. L'abstraction des relations logico-arithmétiques* [Research on reflective abstraction: I. Abstraction of logico-arithmetical relations]. Paris: Presses Universitaires de France.

Piaget, J. (1977b). *Recherches sur l'abstraction réfléchissante: II. L'abstraction de l'ordre des relations spatiales* [Research on reflective abstraction: II. Abstraction of the order of spatial relations]. Paris: Presses Universitaires de France.

Piaget, J. (1979). Discussion. In M. Piattelli-Palmarini (Ed.), *Théories du langage, théories de l'apprentissage* [Theories of language, theories of learning] (pp. 226–238). Paris: Seuil.

Piaget, J. (1981a). *Intelligence and affectivity: Their relationship during child development* (T. A. Brown & C. E. Kaegi, Eds. & Trans.). Palo Alto, CA: Annual Reviews. (Original work published 1953/1954)

Piaget, J. (1981b). *Le possible et le nécessaire: I. L'évolution des possibles chez l'enfant* [Possibility and necessity: The role of possibility in cognitive development]. Paris: Presses Universitaires de France.

Piaget, J. (1983). *Le possible et le nécessaire: II. L'évolution du nécessaire chez l'enfant* [Possibility and necessity: The role of necessity in cognitive development]. Paris: Presses Universitaires de France.

Piaget, J., & García, R. (1991). *Toward a logic of meanings* (P. M. Davidson & J. Easley, Eds. & Trans.). Hillsdale, NJ: Lawrence Erlbaum Associates. (Original work published 1987)

Piaget, J., Grize, J.-B., Szeminska, A., & Bang, V. (1968). *Épistémologie et psychologie de la fonction* [Epistemology and psychology of function]. Paris: Presses Universitaires de France.

Piaget, J., Sinclair, H., & Bang, V. (1968). *Épistémologie et psychologie de l'identité* [Epistemology and psychology of identity]. Paris: Presses Universitaires de France.

Piatelli-Palmarini, M. (1979). Introduction. In M. Piatelli-Palmarini (Ed.), *Théories du langage; Théories de l'apprentisage* (pp. 19–48). Paris: Éditions du Seuil.

Popper, C. W. (1988). Disorders usually first evident in infancy, childhood, or adolescence. In J. A. Talbott, R. E. Hales & S. C. Yudofsky (Eds.), *Textbook of psychiatry* (pp. 649–735). Washington, DC: American Psychiatric Press.

Popper, K. (1974). *Unended quest: An intellectual autobiography.* La Salle, IL: Open Court.

Quine, W. V. (1969). Epistemology naturalized. In *Ontological relativity and other essays* (pp. 69–90). New York: Columbia University Press.

Sherman, C. (2001). Resident training shifts focus to psychotherapy. *Clinical Psychiatry News, 29*(1), 1–2.

Tooby, J., & Cosmides, L. (1995). Mapping the evolved functional organization of mind and brain. In M. S. Gazzaniga (Ed.), *The cognitive neurosciences* (pp. 1185–1197). Cambridge, MA: MIT Press.

Valenstein, E. S. (1998). *Blaming the brain.* New York: The Free Press.

WAYS OF UNDERSTANDING

2

Understanding, Explanation, and Reductionism: Finding a Cure for Cartesian Anxiety[1]

Willis F. Overton
Temple University

This chapter is about the historical changes that have occurred in scientific methodology as it applies to the empirical sciences, especially since the 1950s. Methodology is complementary to, but distinct from, methods. A methodology describes the general rules of science that guide and constrain the elaboration of methods and measurement models, which are the specific techniques for designing, conducting, and evaluating empirical inquiry. My focus in this chapter is on a rule that was central to the methodology called *neopositivism* and has continued to influence the descendants of neopositivism: the rule of *reductionism*.

Clarity demands that any discussion of reductionism include a distinction between analysis and reductionism. Analysis and synthesis stand in a dialectical relationship of parts and wholes. Analysis is about the differentiation of parts of a whole; synthesis is about the integration by the whole of the parts. In contrast, reductionism and synthesis stand in destructive, not dialectic, opposition. Any reductionism worthy of the name does not aim at analyzing how wholes are put together from parts, but rather at explaining wholes away. Reductionism constitutes, therefore, what Dewey (1929) viewed as an adolescent quest for absolute certainty at the expense of com-

---

[1]An earlier version of this chapter was presented at the annual meetings of the Jean Piaget Society, Mexico City, Mexico, June 1999.

plex understanding.[2] The history of analysis is as long as the history of mankind and there are precursors to reductionism that go back to pre-Socratic Greek distinctions between appearance and reality. However, reductionism as a final solution to ontological and epistemological uncertainty has a much shorter history.

It may be profitable to begin a consideration of reductionism in the context of the thought of the later Wittgenstein (1958)—the Wittgenstein of *Philosophical Investigations*. Within this frame, it becomes possible to recognize that reductionism is just a picture, a part of a story, a feature of a particular Wittgensteinian language game. This language game is called "The Story of Empirical Science as Narrated Through the Imagery of Modernity." The story is captivating and comforting, but it also produces problems because there has been a tendency to get so caught up in this particular language game, so ensnared in it, so captured by it, that it is often though not to be a game at all, not a story, but a mirror reflection of the way things really are and always will be. Some come to believe, with great passion, that, if it is a story, it must be a story of fact and not of fiction. But here let me just note that the notion that some things are absolute facts and some things are absolute fiction is itself a part of the very same language game. It is a language game that splits all of our phenomenal experience into necessarily being this or that, into either-one-*or*-the-other, and—having so split the world—it directs us to choose which of the split alternatives constitutes the absolute certainty of the Real and which constitutes the chimera of mere appearance.

There are, of course, those of us who would argue that the story containing reductionism lacks intelligibility and coherence. We would argue that it is a degenerate language game containing lessons that will ultimately harm those who play it. It is a language game that requires modification or replacement as we enter the millennium. An alternative narrative is one that eschews absolute certainty and split-off, either-or dichotomies, that celebrates a dialectical understanding of the world—an understanding composed of relational categories that entail both complementarity and distinctiveness. However, giving up the promise of absolute certainty is not an easy thing, for it raises the specter of absolute relativism and the fear of absolute relativism can unleash powerful resistant forces in both the individual and the community. The psychoanalyst R. D. Laing (1960), among others, described madness and the process of going mad as the stark terror

---

[2]The concept of *methodological reductionism* used by Gottlieb and his colleagues (Gottlieb, Wahlsten, & Lickliter, 1998) to reference their systems approach to development might be considered an exception to this rule. Methodological reductionism, however, entails the analysis of parts in relation to wholes and the reciprocal relationship of parts and wholes, rather than the classical forms of reductionism, which they explicitly reject.

that arises in the context of a sense of absolute relativism. The erosion of a fundamental certainty of being and certainty of continuity of being was termed *ontological insecurity* by Laing. In the 17th century, René Descartes sought to save Western civilization from ontological insecurity by arguing for the necessity of an absolute foundation to knowledge as the base for absolute certainty.

It is against this backdrop of potential terror of relativism—this potential Cartesian anxiety (Bernstein, 1983)—that any language game, and particularly the language game called *empirical science*, must be articulated. As a consequence, an important question to be faced in today's postmodern era is whether it is possible to describe a methodology of science that abandons the quest for absolute certainty while at the same time avoiding the anxious terror engendered by relativism. The thesis to be developed in this chapter is that such an articulation is available and it is discovered in a relational scientific methodology that represents a coordination of physical sciences' methodology of causal explanation and behavioral and social sciences' methodology of hermeneutic understanding.

I will describe some of the main features of this integrated methodology of the empirical sciences by first briefly sketching a history of the rules of reductionism, causal explanation, and inductivism as these developed in the culture of modernity. Following this, I will present a short history of hermeneutic understanding and its role in the story of science, again, as told in the context of the modern project. Finally, I will examine the outlines of the integrated relational methodology that emerged and continues to evolve out of the revolutionary events of the 1950s.

SPLIT SCIENTIFIC METHODOLOGY

The critical place to begin the story of contemporary scientific methodology is in the 17th century with the dawn of the modern age or modernity. The narrative of modernity is defined by both a quest for absolute certainty of knowledge (Toulmin, 1990) and an effort to expand individual freedom, especially freedom of thought. Building knowledge on rational and reasoned grounds, rather than on the grounds of authority and dogma, was understood as the key to each of these goals. The early protagonists who developed the basic story line were Galileo Galilei and his physics of a natural world disconnected from mind, René Descartes, whose epistemology elevated disconnection to a first principle, and Thomas Hobbes, who saw both mind and nature in a vision of atomistic materialism. Of the three, Descartes was to have the greatest and most lasting impact on the text and subtexts that we now refer to as modern scientific methodology.

Splitting and Foundationalism

Descartes' major contributions entailed the insertion and articulation of splitting and foundationalism as key interrelated themes into the story of scientific knowing. *Splitting* is the formation of a dichotomy—of an exclusive either-or relationship—and *foundationalism* is the claim that one or the other elements of the formed dichotomy constitutes the ultimate real. Nature and nurture, idealism and materialism (form and matter), reason and observation, subject and object, constancy and change, biology and culture, and so forth can all be—and under the influence of Cartesian epistemology are—thought of as split-off competing alternatives. Choose the one as the real—as the foundation—and it follows under a split interpretation that the other is mere appearance or epiphenomenal.

The foundation here is the final achievement of absolute certainty and the end of doubt. The foundation is not a vantage point, standpoint, or point of view and certainty and doubt are not dialectically related as an identity of opposites. Descartes' foundationalism describes the final, fixed, secure base. It constitutes an absolute, fixed, unchanging bedrock—a final Archimedes point (Descartes, 1969).

With splitting and foundationalism in place, the theme of reductionism is firmly planted in the story and virtually all change to the present day represents elaboration and variation. Eliminative reductionism, ontological reductionism, property-ontological reductionism, theoretical reductionism, definitional reductionism, causal reductionism (Searle, 1992), radical or leveling reductionism, microreductionism, smooth reductionism, semantic reductionism (Shanon, 1993), and that ever-favorite biosociological reductionism (Bunge & Ardila, 1987)—while each making interesting and valuable discriminations to the plot line—add little to the theme.

Materialism and Objectivism

Cartesian splitting and foundationalism came to operate as a permanent background frame for modernity's scientific story. However, the specification of the nature of the ultimate foundation remained at issue. It was left to Hobbes and later empiricists to operate within the frame of subject split from object, mind split from body, and ideas split from matter, and to build into this frame the materialist identification of atomistic matter as the ultimate ontological foundation—the Real. Furthermore, the epistemological rhetoric of Locke, Berkeley, and Hume operated to suppress subjectivity, mind, or ideas, thereby creating objectivism, or the belief that the ultimate material reality exists as an absolute—independent of mind or knower (Searle, 1992). This constituted, as Putnam (1990) said, an epistemological God's-eye view.

Objectivist matter thus came to constitute the ontological Real to which the manifold of common-sense experience would be reduced to arrive at the goal of science, a systematized body of certain empirical knowledge. It must be cautioned at this point that there is a critical distinction to be made between the use of the term *real* in everyday common-sense life and the foundational Real. No one argues, or has ever argued, that there is a lack of reality or realness in the experienced everyday world. This is common-sense realism. Common-sense realism accepts the material existence of a real, actual, or manifest world and all ontological or epistemological perspectives treat people, animals, and physical objects as having such a real existence. The ontological issue of the Real with a capital "R" (Putnam, 1987) is a very different issue. It concerns the current issue of having an absolute base or foundation from which everything else emerges. In this limited sense, the *Real* is defined as that which is not dependent on something else and cannot be reduced to something else.

Support for the materialist foundation arose and was further defined by Newton's contributions. Central among these contributions was the redefinition of the nature of matter in a way that conceived of all bodies as fundamentally inactive. Prior to Newton, matter was understood as inherently active. Matter had been conceived of in terms of the relation of being (static, fixed) and becoming (active, changing). Newton, however, through his concept of inertia, split activity and matter and redefined matter as inactivity (Prosch, 1964).

The redefinition of bodies as inert matter and the assumption of the atomicity of matter (i.e., bodies are ultimately aggregates of elemental matter that is uniform in nature and, in combination, yields the things of the world) were basic for Newton's formulation of his laws of motion. However, they were also ideas that a later generation generalized into a metaphysical world view that identified the nature of the Real as fixed inert matter and only fixed inert matter. This world view has been called the "billiard ball" notion of the universe, "the notion that basically everything ... was made up of small, solid particles, in themselves inert, but always in motion and elasticitly [sic] rebounding from each other ... and operating mechanically" (Prosch, 1964, p. 66). With these themes at hand—splitting, foundationalism, materialism, objectivism—it was a short step to the formulation of a complete scientific methodology, termed *mechanical explanation*, that, with relatively minor modifications, has extended to the present day as the basic methodology of neopositivism and later instrumentalism, conventionalism, and functionalism.

Mechanical Explanation

The methodology of mechanical explanation continues the splitting process by dichotomizing empirical science into two airtight compartments: description and explanation. There are three steps to mechanical explanation.

The first step is considered descriptive and the second two are considered explanatory.

Step 1: Reduction Description. The first step of mechanical explanation entails addressing the common-sense object of inquiry and reducing it to the absolute material, objective, fixed, unchanging, foundational elements or atoms. Terms like *reductionism, atomism, elementarism,* and *analytic attitude* all identify this step. In psychology for many years the atoms were stimuli and responses. Today they tend to be neurons and behaviors or contextual factors and behaviors—the story line changes but the themes remain the same.

I briefly consider here the impact of this first step on developmental inquiry. Immediately, stages of development and mental organizations that change during development become suspect as being somehow derivative. At best, under this story line, they can only function as summary statements for an underlying, more molecular Real. In fact, the drive throughout this step is toward the ever more molecular in the belief that it is in the realm of the molecular that the Real is found. This is particularly well illustrated in the recent enthusiasm for a so-called microgenetic method (e.g., Kuhn, García-Mila, Zohar, & Anderson, 1995; Siegler, 1996) as a method that offers "a direct means for studying cognitive development" (Siegler & Crowley, 1991, p. 606). In this approach, an intensive trial-by-trial analysis reduces the very notion of development to the molecular bedrock of visible behavioral differences as they appear across learning trials.

It is important to recognize that the aim of Step 1 is to drive out interpretations from the common-sense phenomena under investigation. Under the objectivist theme, common-sense observation is error laden and it is only through ever more careful neutral observation that science can eliminate this error and ultimately arrive at the elementary bedrock that constitutes the level of fact or data.

Step 2: Causal Explanation. Step 2 of mechanical explanation begins to move inquiry into the second compartment of compartmentalized science—explanation. Step 2 consists of the instruction to find the relations among the elements described in Step 1. More specifically, given our objects of study—behavior and behavior change—this step directs inquiry to locate antecedents. These antecedents, when they meet certain criteria of necessity and sufficiency, will be termed *causes* and the discovery of cause defines explanation. The antecedents are also often referred to as *mechanisms*, but the meaning is identical.

This is the most extraordinary feature of the whole narrative. The word *explanation* comes to be defined as antecedent-consequent relation, or the efficient-material cause of the object of inquiry, and *science* comes to be defined as the (causal) explanation of natural phenomena. It is critically important to remember here that Aristotle (Randall, 1960) had earlier produced a story of scientific explanation that entailed a complementary relation among four types of explanation. Two of these were causal explanations (i.e., antecedent material and efficient causes). Two, however, were explanations according to the pattern, organization, or form of the object of inquiry. Aristotle's *formal* (i.e., the form or organization of the object of inquiry) and *final* (i.e., the end or goal of the object of inquiry) explanations were explanations that made the object of inquiry intelligible and gave reasons for the nature and functioning of the object. Today, the structure of the atom, the structure of DNA, the structure of the solar system, and the structure of the universe are all familiar examples of formal pattern principles drawn from the natural sciences. Kinship structures, mental structures, mental organization, dynamic systems, attachment behavior systems, structures of language, ego and superego, dynamisms, schemes, operations, and cognitive structures are familiar examples of formal pattern principles drawn from the human sciences. Similarly, reference to the sequence and directionality found in the second law of thermodynamics, self-organizing systems, the equilibration process or reflective abstraction, the orthogenetic principle, or the epigenetic principle are all examples of final pattern principles.

Both formal and final pattern principles entail interpretations that make the phenomena under investigation intelligible. Both, within the Aristotelian (Randall, 1960) relational scheme, constitute legitimate explanations. However, within the split story of mechanical explanation, as guided by reductionism and objectivism, formal and final principles completely lose any explanatory status. At best, within the mechanical story, they may reappear in the descriptive compartment as mere summary statements of the underlying molecular descriptive Real discussed in Step 1.

Step 3: Induction Of Interpretation-Free Hypotheses, Theories, And Laws.
Step 3 of mechanical explanation installs induction as the foundational logic of science. Step 3 establishes the prescription that ultimate explanations in science are found in fixed, unchanging laws and these are to be inductively derived as empirical generalizations from the repeated observation of cause-effect relations found in Step 2. Weak generalizations from Step 2 regularities constitute interpretation-free hypotheses. Stronger generalizations constitute interpretation-free theoretical propositions. Theoretical propositions joined as logical conjunctions (i.e., *and* connections) constitute interpretation-free theories. Laws represent the strongest and final inductions.

Deduction later re-enters modernity's story of science as a split-off heuristic method of moving from inductively derived hypotheses and theoretical propositions to further empirical observations. When later editions of the story introduced a Hypothetico-Deductive Method, it was simply more variation on the same theme. The hypothesis of hypothetico has nothing to do with interpretation, but is simply a data-driven empirical generalization that then serves as a major premise in a formal deductive argument. Similarly, when instrumentalism moved away from the Hypothetico-Deductive stance to the employment of models, models themselves functioned merely as the same type of interpretation-free heuristic devices.

Another important variation—but a variation nevertheless—on this same theme was called the *covering law model* of scientific explanation. This was introduced by Carl Hempel (1942, 1967) and became the prototype of all later explanations formulated within this language game (cf. Suppe, 1977). The covering law model was particularly important for developmental inquiry because it treated historical events as analogous to physical events in the sense that earlier events were considered the causal antecedents of later events (Ricoeur, 1984).

Here, then, is the basic outline of the quest for absolute certainty according to modernity's story of scientific methodology: Step 1, reduce to the objective (interpretation-free) observable foundation; Step 2, find the causes; Step 3, induce the law. As noted, variations appear throughout history. In fact, it would be misleading not to acknowledge that *probability* has replaced *certainty* as the favored lexical item in the story as it is told today. Indeed, induction is itself statistical and probabilistic in nature. However, this change represents much more style than substance, as the aim remains to move toward 100% probability, thereby arriving at certainty or its closest approximation. This type of fallibilistic stance continues to pit doubt against certainty as competing alternatives, rather than understanding doubt and certainty as a dialectic, framed by the concept of plausibility.

More generally, all of the variations that have been introduced since the origin of Newtonian explanation—including those formulated under the methodological banners of neopositivism, instrumentalism, conventionalism, and functionalism—have in no way changed the basic themes. To a significant degree, we remain prisoners of the mechanical language game.

Recognizing that we remain prisoners of neopositivism's language game does not mean that there has been any lack of critics of this narrative. The movement from Leibniz to Kant to Hegel—the whole German Enlightenment—along with the later neo-Kantian revival can be seen as an attempt to heal the Cartesian splitting found in foundationalism, materialism, and objectivism. This critical effort sought to heal fundamental splits by recasting the dichotomous bifurcations found, for example, in subject versus object, mind versus body, cause versus reason, and interpretation versus observation, as dialectic complementary reflections of the same underlying identity. However, until the 1950s these and other critiques—including Dewey's (1929/1960) attack on certainty in his work entitled *The Quest for Certainty*—

had little influence in the natural sciences or in the line of psychology that locates itself in the natural sciences.

Hermeneutic Understanding

Historically, a contrasting language game was developed parallel to and as a reaction against neopositivism's quest for reductionistic causal explanation. This alternative picture arose within the hermeneutic tradition and it championed understanding, in contrast to explanation, as the methodology of science, or at least as the scientific methodology for the behavioral and social sciences, including the humanities.

Interpretation. Broadly, *hermeneutics* is the theory or philosophy of the interpretation of meaning. Hermeneutics elevates to a heroic role the very concept that mechanical explanation casts as demon error: interpretation. For our purposes, we can pass by the periods of classical, biblical, and romantic hermeneutics and even pass by Vico's historical hermeneutics. Our brief focus here is on the effort that Dilthey (1972) promoted at the turn of the present century to construct a methodology for the social sciences. This was termed the methodology of understanding. Within this methodology, *understanding* operates as an epistemological rather than a psychological concept and, most importantly, interpretation operates as the methodology that results in understanding.

Action Theory. As a methodology of the social and behavioral sciences, understanding is closely related to action theory. Action theory, which, lest we forget, characterizes Piaget's (1952, 1954, 1962) work, is a person-centered approach to inquiry into processes and operations of the living embodied agent (Overton, 1999). Action theory stands in contrast to variable-centered approaches to human behavior, which are externalist and event-oriented in their focus. Ricoeur (1991) clearly outlined—in the context of Wittgenstein's (1958/1953) language games—the distinction between variable-centered events and person-centered actions and in this outline suggested the distinction between explanation and understanding:

> It is not in the same language game that we speak of events [variables] occurring in nature or of actions performed by people. For, to speak of events [variables], we enter a language game including notions like cause, law, fact, explanation and so on.... It is ... in another language game and in another conceptual network that we can speak of human action [i.e., a person-centered frame]. For, if we have begun to speak in terms of action, we shall continue to speak in terms of projects, intentions, motives, reasons for acting, agents [interpretation, understanding], and so forth. (Ricoeur, 1991, pp. 132–133)

Within this dichotomous situation, *Verstehen*, or understanding, was conceived of as a competing alternative account of human functioning to that found in the natural sciences of the inorganic world. This account relies heavily on the intentional quality of action. To intend, is to do something "for the sake of." Intention thus implies order and direction and a methodology designed to account for action must entail inferences about patterns of action and, more generally, teleology. Note here, however, that this focus on action patterns, action organization, or the form of the object of inquiry is little different from Aristotle's formal and final explanations as they were designed to make the object of inquiry intelligible and gave reasons for the nature and functioning of the object.

At this point, a dichotomy of two competing alternative accounts of human functioning and human development thus stood as guardians against Cartesian anxiety, the natural science game of Aristotelian (some would say Galilean) efficient and material cause, and the human science game of Aristotelian formal and final understanding. Efficient and material causal explanation stands squarely committed to a materialist foundationalism. Formal and final pattern understanding, although more ambiguous about foundationalism, was sufficiently identified with an absolute idealism to assuage those who might fear a fall into the terror of relativism.

TRANSITION TOWARDS A NEW METHODOLOGY: THE 1950S

The concepts of *cause* and *interpretation* became the central battlegrounds in this struggle between explanation and understanding. Into the early 1950s it seemed increasingly clear that, at least as far as psychology was concerned, the reductionistic causal explanation of neopositivism-conventionalism-instrumentalism-functionalism had won the day as the methodology of choice. In fact, this increasingly anachronistic methodology, even today, continues to be used as virtually the exclusive doctoral training paradigm in most domains of psychology, including developmental psychology.

However, despite popular stories about the balanced culture and political climate of the 1950s, these years marked the beginning of an explosion of new ideas concerning scientific methodology and the implications of these ideas have yet to work themselves completely to fruition. These ideas arose from diverse narrative streams including analytic philosophy, the history and philosophy of the natural sciences, the philosophy of behavioral and social sciences, and hermeneutics. Despite their often complementary and reciprocally supportive nature, these narratives have frequently failed to connect or enter into a common dialogue, yet their cumulative effect has been to forge at least the outline of an integrated story of scientific methodology that moves beyond the split Cartesian dichotomies of natural science versus social science and explanation versus understanding. This language game, which might be called the *amodern* (Latour, 1993) story of scientific methodology, articulates and elaborates a relational perspective in which these antinomies are coordinated as distinct moments of an identical underlying activity termed empirical science.

Let me briefly point to some of the central characters in the 1950s revolution. First, representing analytic philosophy, there was the later Wittgenstein, whose seminal book *Philosophical Investigations* was originally published in 1953, and following from this point there was Wittgenstein's pupil Georg Henrik von Wright (e.g., 1971) as well as Hilary Putnam (e.g., 1987). Representing hermeneutics, there was Hans-Georg Gadamer, whose *Truth and Method* was first published in 1960, and later Jürgen Habermas (e.g., 1984), Richard Bernstein (e.g., 1983), and Paul Ricoeur (e.g., 1984). Representing the natural sciences were Steven Toulmin, whose *Philosophy of Science* was published in 1953, and N. R. Hanson, whose *Patterns of Discovery* was published in 1958. These were later followed by Thomas Kuhn (1962), Imre Lakatos (e.g., 1970), Larry Laudan (e.g., 1977), and, most recently, Bruno Latour (e.g., 1993). Representing the social sciences, Elizabeth Anscombe's *Intention* was published in 1957, as were William Dray's *Laws and Explanation in History* (1957), and Charles Frankel's *Explanation and Interpretation in History* (1957). These were followed by Peter Winch, whose *The Idea of a Social Science and Its Relation to Philosophy* was published in 1958, and later Charles Taylor (e.g., 1964).

RELATIONAL SCIENTIFIC METHODOLOGY

The story of this outline of an integrated relational methodology of the sciences is obviously detailed and complex (see Overton, 1998). Here I will outline the outline by focusing on a few central figures and their contributions. These include Wittgenstein's *Philosophical Investigations* (1958), Gadamer's *Truth and Method* (1989), Hanson's *Patterns of Discovery* (1958), von Wright's *Explanation and Understanding* (1971), Ricoeur's *Time and Narrative* (1984), and Latour's *We Have Never Been Modern* (1993).

Wittgenstein (1958) and Gadamer (1989) provided the basic scaffolding for the construction of this relational methodology. Wittgenstein's fundamental contribution entailed opening the door to the recognition that it is a profound error to treat the activities of science as providing veridical descriptions of a foundational Real. More positively, Wittgenstein's contribution lies in his suggestion that science is the product of some of the same human actions that underlie the conceptual constructions of our form of life, or *Lebenswelt*. Gadamer's contribution was a systematic demonstration that this move beyond objectivism and foundationalism did not necessitate a slide into relativism and Cartesian anxiety.

Hanson's (1958) analysis of the history of the physical sciences was significantly influenced by Toulmin (1953) and by the later Wittgenstein (1958). In this work, Hanson drew three conclusions about the actual practice of the physical sciences as distinct from the classical language game in which they are described. These conclusions themselves provided a blueprint for the new relational methodology. The conclusions were that: (a) there is no absolute demarcation in the physical sciences between interpretative theory and observation or between interpretative theory and facts or data, a notion that was captured in his now-famous aphorism, "all data are theory laden"; (b) scientific explanation consists of the discovery of patterns, as well as the discovery of causes (see also Toulmin, 1953, 1961); and (c) the logic of science is neither a split-off deductive logic nor a split-off inductive logic, but is rather abductive (retroductive) in nature.

Interpretation and Observation

Hanson's (1958) first conclusion, that "all data are theory laden," became the core principle of the new relational methodology. The idea here of a reciprocal complementarity—a dialectic—between interpretation and observation heals the Cartesian split and thereby destroys any possibility of foundationalism or reductionism. Interpretation and observation, along with other fundamental bipolar concepts, cease being competing alternatives or exclusive dichotomies. Interpretation and observation are relational concepts, not the names for split-off natural entities. They are relational concepts in the same sense that Hegel's (1807) master-slave dialectic entails relational concepts, where it is impossible to define freedom without reference to constraints or to define constraints without reference to freedom.

Interpretation and observation are relational concepts in exactly the sense that Escher's famous sketch "Drawing Hands" is relational, as shown in Fig. 2.1. Here, as I have discussed elsewhere (Overton, 1998, 1999), at any moment the relational stance operates in a fashion roughly analogous to the sketch, in which a left and a right hand are shown in a posture such that each hand is simultaneously drawing and being drawn by the other. The hands are identical to each other in the sense that each is drawing and each is being drawn. At the same time, each hand preserves its own identity in the sense that there are distinctly both a left and a right hand. In this relation, neither is foundational and yet each maintains a distinct identity. Having taken this stance, there can be no question about which of a pair of bipolar concepts is more basic or which of the two is foundational for the other. At the same time, the relational stance allows the investigator to take the point of view from the pole of a focus on either interpretational features

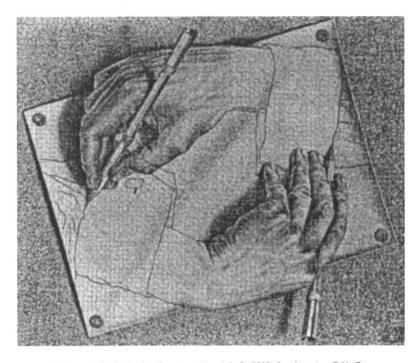

FIG. 2.1. M. C. Escher's "Drawing Hands" © 2002 Cordon Art B.V. Baarn-
Holland. All rights reserved.

(e.g., Escher's left hand) or observational features (e.g., Escher's right
hand). The *or* in this latter case is the inclusive *or* rather than the exclusive
or of the either-or dichotomy. In other words, the inclusive *or* implies that,
given the unity of the system under examination, one line of sight is as valid
as any other line of sight. Taking one or another point of view constitutes a
starting point that will eventually and necessarily implicate the others. To
ask which hand is causing the drawing or is the mechanism of drawing and
which hand is being drawn is senseless. Similarly, to ask whether the right
or left is more Real, more foundational, is senseless. Hegel (1807, 1830) referred to this flow of categories where rigid either-or splits are broken
down as the identity of opposites. Left hand and right hand are opposites
and yet each defines the other. We can explore their oppositeness by taking
a particular point of view—by standing at the left hand or standing at the
right hand—but a point of view or standpoint is understood in the context of
the acceptance that there is no ontological split. Disconnected items represent an abstraction that may prove useful for certain human purposes of inquiry, but such points of view in no way deny the underlying holism.

This feature of the new relational methodology was further supported
and extended by two features of Gadamer's (1989) philosophical hermeneu-

tics. The first was his insistence that the alternating to-and-fro motion exhibited in play presents a favorable ontological alternative to Cartesian
foundationalism. It is this ontological theme of to-and-fro movement that
grounds and sustains the relational methodology. As a consequence, scientific activity, regardless of whether that activity is in the natural or the behavioral and social sciences, becomes grounded in the to-and-fro (left hand-
right hand) movement of interpretation-observation.

Gadamer's (1989) second contribution consists of his articulation, following Heidegger (1962), of the hermeneutic circle. In this articulation, the hermeneutic circle comes to describe the basic form of how interpretation and
observation move to and fro, that is, the circle describes the basic structure
of the new scientific methodology.

Inquiry moves in a circular movement from phenomenological, common-
sense understanding of an object of inquiry to the highly reflective and organized knowledge that constitutes scientific knowledge. The whole, the general field of inquiry, such as human development, is initially approached with
the meanings, or prejudices, that constitute both common-sense observations and background presuppositions. These are the initial meanings of
what hermeneutics terms the *pre-understanding*. These anticipatory meanings, called "the horizon of a particular present" by Gadamer (1989, p. 306),
are projected onto the phenomenon of inquiry. As a consequence, they form
an early stage in inquiry. However, the object of inquiry is not merely a fig-
ment of projection. The object of inquiry is itself an internally coherent whole
and, consequently, it reciprocally operates as a corrective source of further
projections of meaning. In this circle, interpretation identifies what will and
what will not ultimately count as observations and observations determine
what will and will not count as interpretation. Interpretation without observation is empty; observation without interpretation is blind.

Through this circle of projection (interpretation) and correction (observation, i.e., Escherian left hand-right hand), inquiry advances. Importantly,
the notion of an advance or progress in knowledge is appropriate here because the hermeneutic circle is never a closed circle. The hermeneutic circle represents (following Hegel's [1807, 1830] dialectic) the open cycle
whose action creates a continuing directional spirality to knowing. As
Gadamer (1989) stated, "The circle is constantly expanding, since the concept of the whole is relative, and being integrated in ever larger contexts always affects the understanding of the individual part" (p. 190).

It was the dialectic cycle of interpretation and observation that later
grounded and sustained Thomas Kuhn's (1962) notion of interpretative par-
adigms in the natural sciences and Lakatos' (1970) and Laudan's (1977) later
discussions of the centrality of ontological and epistemological background
presuppositions in any research program or tradition. It is the failure to
play this cycle game that accounts for the joy among later postmodern

deconstructionists in their belief that the overthrow of interpretation-free observational science meant the nihilistic freedom of absolute relativism. It is the failure to play the cycle game that also accounts for the Cartesian terror, followed by dogmatic reactionary criticisms, among many natural scientists who came to fear that the radical postmodernists might be right.

Causality and Action Patterns

Hanson's (1958) second conclusion—that pattern and cause have always operated as explanations in the physical sciences—subverts the split stories of a clear-cut line of demarcation between the natural and social sciences. If natural science inquiry has, throughout the modern period, centrally involved both pattern and causal explanations, then understanding and explanation need not be dichotomous, competing, alternative language games. Pattern or action-pattern explanation, which entails intention and reasons, and causal explanation, which entails necessary and sufficient conditions, here become—as with Aristotle—relational concepts (Escherian left and right hands). Explanation then, defined as "intelligible ordering" (Hanson, 1958), becomes the superordinate concept that joins dynamic patterns and cause.

The challenge within this relational methodology is to establish a justifiable coordination of the two modes of explanation. Von Wright (1971) presented a richly detailed and complex effort in this direction and Ricoeur (1984) later built upon and expanded this effort. Both focused on explanation in the behavioral and social sciences.

Von Wright (1971) and Ricoeur (1984) each suggested that the coordination be made along the lines of an internal-external dimension. *Internal* here refers to the domain of the psychological person-agent or psychological action system. *External* refers to movements or states. Following from a critical distinction made earlier by Anscombe (1957), any given behavior can be considered internal under one description and external under another description. Thus, any specific behavior may be, to quote von Wright, "intentionalistically understood as being an action or otherwise aiming at an achievement, or . . . as a 'purely natural' event, i.e., in the last resort muscular activity" (p. 128).

Within this framework, causal explanations, understood as Humean causes defined by the logical independence or contingency relationship between cause and effect, account for external movements and states. Action-pattern explanation (i.e., action, action systems, intention, reason) accounts for the meaning of an act.

The situation here is actually quite clear if one reflects on it for a moment. Imagine the following behavior for two figures, A and B. Figure A moves across a space and a part of Figure A comes into contact with Figure B. In this case, there are states and movements and causal explanation is quite appropriate. The intervening states that identify the movement can readily be considered a series of sufficient and necessary conditions leading to the last state in the series. This can even be demonstrated in a true experimental design.

Although this explanation might be satisfactory if the figures were inorganic objects, the situation changes when the figures are identified as people. In this latter case, it is unlikely that one will be satisfied with the causal explanation because no real psychological sense of the meaning of these movements has been provided. If, however, the figures are identified as people and I further indicate that the movement of Figure A to B is the action of a man who walks across the room and caresses his wife's cheek, explanation begins to operate in the context of action, intention, reasons, and, broadly speaking, meaning. The two moments of explanation—causal explanation on the one hand and action-pattern explanation on the other—explain different phenomena. They have distinct referents: movement and states in causal explanation and meaning in action-pattern explanation. Because they have different referents, different *explananda*, they are compatible. However, they do not replace each other. That is, speaking of reductionism, one cannot be reduced to the other. Action is not a cause of movement, but rather a part of movement. Cause cannot explain action, but action is required to initiate movement (von Wright, 1971).

There are a number of implications that can be drawn from this analysis of the coordination of explanatory types. One is that it demonstrates that, in principle, it is not possible to explain phenomena of consciousness via brain or neurobiological explanations. Consciousness is internal as defined above; consciousness is about psychological meaning and must be explained by action-pattern explanation. The brain is external; it is about states and movements, not psychological meaning. Neurobiological causal explanation complements action-pattern explanation, but can never present the mechanism of consciousness.

A second important implication is that, when one considers the distinction between person-centered and variable inquiry (Overton, 1999), it becomes clear that action-pattern explanations are the focus of the former and causal explanations the focus of the latter. Piaget's (1952, 1954, 1962) theory, for example, is a person-centered theory. Person (child-adult), agent (system, i.e., the epistemological subject), action, embodiment, and intention are core concepts that identify Piaget's focus on development. Piaget, indeed, at least implicitly recognized the coordination of explanatory types and appropriately focused his efforts on explanation via formal action pattern (schemes, operations) and final action pattern (the equilibration process, reflective abstraction). Many, if not all, of the misunderstandings of Piagetian theory that Lourenço and Machado (1996) articulated are derived from the fact that attacks on Piagetian theory have invariably come from those who remain locked into the positivist story of exclusive causal explanation.

There are other implications to be drawn from a relational coordination of explanatory types, but another important question needs to be addressed here. This is the question of how exactly one would go about creating action-pattern explanation. Universally, students are instructed in how to work with causal explanation at least from the time they enter Psychology 101: Learn experimental research design, do an experiment! When it can be shown, under controlled conditions, that an added stimulus (antecedent, independent variable) invariably leads to the behavior of interest (consequent, dependent variable), this demonstrates that the stimulus is the sufficient cause of the event. This provides the rationale for training and enrichment experiments. On the other hand, when it can be shown, under controlled conditions, that, when a stimulus is subtracted or removed and the event does not occur, this demonstrates that the stimulus is the necessary cause of the event. This provides the rationale for deprivation experiments. Correlations are also discussed in this context and, although it is made explicit that correlation is not causation, the same message treats correlation as a step in the direction of causal explanation.

However, what are inductees into scientific method told about how to work with action-pattern forms of explaining? Generally, nothing. Sometimes, especially if the instructor values the story of modernity, students are told that it is a bad thing and to stay away from it because it involves interpretation and interpretation is a lot like speculation and speculation leads to mystery, miracles, spiritualism, and subjectivist relativism. Yet the student is virtually never told how to deal with action-pattern explanation if they choose to. I provide instruction in action-pattern explanation here, but to articulate the specifics of action-pattern explanation, but it is first necessary to turn to Hanson's (1958) third conclusion about the actual operation of science.

Abduction/Transcendental Argument

Hanson (1958) concluded that neither split-off induction nor split-off deduction constitutes the logic of science. Each of these enters the operation of science, but Hanson argued that the overarching logic of scientific activity is abduction. Abduction (also called *retroduction*) was originally described by the pragmatist philosopher Charles Sanders Pierce (1992). In a contemporary version, this logic is defined as "inference to the best explanation" (Fumerton, 1993; Harman, 1965).

Abduction operates by arranging the observation under consideration and all background ideas (including all metatheoretical assumptions and theoretical models) as two Escherian hands (Fig. 2.1). The possible coordination of the two is explored by asking what, given the background ideas, must necessarily be assumed in order to have that observation. The inference to, or interpretation of, what must, in the context of background ideas, necessarily be assumed then constitutes the explanation of the phenomenon. This explanation can then be assessed empirically to ensure its empirical valitity (i.e., its support and scope of application). An important relational feature of this logic is that it assumes the form of the familiar hermeneutic circle by moving from the phenomenological level (the common-sense object) to explanation and back in an ever-widening cycle. The difference between this and the previously described hypothetical-deductive explanation is that in abduction, all background ideas, including metatheoretical assumptions, form a necessary feature of the process and the abductive explanations themselves become a part of the ever-widening corpus of background ideas, as shown in Fig. 2.2.

The basic logic of abduction operates as follows: (a) Step 1 entails the description of some highly reliable phenomenological observation (i.e., O is the case); (b) for Step 2, with O as the explanandum, an inference or interpretation is made to an action-pattern explanation (E) resulting in the conditional proposition "If E is the case, then O is expected"; (c) Step 3 entails the conclusion that E is indeed the case. Thus, the logical form of the argument is:

1. O (Phenomenological observation) is the case.
2. If E (action-pattern explanation) is the case, then O is expected.
3. Therefore, E is the case.

Examples of this action-pattern explanation or, more specifically, the one I describe next, are found throughout any work that takes a person-centered approach to developmental inquiry. Piaget's (e.g., 1965) work is particularly rich in abductive explanation. Consider the following example: There is the phenomenal observation (O) that it is the case that certain persons (i.e., children generally beyond the approximate age of 7 years) understand that concepts remain quantitatively invariant despite changes in qualitative appearances (conservation). Piaget then inferred a certain type of action system (E) having specified features including reversibility (concrete operations), thus, the conditional "If concrete operations (E), then conservation (O) is what would be expected." The conclusion, given the O, is: "Therefore, concrete operations explains the understanding of conservation."

In fact, many of Piaget's synchronous explanations are of this type, but so too is his main diachronic (i.e., developmental) explanation. Here, given the phenomenological observation that novel acts appear across time, Piaget inferred a principle, reflective abstraction-equilibration, that demonstrates how this transformed or emergent action is possible.

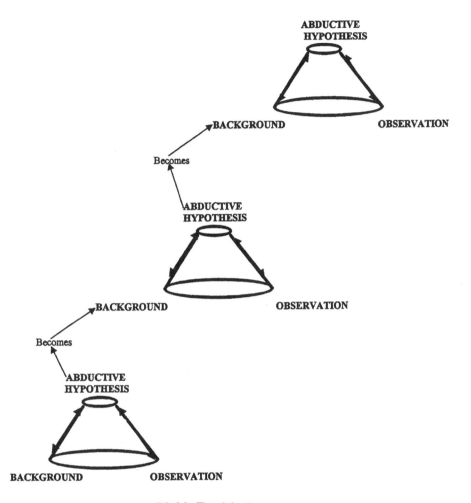

FIG. 2.2. The abductive process.

As Fumerton (1993) pointed out, it is obvious that, if the conditional in Step 2 is read as material implication, the argument would be hopeless because it would then describe the fallacy of the affirmed consequent (i.e., it would be viciously circular). Quite correctly, Fumerton recognized that the "If . . . then" relation asserts some other sort of connection. Specifically, the connection is one of meaning relevance between E and O, where relevance is defined in terms of the intelligibility of the relation between E and O (Overton, 1990).

It is also the case that there must be criteria established that would allow us to choose among alternative Es, the best E. This is no major hurdle, however, because many of the criteria for theory or explanation selection that have been available under the traditional science language game can, with profit, be used here. These criteria include the scope of the explanation, the explanation's depth, coherence, and logical consistency, the extent to which the explanation reduces the proportion of unsolved to solved conceptual or empirical problems in a domain (Laudan, 1977), and, last but not least, the explanation's empirical support and empirical fruitfulness. Note here that scope, empirical support, and fruitfulness themselves bring the circle back to the observational world and thus keep the cycle open. Action-pattern explanation or theory, in fact, determines what will count as further observations and the empirical task is to go into the world to discover whether these observations can be found. Thus, the cycle continually moves from common-sense observations and background presuppositions to action-pattern explanations, returning then to more highly refined observations and back again to explanation.

A form of abduction was brought to prominence by Kant (1781) and has recently been elaborated by Charles Taylor (1995; see also Grayling, 1993; Hundert, 1989) and used in the arena of cognitive development by Russell (1996). This is the transcendental argument and its form is:

1. (We) have a (reliable) phenomenological experience with characteristic a.
2. (We) could not have an experience with characteristic a unless (our) consciousness had feature b.
3. Therefore, (our) consciousness necessarily has feature b.

The transcendental argument is designed to answer "How possible?" questions (von Wright, 1971) with respect to consciousness or psyche. In other words, given some highly reliable phenomenological observation or phenomenological experience such as conservation, what must we necessarily assume (i.e., what kind of action-pattern explanation) about the nature of our consciousness? What are the necessary conditions of intelligibility? Here, again, we begin with the explanandum, make a regressive argument to the effect that a stronger conclusion must be so if the observation about experience is to be possible (and being so, it must be possible). This then leads to the stronger conclusion.

This, then, is the answer to the question of how one does pattern explanation in the behavioral and social sciences. The procedure for action-pattern explanation is found in abduction and the rules of the transcendental argument, and in the criteria that establish a particular abductive transcendental explanation as the best or most plausible of alternative explanations. Rozeboom (1997) provided a richly detailed operational analysis of this process, along with practical advice on statistical and research strategies associated with the process.

In conclusion, let me note that there is much more to the story of the new relational methodology and much of this is given in the detailed elaboration of research methods and measurement models as the specific techniques for designing, conducting, and evaluating the empirical inquiry that adjudicates best explanation. Within this relational context, where interpretation and observation function as a complementary identity of opposites, the broad question of the validity of our scientific observations becomes a central issue. Validity has always been a concern of scientific methodology, but in the story of empirical science as narrated through the imagery of modernity, validity had nothing to do with interpreted meaning. In that story, validity became a content issue dependent to a great degree on the outcome of experimental design. In the relational story, the validity of our scientific observations, or what Messick (1995) called "score validity," becomes a complementary process involving, on the one Escherian hand, the distinctive features of construct validity as it involves interpretative meaning and, on the other Escherian hand, content validity as it involves denotative meaning. This elaboration, however, takes us away from the primary purpose of this essay.

I hope that the relational themes of the hermeneutic cycle of interpretation-observation, the dialectic of causal and action-pattern explanation, and the procedural cycle of the transcendental argument suggest the possibility of producing a relatively stable organized body of empirical scientific knowledge that avoids both the constriction of absolute certainty and the Cartesian terror of absolute relativism. Latour (1993), in his analyses of scientific activity, concluded that the language games of both modernity and postmodernism distort the meaning of the practice of science. Latour maintained that scientific activity, like other activities, most adequately resides in a stable, changing world of relative relativism and this is the world of the relational methodology.

AUTHOR NOTE

Department of Psychology, Temple University, 1701 N. 13th St., Rm. 567, Philadelphia, PA, 19122-0685, USA.

REFERENCES

Anscombe, G. E. M. (1957). *Intention*. Oxford: Basil Blackwell.

Bernstein, R. J. (1983). *Beyond objectivism and relativism: Science, hermeneutics, and praxis*. Philadelphia: University of Pennsylvania Press.

Bunge, M., & Ardila, R. (1987). *Philosophy of science*. New York: Springer.

Descartes, R. (1969). *The philosophical works of Descartes* (Vols. 1–2, E. S. Haldane & G. R. T. Ross, Trans.). Cambridge, England: Cambridge University Press.

Dewey, J. (1929/1960). *The quest for certainty.* New York: G. P. Putnam's Sons.

Dilthey, W. (1972). The rise of hermeneutics. *New Literary History, 3,* 229–244.

Dray, W. H. (1957). *Laws and explanation in history.* Oxford, England: Oxford University Press.

Frankel, C. (1957). Explanation and interpretation in history. *Philosophy of Science, 24,* 137–155.

Fumerton, R. (1993). Inference to the best explanation. In J. Dancy & E. Sosa (Eds.), *A companion to epistemology* (pp. 207–209). Cambridge, MA: Basil Blackwell.

Gadamer, H. G. (1989). *Truth and method* (2nd ed., J. Weinsheimer & D. Marshall, Trans.). New York: Crossroad. (Original work published 1960)

Gottlieb, G., Wahlsten, D., & Lickliter, R. (1998). The significance of biology for human development: A developmental psychobiological systems view. In R. M. Lerner (Ed.), *Theoretical models of human development: Vol. 1. Handbook of child psychology* (5th ed., pp. 233–273). New York: Wiley.

Grayling, A. C. (1993). Transcendental arguments. In J. Dancy & E. Sosa (Eds.), *A companion to epistemology* (pp. 506–509). Cambridge, MA: Basil Blackwell.

Habermas, J. (1984). *The theory of communicative action. Vol. 1. Reason and the rationalization of society* (T. McCarthy, Trans.). Boston: Beacon Press.

Hanson, N. R. (1958). *Patterns of discovery.* New York: Cambridge University Press.

Harman, G. (1965). The inference to the best explanation. *Philosophical Review, 74,* 88–95.

Hegel, G. W. F. (1807). *Phenomenology of spirit.* New York: Oxford University Press. (trans. A. V. Miller).

Hegel, G. W. F. (1830). *Hegel's logic: Being part one of the encyclopedia of the philosophical sciences.* New York: Oxford University Press. (trans. W. Wallace).

Heidegger, M. (1962). *Being and time.* New York: Harper and Row. (translated by J. Macquarrie and E. Robinson)

Hempel, C. G. (1942). The function of general laws in history. *The Journal of Philosophy, 39,* 39–48.

Hempel, C. G. (1967). Scientific explanation. In S. Morgenbesser (Ed.), *Philosophy of science today* (pp. 79–88). New York: Basic Books.

Hundert, E. M. (1989). *Philosophy, psychiatry, and neuroscience: Three approaches to the mind.* New York: Oxford University Press.

Kant, I. (1781). *Critique of pure reason* (trans. F. Max Muller). New York: Anchor Books edition, 1966.

Kuhn, D., García-Mila, M., Zohar, A., & Andersen, C. (1995). Strategies of knowledge acquisition. *Monographs of the Society for Research in Child Development, 60*(4, Serial number 245).

Kuhn, T. S. (1962). *The structure of scientific revolutions.* Chicago, IL: University of Chicago Press.

Laing, R. D. (1960). *The divided self.* New York: Pantheon Books.

Lakatos, I. (1970). Falsification and the methodology of scientific research programmes. In I. Lakatos & A. Musgrave (Eds.), *Criticism and the growth of knowledge* (pp. 91–196). New York: Cambridge University Press.

Latour, B. (1993). *We have never been modern.* Cambridge, MA: Harvard University Press.

Laudan, L. (1977). *Progress and its problems: Towards a theory of scientific growth.* Berkeley: University of California Press.

Lourenço, O., & Machado, A. (1996). In defense of Piaget's theory: A reply to 10 common criticisms. *Psychological Review, 101,* 143–164.

Messick, S. (1995). Validity of psychological assessment: Validation of inferences from persons' responses and performances as scientific inquiry into score meaning. *American Psychologist, 50,* 741–749.

Overton, W. F. (1990). Competence and procedures: Constraints on the development of logical reasoning. In W. F. Overton (Ed.), *Reasoning, necessity, and logic: Developmental perspectives* (pp. 1–32). Hillsdale, NJ: Lawrence Erlbaum Associates.

Overton, W. F. (1998). Developmental psychology: Philosophy, concepts, and methodology. In R. M. Lerner (Ed.), *Theoretical models of human development: Vol. 1. Handbook of child psychology* (5th ed., pp. 107–188). New York: Wiley.

Overton, W. F. (1999, September). *The growing mind: Action, agency, embodiment, and metaphor.* Paper presented at the German (-speaking-) Psychological Society EPSY/PADPSY Conference, Fribourg, Switzerland.

Piaget, J. (1952). *The origins of intelligence in children.* New York: W. W. Norton & Company.

Piaget, J. (1954). *The construction of reality in the child.* New York: Basic Books.

Piaget, J. (1962). *Play, dreams and imitation in childhood.* New York: W. W. Norton & Company.

Piaget, J. (1965). *The child's conception of number.* New York: W. W. Norton & Company.

Pierce, C. S. (1992). *Reasoning and the logic of things: The Cambridge Conference lectures of 1898.* Cambridge, MA: Harvard University Press.

Prosch, H. (1964). *The genesis of twentieth century philosophy.* New York: Doubleday.

Putnam, H. (1987). *The many faces of realism.* Cambridge, England: Cambridge University Press.

Putnam, H. (1990). *Realism with a human face.* Cambridge, MA: Harvard University Press.

Randall, J. H. (1960). *Aristotle.* New York: Columbia University Press.

Ricoeur, P. (1984). *Time and narrative* (Vol. 1, K. McLaughlin & D. Pellauer, Trans.). Chicago: University of Chicago Press. (Original work published 1983)

Ricoeur, P. (1991). *From text to action: Essays in hermeneutics* (Vol. 2, K. Blamey & J. B. Thompson, Trans.). Evanston, IL: Northwestern University Press. (Original work published 1986)

Rozeboom, W. W. (1997). Good science is abductive, not hypothetico-deductive. In L. L. Harlow, S. A. Mulaik, & J. H. Steiger (Eds.), *What if there were no significance tests?* (pp. 335–391). Mahwah, NJ: Lawrence Erlbaum Associates.

Russell, J. (1996). *Agency: Its role in mental development.* East Sussex, England: Lawrence Erlbaum Associates (UK), Taylor, & Francis.

Searle, J. (1992). *The rediscovery of the mind.* Cambridge, MA: MIT Press.

Shanon, B. (1993). *The representational and the presentational: An essay on cognition and the study of mind.* New York: Harvester Wheatsheaf.

Siegler, R. S. (1996). *Emerging minds: The process of change in children's thinking.* New York: Oxford University Press.

Siegler, R. S., & Crowley, K. (1991). The microgenetic method: A direct means for studying cognitive development. *American Psychologist, 46,* 606–620.

Suppe, F. (Ed.). (1977). *The structure of scientific theories* (2nd ed.). Urbana: University of Illinois Press.

Taylor, C. (1964). *The explanation of behaviour.* New York: The Humanities Press.

Taylor, C. (1995). *Philosophical arguments.* Cambridge, MA: Harvard University Press.

Toulmin, S. (1953). *The philosophy of science.* New York: Harper & Row.

Toulmin, S. (1961). *Foresight and understanding.* New York: Harper & Row.

Toulmin, S. (1990). *Cosmopolis: The hidden agenda of modernity.* Chicago, IL: University of Chicago Press.

von Wright, G. H. (1971). *Explanation and understanding.* Ithaca, NY: Cornell University Press.

Winch, P. (1958). *The idea of a social science and its relation to philosophy.* London: Routledge & Kegan Paul.

Wittgenstein, L. (1958). *Philosophical investigations* (3rd ed., G. E. M. Anscombe, Trans.). Englewood Cliffs, NJ: Prentice-Hall. (Original work unpublished, first translation published 1953)

3

Evolution, Entrenchment, and Innateness

W. C. Wimsatt
The University of Chicago

INTRODUCTION

This is part of a larger project to reintegrate development into evolutionary theory, through models of generative developmental structure and their fitness consequences. It suggests handles on some problems in the biological and human sciences not solvable with or easily accessible to a genetic approach. I seek to generate an adequate model of cultural evolution—which must include or interface closely with a theory of cognitive development in the broadest sense, intersecting all cognitive, conative, and affective skills, and the domains of their employment, both throughout the life cycle, and in broader social, cultural, and institutional contexts. This approach also suggests a new and different approach to the phenomena that have motivated the innate-acquired distinction. Part I gives an orientation to generative entrenchment and to why it is so important to a theory of evolving systems. In Part II, I focus on the classical "innate-acquired" distinction and provide a new and richer account in terms of generative entrenchment of the phenomena invoked in its support. The new analysis is compared with traditional accounts of "innateness" as "genetic" or "canalized." I conclude that the old "innate-acquired" distinction should be retired, but its conceptual niche is not dispensable, and is fruitfully filled by the new concept.

PART I   THE EVOLUTION OF GENERATIVE SYSTEMS

Engineering a Dynamical Foundationalism

Consider a common observation from everyday engineering. Trying to re-build foundations after we have already constructed an edifice on them is demanding and dangerous work. It is demanding: Unless we do it just right, we'll bring the house down, and not be able to restore it on the new founda-tions. It is dangerous: the probability of doing just that seems very great, and there are seldom strong guarantees that we are doing it right. We are tempted to just "make the best of it," doing what we can to "patch" prob-lems at less fundamental levels. This is not just back-sliding. The difficulty of the task makes it well-founded advice. These are the phenomena to be explained and exploited. They are very general and have many and diverse consequences for the nature and possibility of change in complex systems.

This is as true for theories or for any complex functional structures—bio-logical, mechanical, conceptual, or normative—as it is for houses. This is why evolution proceeds mostly via a sequence of layered kluges. Scientists rarely do foundational work, save when their house threatens to come down about their ears. (Philosophers like to mess around with foundations, but usually when working on someone else's discipline!) Neurath's image of this activity as rebuilding the boat while we're in it is heroic. (Not an activity one recom-mends lightly!) If we must, actual revisions are preceded by all sorts of vicari-ous activity. We'd prefer to redesign a plan, rebuild only after we're satisfied with the revisions, keep in touch during the reconstruction for problems that inevitably come up, and move in only after the rebuilding is done—complete with local patches and in course corrections. Jokes about construction proj-ects executed by theoreticians, or architects who don't visit the site are le-gion—rich folk-wisdom about the difficulties of foundational revisions, or in getting from new foundations to the finished product.[1]

This bias against doing foundational work is a very general phenome-non. Big scientific revolutions are relatively rare for just that reason—the more fundamental the change, the less likely it will work, and the broader its effects; so the more work it will make for others, who therefore resist it

---

[1]We do sometimes have to live in the house while it is being rebuilt. But this only works be-cause the conceptual organization of science, and of engineering practice, is usually robust, modular, and local, each of which reduces generative entrenchment. Shaking (local) founda-tions usually doesn't bring the house down, and we still have a place to stand (on neighboring timbers) while we do it. For a sense of life at the critical edge, read Rhodes (1986) on revising the-ory and practice in the design, construction, and testing of the first nuclear reactor and atom bomb, or Feynman's view (Gleick, 1992) of the groping development of theory and computation at Los Alamos when they had to have accurate results without direct experiments.

actively. The last two facts are institutional, social, or social psychological, but the first two aren't. They are broad, robust, and deeply rooted logical, structural, and causal features of our world—unavoidable features of both material and abstract generative structures.

Major changes in perspective are rarer later in life.[2] We get more conservative as we age. Behavioral and mental habits "build up," and "increase in strength," as we add commitments and increasingly "channel" possibilities and choices. These marked metaphors delimit proto-theories likely to leave their issue in any future theoretical accounts. They will because they reflect deep truths about the characteristic architecture of our behavior. Biological evolution shows related features even more strongly and deeply than the cognitive or cultural realms. Von Baer's "law" that earlier developmental stages of diverse organisms look more alike than later ones is broadly true (with some revealing exceptions)[3] and reflects this deep structural truth. It is most fundamentally an expression of the evolutionary conservatism of earlier developmental features. More usually depends on them, so mutations affecting them are more likely to be strongly deleterious or lethal. So they persist relatively unchanged.

Differential dependencies of components in structures—causal or inferential—are inevitable in nature. Their natural elaboration generates foundational relationships. New systems in which some elements play a generative or foundational role relative to others are always pivotal innovations in the history of evolution, as well as—much more recently—in the history of ideas. Mathematics, foundational theories, generative grammars and computer programs attract attention as particularly powerful ways of organizing complex knowledge structures and systems of behavior. Generative systems would occur and be pivotal in any world—biological, psychological, scientific, technological, or cultural—where evolution is possible. Generative systems came to dominate in evolution as soon as they were invented for their greater replication rate, fidelity, and efficiency. We must suppose that even modest improvements in them spread like wildfire.

The emergence and spread of informational macromolecules RNA and DNA were two of the most irreversible reactions in the history of life. Others followed: eucaryotic cells, multicellularity, and sociality broadened the possibilities. Skipping to the cultural level, spoken language, the advent of written and alphabetic languages, printing and broader literacy, and other means of increasing reliability of transmission (teaching) and accumulation of increasingly complex information should have spread rapidly under

---

[2]Although his ultimate conclusion favors the account in terms of generative entrenchment given here, Hull's careful review, analysis, and discussion (1988, pp. 379–382) of "Planck's Platitude" (that older scientists are slower to accept new theories) shows how dangerous easy generalizations are in this area.

[3]I have argued elsewhere (Wimsatt, 1991, 1994, 2003) that there are no interesting exceptionless causal regularities in the complex sciences.

suitable circumstances. Diamond (1997) attempts global and integrated explanations of the rise and character of civilizations essentially from this perspective, providing a mix of contingencies and autocatalytic and hierarchially dependent processes showing rich signs of generative entrenchment. Adaptations (beginning with agriculture) causing and supporting increasing population densities, cities, and role differentiation and interdependencies make generative entrenchment inevitable. Many levels of adaptation, mind, and culture have yielded similar inventions—new generative foundations. Campbell (1974) distinguishes 10 levels of "vicarious selectors"—all prima facie suitable candidates. For each, a similar dominance and irreversibility, product of runaway positive feedback processes, results in a contingent—but once started, increasingly unavoidable—freezing in of everything essential to their production.

There are generalizeable and important things you can say about these change processes. The generative role of entities is important to whether we keep them around. Golden or not, if you like eggs, protect the goose! Generative role is central to explaining what changes and what remains the same, the magnitude and rates of change, and ultimately, the basic features of all of our generative structures. Classical foundationalists had it half-wrong: generative foundations are not architectonic principles for a static metaphysics, epistemology, or methodology. But they also had it half-right: generative foundations are the deepest heuristics for a dynamic evolutionary one. Once in place, generative elements can be so productive and become so rapidly buried in their products that they become foundational and de facto unchangeable. Foundations and foundationalisms everywhere—logical, epistemological, cognitive, physicalistic, cultural, or developmental and evolutionary—owe their existence, form, motivation, and power to the invention and evolution of generative structures.

Darwin's Principles Embodied in Generative Structures

For greatest generality, consider an abstract characterization of evolving structures. We add theoretical power to the normal framework of "Darwin's principles" by considering the generative role of entities in the adaptive structure of replicating and evolving systems. In evolving systems, it is the generative role of elements that causes resistance to their change, or can lead to rapid adaptive radiations if they are relatively unburdened (Riedl, 1978; Wimsatt & Schank, 2001). The anchoring against change in structures of widely used elements requires few assumptions: We begin with "Darwin's principles" (Lewontin 1970).[4] Evolving structures must:

---

[4]Campbell (1974) suggests a closely related set of requirements, "blind variation and selective retention," which he applied first to learning trials, culture, and finally to all aspects of a broader selection theory.

1. Have descendants that differ in their properties (variation)
2. Have at least some properties that are heritable (heritable variation)
3. Have varying causal tendencies to have descendants (heritable variation in fitness)

But as a deep empirical fact, every non-trivial evolutionary system also meets two additional conditions (Wimsatt, 2001).
These structures must also:

4. Have a developmental history because they are generated over time (generativity)
5. Have some elements which have larger or more pervasive effects than others in that production (differential entrenchment).

Then different elements in the structures have downstream effects of different magnitudes. The generative entrenchment of an element is the magnitude of those effects in that generation or life cycle. Elements with larger degrees of generative entrenchment are generators. This is a degree property.

So why add conditions (4) and (5) to the widely accepted (1–3)? Because any non-trivial physical or conceptual system satisfying (1–3) will do so via causal (phenotypic) structures satisfying (4) and (5). Condition (5) is satisfied for any heterogeneous structure: they all have parts with different consequences from their activities and from their failures. Imagine a machine or system whose breakdowns are equally severe for each kind of failure, in any part, under all conditions. (Logical idealizations aside, there aren't any!) Any differentiated system—biological, cognitive, or cultural—exhibits different degrees of generative entrenchment among its parts and activities.[5] But even if a system violating (5) could exist, with all parts having effects of the same magnitude, it would be evolutionarily unstable. With any fluctuations, it would undergo self-amplifying natural and unavoidable symmetry-breaking transitions through mutation and selection processes, and would evolve towards systems that increasingly satisfy (5; Wimsatt & Schank, 1988; Wimsatt, 2001). So evolutionary systems will satisfy (4) and (5). They will thereby have a development, and if they can reproduce and pass on their set of generators, they will have a heredity.

Heredity and development are co-generative: without a minimally reliable heredity, you cannot maintain a complex developmental phenotype, but developmental architecture can increase the efficacy and reliability of hereditary transmission. Heredity and development thus bootstrap each

---

[5]On functional differentiation, aggregativity, and emergence, see Wimsatt (1997b, 1997a, and 2003, respectively).

other—as emerging genotype and phenotype—through evolution.) This condition is as true for the transmission of culture as it is for the transmission of biological order. Evolution requires only that generators retain their generative powers (in context, within a tolerable range) under a sufficient fraction of accessible small changes in their structure (qualifications indicate tradeoffs among parameters of the process). Then they will also show phenotypic variations that inevitably (by Darwin's argument) yield fitness differences, natural selection, and evolution.

"Darwin's principles" never mention genes. Neither do the new additions. This expanded list of conditions gives heredity and development without ever introducing the usual replicator-interactor distinction of Hull (1980). Instead, I borrow Griesemer's account of reproduction, rooting heredity within an account of evolution as a lineage of developments (Griesemer, 1999a, 1999b) This reintegrates development into our accounts of the evolutionary process. Genes are agents in these accounts (in biology), not the privileged bearers of information, but co-actors with developing phenotype and its environments as bearers of relationally embodied information. I proposed (in Wimsatt, 1981b; see also Callebaut, 1993, pp. 425–429) that generative entrenchment be used to individuate genes in terms of their heterocatalytic role—by their phenotypic activity—rather than talk of copying (an abstraction of their autocatalytic role) as replicator based accounts try to do.

Heterocatalytic gene-like things picked out by the generative entrenchment criterion in biology include some but not all genes, some things that are not genes, and most often, heterogeneous complexes of both. In some domains (like cultural evolution) gene-like things may be individuated by generative entrenchment criteria when autocatalysis is too distributed and diffuse to track compact lineages through it.[6] (How does a scientific theory make a copy of itself? Very indirectly!) Kenneth Boulding commented that: "A car is just an organism with an exceedingly complicated sex life."[7] A technological virus, it takes over a complex social structure and redirects resources to reproduce more of its own kind. Our economic system has fostered an environment—a "culture dish" in which the invention, mutation, and expansion of such cultural viruses is encouraged, many environmentalists would say, until it has assumed cancerous proportions (see also Sperber, 1995).

Consider the evolutionary consequences of generative entrenchment: If an adaptive structure meeting (1–5) is adapted to its environment or task,

---

[6]A "heterocatalytic" account of (biological) genes richly elaborated by Neumann-Held (2001) argues that this is true of biological genes as well (see also Moss, 2001, who raises even more problems).

[7]Notes of Boulding's lecture at Cornell University, 1974–1975.

then modifications of more deeply generatively entrenched elements will have higher probabilities both of being maladaptive, and of being more seriously maladaptive. Parts of an adaptive structure are inevitably co-adapted to each other, as well as to different components of the environment. Larger changes in this structure must meet more design constraints, and fewer will do so. Mutations in deeply generatively entrenched elements have large and diverse effects, and are much more likely to be severely disadvantageous or lethal. These probabilities of failure are more extreme—in the simplest models, exponentially so—either for larger structures (e.g., if they grow by adding elements downstream), or as one looks to more deeply entrenched elements in a given structure. Either change increases the degree of "lock in" of entrenched elements.[8]

This differential evolutionary conservatism is the basis of von Baer's "law," that things earlier in development are more similar across diverse kinds of animals than things that appear later, or "differentiation proceeds from the general to the particular." Generally speaking, things earlier in development have much higher probabilities and degrees of generative entrenchment. There are exceptions—things that appear early and are not deeply generatively entrenched, and things which appear late and are, so this is a probabilistic generalization, but the strong association remains. Simple analytical models (Wimsatt, 1986) and more realistic structures and simulations of them (Rasmussen, 1987; Schank & Wimsatt, 1988; Wimsatt & Schank, 1988) confirm these arguments. All show that parts with greater generative entrenchment tend to be much more conservative in the evolution of such systems. Changes accumulate elsewhere while these deeper features are relatively "frozen" over evolutionary time.

Crucial for cultural evolution are the many ways we have for modulating or weakening generative entrenchment temporarily or for some purposes so we can (occasionally) make deeper modifications and get away with it (Wimsatt, 1987, 2003). (Most ways of facilitating deep modification are not applicable to or are present only in much weaker versions in biology. For this and other reasons, cultural evolution generally proceeds much faster than biological evolution.)

So one should be able to predict which parts of such structures are more likely preserved, or changed—and over broader time scales, their relative rates of change—in terms of their generative entrenchment. What kinds of structures? They could be propositions in a generated network of inferences, laws or consequences in a scientific theory, experimental procedures or pieces of material technology, structures or behavioral traits in a

---

[8]"Lock in" is Brian Arthur's (1994) term for the same process—explored in economic models of the development of technology, the formation of cities, and other cases where increased adoptions reduce the relative cost of doing so to others, generating a positive feedback loop.

developing phenotype, cultural institutions or norms in a society, or the dynamical structures, biological and cognitive, driving cognitive development. In this dynamical foundationalism, a larger generative role for an entity makes it more foundational (in role and properties), more likely to persist to be observed and, (for some fraction of them) to grow. And, if the generatively entrenched thing is more robust than its alternatives (Wimsatt, 1981a), it is more likely to have been there from the beginning and appear to have an almost unconditional necessity. Thus, an element is foundational in terms of its dynamical properties, so this kind of foundationalism, far from being static, encourages and contributes to the study of processes of change—at all levels.

This model applies in diverse disciplines. In developmental genetics, Rasmussen (1987) predicted the broad architecture of development in Drosophila melanogaster from the effects of its mutants and comparative phylogenetic data. Schank and I applied it to problems in biological evolution and development ranging from the architecture of gene control networks (1988), to the role of modularity in development (2000), and to the evolution of complexity (Wimsatt & Schank, 1988). I reconsider below the traditional innate/acquired distinction (Wimsatt, 1986). Crossing the disciplinary spectrum, Turner (1991) used generative entrenchment to analyze the distinction between literal and figurative meaning, and Griffiths (1996) argued for its use in justifying a limited essentialism. It has powerful implications for scientific change (Wimsatt, 1987—partially described in Callebaut, 1993, pp. 331–334; 378–383; 425–429, 2003; Griesemer & Wimsatt, 1988).

The form of adaptive structures affects the foci and relative rates of their evolution. Evolution also acts on that form. Tracing feedbacks from developmental pattern to evolutionary trajectory and back again should allow identification of pivot points where relative stasis or elaboration can cause major changes in evolutionary direction. These are second-order effects, but not less important for that. They give "dynamical foundationalist" theories greater explanatory power than one might at first suppose. Campbell's (1974) "vicarious selectors" have demonstrated abilities to create or make possible new effectively autonomous higher-level dynamics (see "dynamical autonomy" in Wimsatt, 1981a, 1994.) Thus perception (a vicarious selector) plus mate-choice can create runaway sexual selection and other dynamics leading natural selection in new directions (Todd and Miller, 1998). Other new directions become possible with cultural evolution (Boyd and Richerson, 1985). These processes interact and build upon each other. As products of generative entrenchment, they provide new opportunities for its action and occasions for its use as a tool of analysis. Differences among these processes in different areas affect how the model must be developed and applied, and the kinds of results expected. Subject area differences in how generative entrenchment models should be developed, and the character and consequences of these elaborating second-order effects, are topics which should provide many areas for further development of this theory.

PART II   GENERATIVE ENTRENCHMENT VERSUS INNATE-AQUIRED

Developmental Constraints, Generative Entrenchment, and the Innate-Acquired Distinction

One of these "second-order" effects provides particularly rich connections with other disciplines (Wimsatt 1986, 1999). Features of generative entrenchment show striking parallels or connections with a distinction commonly drawn in very different terms. The innate-acquired distinction originated in philosophy, with Plato's Meno, and has been a topic of continuing debate there ever since—nicely reviewed by Cowie (1999). Exported from there to ethology as the latter emerged as a science, it has generated a new host of quarrels with equally inconclusive results. It has seemed both central and problematic for millennia. Generative entrenchment can capture phenomena that this distinction has been invoked to explain throughout its range in ethology, cognitive development, linguistics, philosophy, and elsewhere. And it does so without the problematic assumptions that have tarred the innate-acquired distinction. Given the distinction's traditional commerce between biology and psychology, this domain of phenomena occupies a critical transition zone between "strictly biological" and cognitive and cultural processes of development. Any theory providing insights for both biological and cultural evolution through consideration of developmental processes should have rich applications here. If I am right, the rich claims made for "innateness" in philosophy and their easy export to ethology is no coincidence. The uncommon two legs of this controversial distinction have a common root—just not the one so commonly supposed.

I wish to deny that there is anything that is innate as traditionally understood. But the alternative approach I propose captures the phenomena and order this distinction was designed to capture and more as well.

Suppose that to be what is traditionally called innate is to be deeply generatively entrenched in the design of an adaptive structure—to be a functional part of the causal expression of that system, and a relatively deeper one on which the proper operation of a number of other adaptive features depend.[9] I take the notion of adaptive design to be unproblematic—at least

---

[9]Or it may be a relatively ineliminable consequence of such a deeply generatively entrenched trait. This qualification is required for cases where an entrenched and adaptive trait may have maladaptive or nonfunctional side effects. This suggests the possibility of "innate" or "intrinsic" flaws or limitations. All designs are compromises among conflicting design constraints and desiderata, and some of them may be ineliminable.

in biology and in the broadly naturalized half of psychology.[10] Generative entrenchment explains more proposed criteria for innateness than any other analysis. (I have found 30 so far, including 9 new ones predicted by this analysis. See Tables 3.1 and 3.2 at the end of the discussion.[11]) Unlike other approaches, generative entrenchment gives a theoretically unified analysis: It explains why the criteria hang together, and why they should be criteria for these phenomena. One might think that to do so well the new analysis must be very conservative. Not so!

We will consider some of the claims commonly made for innate behavior. Selected from a longer list (in Wimsatt, 1986), certain claims are followed by comments on how they fare on two standard competing accounts of innateness, and the generative entrenchment account (Wimsatt 1986, 1999[12]). The "genetic" account claims that something is innate if it is "coded in the genes"—an assertion whose further consequences are less than clear as we will see. The "canalization" account (which better fits many criteria for innateness) claims that innate traits are developmentally buffered, so they appear in a variety of different environments (i.e., Ariew 1996). Not normally claimed in that account (though also required to fit intuitions about innateness) is genetic canalization—the tendency for the trait to appear for different genotypes for that species. Finally, I ask whether the account explains the criterion directly (commonly so for generative entrenchment) or does it require additional hypotheses? (A partial success—it is then consistent with the criterion, but does not explain it.)

E1. Innate behavior for a given species is universal among normal members of that species in their normal environments.

E1a. On the "genetic" account, this indicates that the innate behavior has a genetic basis, but species-universality requires two additional assumptions: that the relevant genes are fixed, and that they have high penetrance. The latter pushes in the direction of canalization or generative entrenchment.

E1b. On the "developmental" account, this indicates that the innate behavior is "canalized" or regulated, so it appears in a range of

---

[10]Wimsatt 1972 and 1997b give extensive analyses of the notion of function and functional organization—the key ideas behind adaptive design—explicating both in terms of selective processes. I presuppose that here.

[11]Conceptual analyses can make predictions just as a theory can. A good analysis of a phenomenon will generate criteria in terms of some deeper understanding of its character, just as a theory of a mechanism can be used to generate good indicators of its presence. Test the analysis by asking knowledgeable observers whether they think the criteria are plausible. My new criteria are successful in this sense (see Wimsatt, 1999).

[12]Also discussed in this paper are 8 criteria for innate knowledge from the philosophical tradition and their close relations with many of the ethological criteria.

TABLE 3.1
Standard Criteria
How Different Analyses of 'Innateness' Deal With Criteria or Characterizations Found in the Ethological Literature

CRITERION FOR "INNATENESS":	Import	Import for GE	CANALIZATION G = genetic E = environmental	GENETIC	GENERATIVE ENTRENCHMENT	COMMENTS:
1. Developmental canalization or fixity	••	••	X	not implied	X	**Defining** criterion for 'canalization' analysis
2. Universality within species	••	••	X (Ariew: no) (G => yes)	x (if fixed)	X	(for 'normal' members of that species)
3. Presence in related species	••	•	(G => more likely)	x	X	treated as weaker 'inductive' criterion
4. Appears early in development or in naive individuals prior to opportunity for learning	••	••	no	no	X (conditional)	Traditionally important, and common, but not necessary or sufficient on GE analysis
5. Simple stimuli→complex char. behavior	••	•	(problematic)	X	X	Presupposed by Chomsky's 'poverty of stimulus' argument
6. Deprivation→major malfunctions	••	•••	(possible: Canaliz. is often GE'd)	X	X	Often ignored in analyses but crucial to Lorenz and pivotal to GE account
7. Releaser elicits activity	••	•	yes?		(x*, case of #5)	From Lorenz's early "hydraulic" model
8. Teaching mechanisms are innate	••	?			X	Nativist counter to empiricism
9. Stereotypy of behavior	•	?	X?	?	x*	Contrasted with flexibility of learning

(Continued)

TABLE 3.1
(Continued)

CRITERION FOR "INNATENESS":	Import	Import for GE	CANALIZATION G = genetic E = environmental	GENETIC	GENERATIVE ENTRENCHMENT	COMMENTS:
10. Parallels between behavior & phylogeny		•	(G => more likely)	?	X	Crucial for Ethologist's focus on behavior
11. Unusually easy, rapid 1-shot learning	•	•	X		X	Contrast with S-R learning paradigm
12. Critical periods for learning	••	••	?		x*	Connected w. poverty of stim. and imprinting
13. Resistance to evolutionary change		••	X?	X?	X	Derived but important property of GE
14. spontaneous prod. of complex behavior	•		homeorhesis (but problematic)		X	not learned, thus innate (related to #5 above)
15. imprinting is irreversible		•			X	Lorenz, 1937
16. imprinting is not repeatable					X	Lorenz, 1937

Note. Relations between criteria and the specified analysis of innateness: X = true by definition; X = explained by; x = consistent with; X = presupposed by; $\mathbf{x}$ = consistent with; $\mathbf{x}$ = explained by with addition of subsidiary hypothesis; * = explicable with addition of Mayr's closed/open program distinction; blank = no relation claimed, but consistent with; 'yes', 'no' indicated explicit claimed connection or denial. Importance of criteria: ••• = ineliminably important; •• = centrally important; • = important.

TABLE 3.2

Criteria Demoted and New Predicted Criteria

How Different Analyses of 'Innateness' Deal With Criteria or Characterizations Found in the Ethological Literature

CRITERION FOR "INNATENESS": DENIED OR NOT CENTRAL ON GE ANALYSIS:	Import	Import for GE	CANALIZATION	GENETIC	GENERATIVE ENTRENCHMENT	COMMENTS:
17. I/A as phylogenetic/ontogenetic acquired	••		no	X	explicable but not central on GE	alt. characterization of I/A; **Definitional?** Q-able whether an independent criterion
18. Mendelian or other simple inheritance	?		possible if NO genetic canalization	yes	no	derived from 'innate = genetic' equation Mayr: segregating behavior in *species* hybrids
19. (currently) selectable (=>heritability ? 0)	?		yes	yes	no?	derived from 'innate = genetic' equation?
20. (physical) modularity of functional trait	?				no?	Emphasized by Chomsky, linguists, and no-one else. [a mistake]
21. Innate as 'internal' to acting object	•	•	yes?	yes	no?	Exception: if internality connects with phylogenetic entrenchment; e.g., cellular traits entrenched by emergence of multicellularity

(Continued)

TABLE 3.2
(Continued)

CRITERION FOR 'INNATENESS':	Import	Import for GE	CANALIZATION	GENETIC	GENERATIVE ENTRENCHMENT	COMMENTS:
PREDICTED ON GE ANALYSIS:						
22. reappearance of early simpler (reflexive) traits after (brain) damage in adult					x	noted by Teitelbaum for rooting and grasping reflexes
23. phylogenetic ancestral traits in hybrids	•	•	X?		X	Darwin's argument that all pigeon varieties are descended from ancestral rock pigeon; relates both to canalization and to generative entr.
24. early devel traits more evol conservative		••			X	connected with GE and von Baer's "law".
25. deeply entrenched generative role	•	•••			X	*Defining* criterion for 'GE' analysis; generativity noted as important by Chomsky
26. existence of supernormal stimuli					X	Like poverty of stimulus, a consequence of simplicity of releasing stimuli
27. analogies in cognitive structures	••	••			X	Centrally important for 'innateness' in mental, and philosophical origin of ethological concept.
28. restricted modes of deep GE modification		•			X	plausible consequence of GE for innateness
29. association between 'habitual' & 'innate'		•	no	no	X	vernacular: plausible on GE account, by analogy; contradicts genetic account
30. arbitrariness or contingency common	•	••	no	no	X	**robust predicted characteristic of evolved GE systems.**

Note. Relations between criteria and the specified analysis of innateness: X = true by definition; X = presupposed by; X = explained by; x = consistent with; x = explained by with addition of subsidiary hypothesis; * = explicable with addition of Mayr's closed/open program distinction; blank = no relation claimed, but consistent with; 'yes', 'no' indicated explicit claimed connection or denial. Importance of criteria: ••• = inelIminably important; •• = centrally important; • = important.

environments. Given substantial genetic variability in virtually all species, genetic canalization is also required for universality across the whole species.

E1c. On the "generative entrenchment" account this follows directly: Strong stabilizing selection produced by the large number of other traits depending on its normal expression guarantees both its effective universality and that any individual lacking it will appear strongly abnormal. But here there is a further important connection I return to next: It is often adaptive for a generatively entrenched feature to be both genetically and environmentally canalized.

E2. Innate behavior appears early in development, before it could have been learned, or in the absence of experience.

E2a. On the "genetic" account this is (incoherently) taken as a basis for saying it is "more genetic," because the environment will have had less time to act. (But then the genes will also have had less time to act!)

E2b. This is not predicted or explained on developmental canalization approach. Ariew (1999) denies it as a characteristic, but this does violence to our intuitions.

E2c. Traits expressed early in development are more likely to have high generative entrenchment, so the association follows directly, though without invoking "absence of experience." On the other hand, things which appear late in development can be regarded as innate on this account if there is still a lot "downstream" depending on them—preserving intuitions we should maintain (e.g., for mating rituals or parental imprinting on offspring). So this rationalizes the very late-emerging examples Ariew would use as counterexamples.

E3. Innate behavior is relatively resistant to evolutionary change. This can be explained most naturally on the generative entrenchment account, from which it follows directly. It is explained (less successfully) on the developmental fixity account (assuming genetic as well as environmental canalization, and strong stabilizing selection). Similarly for the genetic account. But for the other accounts, using strong stabilizing selection of a developmental trait is getting close to assuming high generative entrenchment, so neither of the alternatives do very well.

E4. Critical periods for learning certain information, or unusually rapid or "one-shot" learning indicates the presence of an "innate teaching mechanism." With E2, this is the basis of Chomsky's "poverty of stimulus" argument against behaviorist theories of language learning. It shows obvious generativity, as Chomsky argues, and so relates naturally to a generative entrenchment account. It is more problematic for canalization, which is less explanatory the more complex the generated behavior, and not captured at all on the genetic account.

E5.   Innate information is said to be "phylogenetically acquired" (through selection) and hereditarily transmitted; acquired information is said to be "onto genetically acquired," usually through some variety of learning. Cited often as a criterion, this is usually just treated as a restatement of the 'genetic' criterion. It is also captured by the generative entrenchment account, since highly generative entrenched traits are highly conserved, and thus likely to be phylogenetically old. The canalization account could use a parallel strategy by invoking stabilizing selection.

E6.   Relatively major malfunctions occur if innate features don't appear or aren't allowed to develop. This is a direct consequence of the generative entrenchment account, and not explicable by either canalization or genetic accounts without supposing generative entrenchment.

Since the rise of genetics and evolutionary theory, two common but more problematic criteria have been added, presumably as criteria for a trait's having a genetic basis:

E7.   If a trait shows simple (e.g., Mendelian) patterns of inheritance, it is innate. But this violates E1, since it must thus be a segregating trait and variable in the population.

E8.   If a trait is modifiable through selection, it is innate. Same problem as for E7, but this also violates E3. This criterion would be doubly problematic for a generative entrenchment trait, which would be very difficult to modify through selection because of E6. Yet (stabilizing) selection is clearly very relevant—and expected for a generatively entrenched trait.

Criteria, E7 and E8 are particularly interesting. They are relatively recent (since Mendel and Darwin, respectively). Both conflict with E1, and E8 also conflicts with E3 and E6. So one can't consistently maintain all as criteria for the same concept. Lehrman (1970) individuates two concepts—"genetic" and "canalization" senses of innateness. But he rejects the latter, and interprets the former (which he embraces) in terms of heritability. This has other problems that I will avoid here.[13] On any analysis of innateness, these

---

[13]In arguing for the "canalization" concept, Ariew (1996) nicely points out the problems with heritability in this context.

two criteria (E7 and E8) should be rejected—at least in their present forms. They were likely both added (see e.g., Mayr, 1974) as criteria for a trait having a genetic basis on the assumption that was the appropriate gloss for innateness. Seeing this makes their addition less compelling.

The generative entrenchment analysis has several other interesting features:

1. Generative entrenchment is a degree property—recognized since Lehrman (1970) as required for an acceptable analysis.

2. It captures E2, E4, and E5, which canalization fails to do, or does poorly, although these have been paradigmatic claims for innateness. The genetic account does no better for E2 and E4. Generative entrenchment captures E2 and E5 in radically different ways than traditional analyses, but this is a strength because it thereby avoids other significant problems for traditional accounts.

3. By not viewing innate traits as things which are there before learning, generative entrenchment avoids problems traditional nativists have had with trying to say what learning is and when it begins, in a manner allowing them to distinguish learning from interactions necessary for development. This cluster of issues has probably been the most problematic one for the nativist tradition, so avoiding it is a real plus (for the problems essentially this issue has caused in philosophy, see Cowie, 1999).

4. Criterion E6 often comes up in discussions of innateness but rarely criterially, and is often ignored (but see Lorenz (1965) on "deprivation experiments"). It becomes central to, and is pivotally important on the generative entrenchment account as it helps to explain why E1 and E3 are met.

5. As Griffiths (1996) notes, through criterion E6, generative entrenchment also provides room for a modest essentialism. Because of the causal importance of a generatively entrenched trait, anything lacking it (even if viable), will be seriously (and deleteriously) abnormal. Essentialism also has linguistic tones, a fact explored by Turner (1991) in his use of generative entrenchment to characterize the difference between literal and figurative meaning.

6. This new analysis of "innate" things shows them as comfortably relational, and connected with their environments in ways not captured in prior accounts. The equation of innate with genetic is ill-founded—being genetic is neither necessary nor sufficient for being innate. (Equating 'innate' with 'genetic' is a kind of functional localization fallacy.)

7. Nor does it follow any longer that what is "innate" must be internal to the system. This follows from the relational character of the analysis. *Environmental* features could be equally "innate" (Wimsatt, 1986)—although prop-

erly speaking both internal and environmental features involve disguised relational attributions.[14]

8. This analysis also turns traditional accounts on their heads in another way: things are classified not by where they came from ("phylogenetically acquired" vs. "ontogenetically acquired" information), but in terms of their effects—their generative power. Generative power also supports many of Chomsky's uses of innateness without making assumptions that are developmentally and evolutionarily unsound.

These surprising changes in the account could not be justified but for the remarkable explanatory integration which results. It works not only on internal conceptual grounds (capturing, integrating, and explaining relations between diverse criteria traditionally offered for innateness), but also on external grounds. It preserves the importance of the reconceptualized distinction in disciplines that have found it useful—in part by generating and supporting more of the criteria commonly used for it than any other analysis. At the same time, it is consistent with and richly connected to relevant theory in evolution and development. No extant account does any of these as well.

Nonetheless this is not the old innate-acquired distinction. It captures phenomena for which innateness was traditionally invoked, but along a quite different trajectory, which does not support central nativist claims. These changes are important in making the focal message of this essay unambiguous: *This is not the traditional innate-acquired distinction.*

There is a price however—this account ignores three traditional assumptions about innateness: (1) on the generative entrenchment account a trait is "innate-like" in virtue of its consequences rather than the character of its causes; (2) the generative entrenchment account decouples "innateness"

---

[14]See, for example, advocates of the "developmental systems" perspective (Oyama, 1985; Oyama et al., 2001). What is innate, if anything, are relationships between phenotype and environment which serve to secure and increase fitness and its heritability. We have exploited the biases of the gene-centered perspective since early in this century. Its enormous inertia (generative entrenchment!) forms how we conceptualize all sorts of fundamental relationships in biology. We must stand outside it to see its limits and better assess its true strengths. Most critics urge that the 'innate-acquired' distinction be simply trashed. The radical differences in the analyses suggest this may be necessary for productive thought in the new paradigm.

Generative entrenchment combines elements of genetic and selectionist theories in developmental form. It is essential to the "developmental systems" approach as the closest to a motor driving evolutionary change available to it. Generative entrenchment actually explains trajectories more in terms of highway construction than propulsion technology, but constraints on shorter time scales may act as generative motors on longer ones. A final caution to "developmental systems" theorists: new theories must remain in contact with well-developed tools already in the discipline, (including the many successful theories in genetics and population genetics), or be dismissed either as obvious heresy or a pointless principled worry. But one can use these tools without regarding them as foundational (see Griesemer on reproduction vs. replication, 1999, nd.).

from genetics; and (3), it decouples being "innate" from being internal to the system.[15] How fundamental can you get? Of course, none of these associations are denied *simplicitur*: there is a convincing gloss for why we should have believed each of them to be true. But violating them might seem to make the inductive strategy essential: overwhelm the unintuitive character of the analysis by showing how many distinct criteria it explains.

This is surely a great strength of this account that is not apparent if we look at just a few criteria. Special pleading? But the inductive strategy was not invented for this purpose: I was impressed at the large and diverse array of criteria. Like Lehrman, I thought it likely that there were *at least* two senses of innateness, and I wanted to appreciate the whole range of claims made for it before starting an analysis. I was astounded that so many of the criteria could be captured as consequences of a simple mechanistic analysis turning basically on one criterion with a few appropriate qualifications. (Considered are the 7 philosophical criteria listed in 1986, 1999, as well as the 30 ethological, evolutionary, and cognitive ones given in Tables 3.1 and 3.2.) Particularly interesting is how the new account predicts so many plausible *new* criteria.

The generative entrenchment account is so radically different in approach that it is tempting to see it as a competing eliminative account, but it integrates and preserves so much that if so it is eliminitivism with a difference. Discussions of eliminativism in the philosophy of mind are associated with threats to "urban renew" (bulldoze or demolish) our ordinary conceptions of "folk psychology," replacing them with sub-psychological concepts derived from theories of our neural hardware, whose conceptual basis would necessitate entirely new concepts at the macroscopic level. By implication, we would have to give up many or most of these folk beliefs as false. This has engendered various defenses of folk-psychology, arguing that we can't do without these beliefs and that any conceptual revision adequate to the phenomena would have to preserve them in some form. I have always been sympathetic with these complaints against eliminativism (see discussions of "dynamical autonomy" in my 1981a, 1994). The extreme forms of eliminativism are now being replaced by more tempered views (see my 2003, chap. 9, for a partial analysis and explanation of the early excesses characteristic of reductionistic programs).

---

[15]Analyses advanced by Johnson and Morton (1991) and elaborated by Elman et al. (1996; not the complete account of either) utilizes a hierarchial inclusion model to classify degrees of innateness (in effect, from more to less), with intra-cellular and intra-organismal both classified as (more and less) innate, and then distinguishing species-typical and individual-differentiating environments, which they call 'primal' and 'learning.' There are clear exceptions, but the order delineated here may roughly follow an order from increased to decreased entrenchment (with the evolution of eucaryotes, metazoa, and the successive differentiation through lower taxa of von Baer's law.) So internal/external classifications are not totally irrelevant to the phenomena of the innate/acquired distinction.

But this account of innateness is quite different. It is an eliminativist account that better and more richly anchors more intuitive phenomena which innateness was invoked to explain than innateness itself. Generative entrenchment seems a better concept for organizing this domain of phenomena than innateness, but it is not "sub-personal" and reaches out in new ways that make it better adapted to the future of theory in these areas. If any of the recent eliminativist theories of mind had even nearly the promise of this one of saving so many of the phenomena, they would never have been so roundly attacked.

PART III   SOME ALTERNATIVE ACCOUNTS

A Closer Look at Canalization

Probably the most widely favored attempts to analyze or replace innateness without simply trying to eliminate it (Oyama, 1985) have tried to do so in terms of canalization. (Ariew, 1996, 1999). Canalization (Waddington, 1957; Lerner, 1954) is an important concept both in developmental biology, and for thoughts about the evolution of development. There is growing interest in the experimental assessment of and conditions favoring the evolution of genetic and environmental canalization, and how they interact with each other, with stabilizing selection of different intensities, with inbreeding, and with the evolution of modularity (see e.g., Stearns et al., 1995; Wagner et al., 1997; Rice, 1998; and Schank & Wimsatt, 2000). I want to consider shortly canalization's relation to generative entrenchment, and consider its limitations as a phenomenological concept. The first emphasizes its importance for thinking about the evolution of development, and helps to explain why canalization and generative entrenchment so often go hand in hand. The second suggests a dangerous looseness that is better avoided. Some residual problems with an account of innateness based on canalization are treated in passing.

Relations between Canalization
and Generative Entrenchment

Because canalization involves regulatory phenomena and generative entrenchment induces stabilizing selection for that feature, they should share many criteria: both will resist perturbations tending to push systems having them away from the regulated or generatively entrenched states. Thus many operational tests for either could be expected to be neutral between them. One may wonder how often they are confused—how many things glossed as canalization actually reflect significant generative entrenchment with only modest canalization—for example, significant embryonic mortality of earlier deviant embryos, followed by more modest regulation of smaller and later deviations. And of course slightly different errors could make the reverse happen as well.

But generative entrenchment and canalization are distinct—both as concepts, and also in how they are described. Waddington (and Lerner) characterize canalization phenomenologically as stabilization of an outcome across environmental and genetic variation, respectively. This phenomenological character of the concepts of canalization need not rule out productive experiments or theory, but these concepts must be operationalized, and there may be more play in how they are realized in any situation. generative entrenchment is characterized more mechanistically, in terms of causal dependency relations in the production of phenotypic traits. So as we learn more about the mechanisms, the sophistication of our generative entrenchment accounts and what we can infer from them should automatically rise.

It would usually be adaptive for entrenched things to be canalized. If it is strongly deleterious for an organism to deviate from a state (whether static or developmental), it is advantageous to regulate its production through various means, including redundancy and feedback control (or to abort without expending further resources if not).[16] Thus, one should expect selection for such regulation. This might include some or all of environmental canalization, genetic canalization, and regulation of developmental trajectories (Waddington's 1957 homeorhesis), since assimilated to canalization (Rice, 1998). So, entrenchment breeds canalization.

Canalization should invite accumulation over macro-evolutionary time of features which depend for their proper functioning on maintenance of the canalized state (Wimsatt & Schank, 1988). So canalization breeds generative entrenchment. (You can't come to depend upon things which aren't reliably there.) Stable states may become generatively entrenched, whether we think of them as internal, external, or relational. In perhaps the most extreme version of this, Morowitz (1992) argues that primary metabolism is the entrenched remains of the prebiotic and early biotic "organic soup" in which life first evolved. In subsequent evolution, the external environment was materially internalized, becoming the "milieu interior" to control and regulate diverse organisms' entrenched states, and permit reliable and efficient operation of processes that depended on it.

So canalization and generative entrenchment should each favor selective enhancement of the other. But then we should be very careful with attempts to explain innateness in terms of one while denying any need for the

---

[16]Like all "adaptive design" arguments, this requires detailed qualifications, which won't be provided here.

other. If evolution naturally builds organisms that have both it may be all too easy to utilize the properties of the "silent partner" while making the argument for the preferred criterion. Canalizations and generative entrenchments have obviously been interleaved many times in constructing our layered architecture of kluged exaptations. In the next section we will see various cases where canalization and generative entrenchment are almost inextricably interdigitated.

On the Plasticity of Canalization

As a phenomenological concept, canalization suggests developmental regulation without specifying any mechanisms for it. Waddington (1957) explicates it with specific examples, and the metaphor of the "epigenetic landscape"—a kind of state space representation for developmental trajectories, which I return to below. But nothing in Waddington's characterization tells how wide or deep the "chreodes" (regulatory channels) are, how they are determined, or how they are supposed to relate to intra- or inter-specific differences. This leaves lots of room for interpretation. Consider the treatment of inter and intra-specific variation. One could imagine trimming the canalization chreodes quite narrowly, with canalization quite contextual, minimizing "genetic canalization," and letting canalized states change with different genotypes within the species. We would then have different "innate" phenotypes for different genotypes (Ariew, 1999). Then innateness Mendelizes: One can speak of baldness and blue versus brown eyes as innate traits, and criteria E7 (and E8) are restored. This moves in the direction of merging the canalization account with the genetic.[17] But then it is not clear what function "innateness" serves that "genetic" doesn't already capture. It then becomes only too easy to speak of innate intra-specific differences in all kinds of traits. We've been there before, and it is dangerous and easily misused territory. Chomsky's scientific tastes for species-universals is a better place to draw the distinction: keep "innate" differences at the species level or above. The generative entrenchment account goes even further—using only a winnowed subset of these species-specific traits.[18]

If we ignore genetic canalization[19] and treat garden-variety intra-specific differences as innate, "phenotypic switching" causes problems. Different environments in development can yield characteristically and radically dif-

---

[17]Mendel (1866/1909) made clear that he sought traits that were relatively insensitive to environmental conditions, to get clear ratios and avoid confounding effects of environmental variation. So he too used canalization. This was indeed an elegant aspect of his experimental design.

[18]This as at least partially a tactical decision concerning how to draw the boundary, rather than simply a way of deciding who is right or wrong. Where to draw boundaries is an unavoidable source of argument with a degree property. As should be obvious, I favor the generative entrenchment account over the canalization account on other grounds for reasons stronger than tactics.

ferent adaptive phenotypes in the same species. Presumably we want to classify them as "innate-like" even if they are intra-specific variants. They are generatively entrenched—with lots of downstream consequences. These alternative phenotypes are relatively tightly regulated—with no natural states between—in a threshold-based switching structure. Could we save it for canalization by saying that their disjunction is canalized? But with canalization phenomenological, metaphorically expressed and not anchored to any mechanisms, it threatens a slippery slope away from environmental invariance towards admitting almost anything.

Waddington (1957) speaks of "nudging a ball" into one trough rather than another in the "epigenetic landscape" with a small stimulus early in development. This fits phenotypic switching all right, but metaphorically: it is hard to see how to explicate it without violating canalization. The physical analogy suggests that the magnitude of the nudge together with the height of the chreode walls (together with the timing of events) is what matters. But for biology the character of the stimulus matters more than the size of the nudge. Movement in the visual field works for greylag hatchlings, and conspecific cries do for mallards, but nudges or hot breaths—other forms of energy transfer—don't work for either. Migratory versus non-migratory forms in locust species (Maynard Smith, 1975) and different morphs for caterpillars (Greene, 1989) are mediated by "phenotypic switching" early in development in response to highly specific stimuli which are good predictors of the environments in which the alternative phenotypes are better adapted. The "bithorax" response of developing Drosophila to ether in Waddington's (1957) account of "genetic assimilation" (although maladaptive) or the Baldwin effect both reflect this kind of sensitivity. These are control structures with complex consequences that are both "programmed" and regulated. But the more structure there is to the consequences, the better the generative entrenchment account fits, and the less revealing it is to claim that the behavior is canalized.

Why not be a narrow canalizationist in some environments (to capture Mendelizing and selectable traits in natural populations and steal the ground from genetic accounts), a broad one in others (for species-universality, and other macro-evolutionarily relevant criteria), and a structured one in still others (for phenotypic switching and all kinds of complex adaptive programmed interactions with the environment)? But how do we know when to be which? Without criteria to tell us we don't have an analysis that is of much use. And notice that the second and third alternatives are each sneaking generative entrenchment in the back door—for what else are the releasing parameters and the complex coordinated changes responding to

---

[19]Phenotypic switching is a species-specific adaptation demanding substantial genetic canalization because of genetic variability in almost all species.

them but rich programmatic structures whose architectures and characteristic responses are deeply generatively entrenched?

It is easier to start with a chosen "innate" trait and say how it is canalized
or not, and in what respects, at what times in development, and how all of
this may vary by genotype than it is to start with an idea of canalization and
just using that criterion decide which traits are going to be innate. This
seems a problem for the canalization account: the preceding qualifications
then appear as gerrymandering, and the sense that one has captured the
distinction seems to run out between your fingers. Perhaps this holds for
any category in a science with richly textured objects where a lot of the details matter. But generative entrenchment has more structure, and seems
less prone to this problem than canalization.

A more diffuse but an unnoticed and serious problem remains. Canalization becomes less informative as an explanation as the behavior becomes
more complex and conditional, whereas generative entrenchment, with its
invocation of stabilizing selection, and the accumulation of layered exaptations (which brings in seemingly arbitrary contingency) does successively better.[20] The phenotypic switches discussed previously, or the rig-
idly stereotyped mating rituals of various species seem designed for a
generative entrenchment account. One might on a generative entrenchment account expect evolution to produce a growing succession of initially
arbitrary display, feeding, and appeasement behaviors that are added to
differentiate rituals of closely related species. In these cases, it is obvious
enough that the behavior is canalized, but also that it is generatively entrenched (both relative to the next part of the ritual, and with respect to
mating success). On the generative entrenchment account, entrenched arbitrary contingencies differentiate mating rituals in similar species which
overlap, and the emphasis on dependency structure lead naturally to the
complex interactions through which the behavior is realized. Here the
causal richness and environmental sensitivity of the adaptive design cou-
ples naturally with the definition of generative entrenchment and its designedly relevant causal dependencies.

This points to another important feature of the generative entrenchment
account—one not to my knowledge ever noted before, but a very common
characteristic of phenomena said to be innate. Ethology is full of contingent
and arbitrary differences between species. Whether arising in morphology
or mating rituals, species-specific "contingency" in nature is widely remarked. Generative entrenchment predicts a hierarchy of preserved contin-

---

[20]Generative entrenchment has a complementary, but I think less severe problem: it becomes at least harder to evaluate the more redundancy there is, and redundancy could be
thought of as a variety of canalization.

gencies of varying scope in the history of life and in the physiology of development. Generative entrenchment systems accumulate contingencies (Wimsatt, 2001). Generative entrenchment is probably the most robust explanation for the possibility and ubiquity of this characteristic of evolved systems. Indeed, it may be the only one. This is a new prediction totally unexpected in discussions of innateness.

A final observation indicates significant differences between the generative entrenchment approach and either the genetic or canalization accounts. There is a natural association in common speech (#28 in Table 3.2) between instinctive behavior and things that have become habitual—especially designedly, through practice, and especially if done smoothly, or sometimes stereotypically. Thus, "on hearing the faint click, he instinctively went for his gun"—a plausible description in the middle of any 'dime' Western. There are myriad varieties of this statement. It fits (at least roughly) criteria 5, 7, and 9 from Table 3.1, but without satisfying either the genetic or the canalization accounts. It is complex behavior which must be learned, practiced, even trained for, which has become "chunked," "black boxed" (Latour, 1987), or modularized. It cannot any longer be executed piecemeal, but only as a unit, and must be started "at the beginning," not in the middle—showing that its early pieces (and sometimes its learned "releasers") are generatively entrenched relative to the rest. This example midwifes the transference of the generative entrenchment account from biology and developmental psychology to the unchallenged common minutia and practices—and the most deeply entrenched principles—of science and culture. But that is a story for another time.

CONCLUSION

Canalization seems an intuitive gloss on much of what many past theorists (including Lorenz) had in mind by innateness, but fails to capture some crucially important criteria. Generative entrenchment gives a reconstructive analysis which better fits existing claims (including Lorenz's) than any other, offers new fruitful connections and predictions, and reflects modern accounts of the relation between genes and development. Though not discussed here, it also provides an engine for evolutionary change for the developmental systems view—and thereby strengthens it substantially (Wimsatt, 2001). Particularly intriguing (but only suggested here) is the ease with which the generative entrenchment account captures or explains many of the traditional philosophical criteria (P1-P7) for innateness (Wimsatt, 1986, 1999). This suggests a fruitful naturalistic analysis of a priori/a posteriori and analytic-synthetic distinctions that I will pursue elsewhere. The generative entrenchment account requires breaking some time-honored presuppositions of traditional notions of innateness, but allows making many others in a satisfying and unitary fashion. No analysis can capture all of the criteria, which form an inconsistent set, so the loss of these associations should not be taken as critical. Finally, the strongly relational character of this analysis can torpedo the basis for recurrent nativist claims that something which is innate is therefore independent of environmental involvement or effects. It is time that we stopped basing faulty social analyses on mistaken conceptions of human nature anchored firmly in obsolete biology.

Comments on Tables 3.1 and 3.2

These tables include all criteria I have been able to find in the literature or in conversation with practicing scientists in the disciplines affected. The criteria, my judgements of their importance in general and for the generative entrenchment account, and how or whether they are handled by the canalization, genetic, and generative entrenchment accounts are all tabulated, with comments indicating any special conditions or relevant sources. Most are found widely in the literature, with 1, 2, 4, 5, 12 and 13 probably the most common. Most writers use multiple criteria, often drawing on more than they list explicitly. Thus Lorenz (1965) uses many of them seriatim in his discussions, either criterially or as comments about innateness, and has probably used or discussed almost all of the first 16 at one time or another. Mayr (1974) lists six explicitly (10, 4, 9, 18, 19, 1), but I know no other sources explicitly listing nearly this many. My judgments of importance are not based on a systematic careful survey but "eyeballed" from experience (of now 30 years thinking about these issues). Different individuals may weight different criteria differently—if I am right, indicating how much use they have made of them themselves, and reflecting the role that generative entrenchment plays in their own thinking.

Table 3.1 includes criteria captured by the generative entrenchment account. Table 3.2 indicates further criteria or presuppositions that are either denied (18–21) or regarded as less central (17, 20, 21) on the generative entrenchment account. Criteria 22 thru 30 are new predictions by the generative entrenchment analysis of reasonable criteria for or common properties of things said to be innate.

AUTHOR NOTE

William C. Wimsatt; Department of Philosophy; University of Chicago, 1010 East 59th Street, (C/M:CL17), Chicago, IL 60637, USA. Telephone: (773) 702-8513 or 363-2519; Fax: (773) 702-9861; wwim@midway.uchicago.edu.

Parts of this paper draw on materials also presented in Wimsatt, 1986, 1999a, 1999b, and 2001, and on unpublished material for a forthcoming book (Wimsatt, in progress). Probably the fullest account of this perspective in biology is Arthur (1997). I thank the National Humanities Center and the NEH for time and support in a lovely and productive place during 2000–2001.

REFERENCES

Ariew, A. (1996). Innateness and canalization. *Philosophy of Science, 63,* (Proceedings), S19–S27.

Ariew, A. (1999). Innateness is canalization: In defense of a developmental account of innateness. In V. Hardcastle (Ed.), *Biology meets psychology: Philosophical essays* (pp. 117–138). Cambridge, MA: MIT Press.

Arthur, B. (1994). *Increasing returns and path-dependence in the economy.* Michigan University Press.

Arthur, W. (1997). *The origin of animal body plans: a study in evolutionary developmental biology.* Cambridge, UK: Cambridge University Press.

Boyd, R., & P. Richerson (1985). *Culture and the evolutionary process.* Chicago: University of Chicago Press.

Callebaut, W. (1993). *Taking the naturalistic turn: How to do real philosophy of science.* Chicago: University of Chicago Press.

Campbell, D. T. (1974). Evolutionary epistemology. In P. A. Schilpp (Ed.), *The philosophy of Karl Popper* (Vol. II, pp. 413–463). LaSalle, IL: Open Court.

Darwin, C. (1859). *The origin of species.* London: John Murray (Reprinted by Harvard University Press, 1959.)

Diamond, J. (1997). *Guns, germs and steel: The fates of human societies.* New York: Norton.

Elman, J., Bates, E., Johnson, M., Karmiloff-Smith, A., Parisi, D., & Plunkett, K. (1996). *Rethinking innateness: A connectionist perspective on development.* Cambridge, MA: MIT Press.

Gleick, J. (1992). *Genius: A biography of Richard Feynman.* New York: Pantheon.

Greene, E. (1989). A diet-induced developmental polymorphism in a caterpillar. *Science, 243,* 643–646.

Griesemer, J. R. (1999). Reproduction and the reduction of genetics. In H. J. Rheinberger, P. Beurton & R. Falk (Eds.), *The gene concept in development and evolution* (pp. 240–285). Cambridge, UK: Cambridge University Press.

Griesemer, J. R. (In progress). *Reproduction in the evolutionary process.*

Griesemer, J. R., & W. C. Wimsatt (1988). Picturing Weismannism: A case study in conceptual evolution. In M. Ruse (Ed.), *What philosophy of biology is* (pp. 75–137). Dordrecht: Martinus-Nijhoff.

Griffiths, P. (1996). Darwinism, process structuralism and natural kinds. *Philosophy of Science, 63*(3) Suppl., 1–9.

Griffiths, P., & R. Gray. (1994). Developmental systems and evolutionary explanation. *Journal of Philosophy, 91,* 277–304.

Hull, D. L. (1980). Individuality and selection. *Annual Review of Ecology and Systematics, 11,* 311–332.

Hull, D. L. (1988). *Science as a process.* Chicago: University of Chicago Press.

Johnson, M. H., & Morton, J. (1991). *Biology and cognitive development: The case of face recognition.* Oxford: Blackwell.

Latour, B. (1987). *Science in action.* Cambridge, MA: Harvard University Press.

Lehrman, D. S. (1970). Semantic and conceptual issues in the nature-nurture controversy. In L. R. Aronson et. al. (Eds.), *Evolution and development of behavior* (pp. 17–52). San Francisco: Freeman.

Lerner, I. M. (1954). *Genetic homeostasis* (Reprint). New York: Dover Books.

Lewontin, R. C. (1970). The units of selection. *Annual Review of Ecology and Systematics, 1*, 1–18.

Lorenz, K. Z. (1965). *Evolution and modification of behavior.* Chicago: University of Chicago Press.

Maynard-Smith, J. (1975). *The theory of evolution* (3rd ed). London: Pelican.

Mayr, E. (1974). Behavior programs and evolutionary strategies. *American Scientist, 62*, 650–659.

Mendel, G. (1902). *Experiments in plant-hybridization* (Bateson, Trans.; reprinted 1902). Cambridge MA: Harvard University Press (Originally published German, 1866)

Morowitz, H. (1992). *The origins of cellular life.* New Haven, CT: Yale University Press.

Moss, L. (2001). Deconstructing the gene and reconstructing molecular developmental systems. In S. Oyama, R. Gray & P. Griffiths (Eds.), *Cycles of contingency: Developmental systems and evolution* (pp. 85–98). Cambridge, MA: MIT Press.

Neumann-Held, E. M. (2001). Let's talk about genes: The process molecular gene concept and its context. In S. Oyama, R. Gray & P. Griffiths (Eds.), *Cycles of contingency: Developmental systems and evolution* (pp. 69–84). Cambridge, MA: MIT Press.

Oyama, S. (1985). *The ontogeny of information.* Cambridge, MA: MIT Press.

Oyama, S., Gray, R., & Griffiths, P. (Eds.). (2001). *Cycles of contingency: Developmental systems and evolution.* Cambridge, MA: MIT Press.

Rasmussen, N. (1987). A new model of developmental constraints as applied to the Drosophila system. *Journal of Theoretical Biology, 127*(3), 271–301.

Rhodes, R. (1986). *The making of the atomic bomb.* New York: Simon and Schuster.

Rice, S. H. (1998). The evolution of canalization and the breaking of Von Baer's laws: modeling the evolution of development with epistasis. *Evolution, 52*, 647–657.

Schank, J. C., & Wimsatt, W. C. (1988). Generative entrenchment and evolution In A. Fine & P. K. Machamer (Eds.), *PSA-1986 Vol. II* (pp. 33–60). East Lansing, MI: The Philosophy of Science Association.

Schank, J. C., & Wimsatt, W. C. (2000). Evolvability: modularity and generative entrenchment. In R. Singh, C. Krimbas, D. Paul & J. Beatty (Eds.), *Thinking about evolution: Historical, philosophical, and political perspectives* (pp. 332–335). Cambridge, UK: Cambridge University Press.

Simon, H. A., (1996). *The sciences of the artificial, 3rd ed.* Cambridge, MA: MIT Press. (Originally published in 1969)

Sperber, D. (1995). *Explaining culture.* London: Blackwell.

Stearns, S. C., Kaiser, M., & Kawecki, T. J. (1995). The differential canalization of fitness components against environmental perturbations in Drosophila melanogaster. *Journal of Evolutionary Biology, 8*, 539–557.

Todd, P. and Miller, G. (1998). Biodiversity through sexual selection. In C. Langton (Ed.), *Artificial life, V.* Cambridge, MA: MIT Press/Bradford Books.

Turner, M. (1991). *Reading minds: The study of English in the age of cognitive science.* Princeton, NJ: Princeton Universtiy Press.

Waddington, C. H. (1957). *The strategy of the genes.* London: Routledge.

Wagner, G. P., Booth, B., & Bagheri-Chaichian, H. (1997). A population genetic theory of canalization. *Evolution, 51*, 329–347.

Williams, G. C. (1966). *Adaptation and natural selection.* New Jersey: Princeton University Press.

Wimsatt, W. C. (1972). Teleology and the logical structure of function statements. *Studies in History and Philosophy of Science, 3*, 1–80.

Wimsatt, W. C. (1981a). Robustness, reliability and overdetermination. In M. Brewer & B.Collins (Eds.), *Scientific inquiry and the social sciences* (pp. 124–163). San Francisco: Jossey-Bass.

Wimsatt, W. C. (1981b). Units of selection and the structure of the multi-level genome. In P. D. Asquith & R. N. Giere (Eds.), *PSA-1980, Vol. 2* (pp. 122–183). Lansing, MI: The Philosophy of Science Association.

Wimsatt, W. C. (1986). Developmental constraints, generative entrenchment, and the innate-acquired distinction. In W. Bechtel (Ed.), *Integrating scientific disciplines* (pp. 185–208). Dordrecht: Martinus-Nijhoff.

Wimsatt, W. C. (1987). *Generative entrenchment, scientific change, and the analytic-synthetic distinction.* Invited address at Central Division APA meetings (unpublished)

Wimsatt, W. C. (1994). The ontology of complex systems: Levels, perspectives and causal thickets. In R. Ware & M. Matthen, *Canadian Journal of Philosophy, 20* (Suppl.) 207–274.

Wimsatt, W. C. (1997a). Aggregativity as a heuristic for finding emergence. In L. Darden (Ed.), *Philosophy of Science* (Suppl. to Vol. 4, #4, pp. S372–S384).

Wimsatt, W. C. (1997b). Functional organization, functional analogy, and functional inference. *Evolution and Cognition, 3*(2), 102–132.

Wimsatt, W. C. (1999a). Genes, memes, and cultural inheritance. *Biology and Philosophy, 14,* 279–310.

Wimsatt, W. C. (1999b). Generativity, entrenchment, evolution, and innateness. In V. Hardcastle (Ed.), *Biology meets psychology: Philosophical essays* (pp. 139–179). Cambridge, MA: MIT Press.

Wimsatt, W. C. (2001). Generative entrenchment and the developmental systems approach to evolutionary processes. In S. Oyama, R. Gray & P. Griffiths (Eds.), *Cycles of contingency: Developmental systems and evolution* (pp. 219–238). Cambridge, MA: MIT Press.

Wimsatt, W. C. (2003). *Re-Engineering philosophy for limited beings: Piecewise approximations to reality.* Cambridge, MA: Harvard University Press.

Wimsatt, W. C. (In progress). *The evolution of generative structures: Dynamical foundationalism in biology and culture.*

Wimsatt, W. C., & J. C. Schank (1988). Two constraints on the evolution of complex adaptations and the means for their avoidance. In M. Nitecki (Ed.), *Evolutionary progress* (pp. 231–273). Chicago: University of Chicago Press.

4

Reductionism in Mathematics

Jaime Oscar Falcón Vega
Facultad de Ciencias, UNAM, México DF

Gerardo Hernández
Juan José Rivaud
Sección de Metodología y Teoría de la Ciencia,
Cinvestav, México DF

The term *reductionism* has often faced fashionable enemies (cf. holism, organicism, vitalism, and systems theory). It has, in fact, been an anathema for half a century. Perhaps the first reductionist idea is attributable to Democritus. Not that he claimed for the first time the existence of atoms or that everything was composed of atoms: Both theses had been sustained before by others (Coulston-Gillispie, 1981, pp. 30–35). Rather, the originality of Democritus was that he claimed that knowledge of specific atoms and their differential properties would allow everything in nature, even the soul that we cannot see, to be explained. At about the same time, Aristotle enunciated the first antireductionist dictum: "The whole is not the same as the sum of its parts" (Barnes, 1985, p. 252). A consequence of Aristotle's dictum would be that an organism could not be conceived as nothing more than a random aggregation of organs and systems.

Both reductionist and antireductionist conceptions of the world had important implications with regard to seemingly distant and unrelated topics like the nature of time and space. Since Aristotle's time, science has been faced with an ubiquitous and probably deceptive dichotomy: the whole versus the parts. Instances of this dispute are evident in disciplines as diverse as geometry, cell theory, sociology, anthropology, and evolutionary biology, where individual dynamics are opposed to group dynamics. A list, perhaps stereotyped but nevertheless representative, of such instances can be found in Bertalanffy (1975).

Descartes' mechanism found promising sequels through the achievements of one of his rivals, Newton. Both the driving ideas of Descartes and the methods and techniques of Newton were prominent during the Enlightenment: The aim was to explain every phenomenon in terms of mechanical forces (Hankins, 1985). This new form of reductionism is worth mentioning because it addresses a distinction that has become common in recent years: the distinction between identifying the mechanisms (parts) and forces responsible for the phenomena observed and imposing some prevailing theory as a unique and omnipotent approach to reality. Not only were biological entities and their functioning to be reduced to mechanical components, but chemical and biological theories were also reduced to mechanics. When this was accomplished (if it ever could be), every explanation for the phenomena involved would have to be framed in terms of the mechanical theory invoked. Yet even this ambitious but unrealized program did not put disagreement to rest. After Galileo's and others' demolition of Aristotelian physics, Aristotle's dictum lived on in biology in the form of a nonmechanical vital force that caused organisms to live and grow. In the modern perspective, Aristotle's notion that the parts are not the same as the whole and that wholes have an essence irreducible to their parts might be regarded as corresponding to the notion of structure, understood as the relations among the parts.

Certainly, no one at present would sustain a reductionism that omitted structure. (Dawkins, 1987, termed that form of reductionism "baby-eaters reductionism.") Obviously, many different electrical circuits can be formed from a given set of elements. Such differences are "explained" in terms of the way the parts are assembled, in terms of the configuration of the circuit. It follows, therefore, that, given that the parts are the same, differences in functioning are due to differences in structure. One is tempted to conclude then that, if the properties of each individual component are known and if the way in which all the components are arranged is known, it would, at least in principle, be possible to predict the function of the whole. Advocates of this point of view insist that, if we are not to appeal to some entelechy to explain complex behaviors, explanations must be formulated in terms of the parts and their relations. Antireductionists, on the other hand, insist that not every property of a system can be explained by such decomposition, that is, there are emergent properties, defined as new properties of the system, not present in the components of the system (Bechtel & Richardson, 1993, p. 229). To this, reductionists respond that, even accepting that a particular partition does not explain what appears to be emergent, another, more appropriate partition of the system might account for the properties involved. In other words, what is called *emergent* is never explained by totalities, but by an adequate partition, and what seems to be emergent is only so with respect to a certain partition.

Consider the next example, which is a further elaboration of a classical Kant's example: The number 12 is divisible by 3, but neither 7 nor 5 is, although $7 + 5 = 12$. We could say that being divisible by 3 is an emergent property of adding up 7 and 5. Clearly however, 7 and 5 are not the best choices for decomposing 12 in order to understand its possibility of being divided by 3. This is true enough, but antireductionists would reply that the right decomposition is a result of taking the numerical system as a whole, with all of its operations and relations. Being divisible by 3 (or any other particular number) is not a concept tied to 12 (or any other specific number), but a notion bound to that of being a multiple. However, the notion of multiples of a number ranges over the complete system of natural numbers and it has to do with a classification for numbers, among other things. All this might be clarified by studying the problem in a more general setting (see, e.g., Smith, 19). The point is that, from the reductionist point of view, unexplained processes can only be described, but cannot be understood until an appropriate partition of a system is found. Reductionists would not deny that consideration of the whole might be important as a heuristic method, but they would emphasize that explanation can only be achieved when we use the parts to give an account of the phenomena, although what we will call *mild* reductionists (in contradistinction to baby-eater reductionists) claim that reductive explanations should be made between adjoining levels. Organisms should be understood in terms of systems and tissues, rather than atoms or quarks. There are, however, dramatic exceptions to this rule, for example, explanations of cosmic phenomena, where quarks play a more important role than ecosystems. Despite arguments against great jumps in level, analyses of this dramatic nonadjacent level continue.

Among the many distinct taxonomies for reductionism, we adopt the one derived from Piaget's (1979) analysis of the classification of sciences. According to Piaget, each scientific discipline has a material domain (material even in mathematics, where the subject matter is abstract) and a theoretical domain. Taking this distinction into account, we deal with two forms of reductionism. On the one hand, material reductionism attempts to find elements of the material domain whose properties allow everything that happens in that domain to be inferred (i.e., predicted or deduced). In extreme cases, material reductionism even attempts to explain events in the material domain of one discipline in terms of elements belonging to the material domain of another discipline. In contrast, theoretical reductionism attempts to reduce one theory to another. In some cases, this type of reduction involves demonstrating that some theory is only a special case of another, for example, the reduction of classical mechanics to relativity. In extreme cases, theory reduction involves the absorption of one discipline into another, for example, the reduction of chemistry to physics.[1]

The ways in which material and theory reductionism are manifested in mathematics are particularly instructive in understanding not only how

---

[1]Piaget's ideas about the relations of sciences to one another are also discussed by Brown (chap. 1, this volume).

mathematical knowledge grows, but also the growth of knowledge in other disciplines. As far as theoretical reductionism is concerned, it was developed in mathematics (geometry reduced to algebra, analysis to arithmetic, etc.) from apparently independent sources and relates to one of mathematics' most fundamental instruments—generalization. Although it is has found widespread use in science and has played a major role in mathematics, discussion of theory reductionism will be left to further studies.

In mathematics, material reductionism takes the form of axiomatic method: For any branch of mathematics, there is a (finite) set of axioms and a (finite) set of rules of deduction that account for the whole of the theorems in that field. Because of its impact and acceptance within mathematics, it has been applied in many other fields. In physics, for example, the laws of motion function as axioms that allow phenomena involving objects, masses, forces, and so on, to be deduced much in the same way that the Euclidean axioms deductively determine the properties of geometric figures. Axiomatic reduction has also been used in other fields, including biology.

Reductionism has not been a frequent issue in the philosophy of mathematics, but we believe that it has been present throughout the historic development of mathematics. In fact, reductionism in the form of axiomatic method was the first serious reductionist program in science. We want to show that it has significantly affected the notions of truth and proof in mathematics for several centuries. It is usual to identify axiomatic method and deductive reasoning, but those two concepts are not the same. In this chapter, we attempt to show that deductive thinking was a standard way to do mathematics before Euclid and that it produced important results. Associated with this way of thinking, there were notions of truth and proof that defined this geometry as the immediate predecessor of Euclid's geometry. We then present the axiomatic method as given by Euclid, providing some examples to show that new proofs of already-known results were necessary precisely because the object of geometry itself was different. Euclid believed that he was describing the space and the geometric properties of objects were a consequence of the properties of the space. This is specially exemplified by showing that the symmetry of the figures is explained in terms of the congruence, which is a characteristic of space. We go on to deal with the change of status of some well-known problems and results due to the way Euclid axiomatized geometry. Finally, some consequences of the notion of geometric truth caused by the appearance of non-Euclidean geometry are presented. We claim that non-Euclidean geometry is only possible given the existence of Euclid's axiomatic presentation of geometry. We hope that this short analysis will identify some of the virtues and failures of reductionism associated with axiomatic method in mathematics.

GREEK DEDUCTIVE GEOMETRY AND GEOMETRIC TRUTH

It is often claimed that geometry became a science with Euclid's *Elements* (c. 300 B.C.), the axiomatic method introduced in that work being considered the basis of geometry as a science. There are, on the other hand, people who hold that geometry was a deductive science as early as the sixth century B.C. with Thales and Pythagoras (Heath, 1921, 1926; Knorr, 1975; Szabó, 1978; Tannery, 1912–1934, vols. 1–2; van der Waerden, 1961). We want to begin our discussion by explicating the differences between deductive geometry and axiomatic Euclidean geometry in order to make clear just what Euclidean reductionism is. We start by describing deductive geometry, with special reference to Thales.

Tradition attributes to Thales the proofs of a collection of fundamental results in elementary geometry. (It has, however, been recognized for more than half a century that these results were known to the Babylonians; see Boyer, 1968). Some of the theorems attributed to Thales are as follows:

1. The sum of the inner angles of a triangle is equal to two right angles (Fig. 4.1).

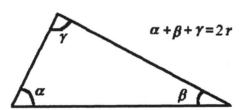

$$\alpha + \beta + \gamma = 2r$$

FIG. 4.1. The sum of the inner angles of a triangle.

2. All angles inscribed in a semicircumference are right angles (Fig. 4.2).

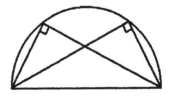

FIG. 4.2. Angles inscribed in a semicircumference.

These theorems, like Pythagoras' theorem (i.e., in a right triangle, the area of the square built along the hypotenuse equals the sum of the areas built along the legs), have the characteristic that it is not enough to look at the figures in order to see the truth of the corresponding propositions; an argument is required in order to be convinced of their truth. (We will come back to this point.)

Other theorems attributed to Thales are:

3. If a triangle has two equal sides (isosceles triangle), then the angles formed by these sides and the base are equal (Fig. 4.3).

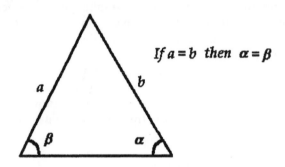

FIG. 4.3. Isosceles triangles.

4. Opposite angles to a vertex are equal (Fig. 4.4).

FIG. 4.4. Opposite angles to a vertex.

Another result of the same type is: Every diameter divides a circle in two equal semicircles. Pointing to the symmetry of the figures can show the truth of these propositions, as in Fig. 4.5. The point we wish to make is that this way of looking at the figures presupposes, in addition to the notion of bilateral symmetry, intentionality. There is no such thing as simply looking. The bilateral symmetry of the isosceles triangle leads to the equality of the angles at its base by folding the paper sheet along the symmetry axis or by rotating the triangle around this axis; the equality of the angles follows from the resulting superposition of the figures. This way of looking presupposes the logic of the equality of figures that can be superposed one on the other. Nevertheless, no further argument is required to establish these results.

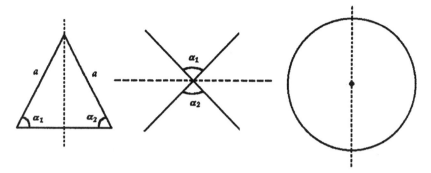

FIG. 4.5. Truth by symmetry.

Another result whose truth can be seen in this way is shown in Fig. 4.6.

5. If we draw a transversal line to two parallel lines, then the alternate angles α and α' are equal (Fig. 4.6).

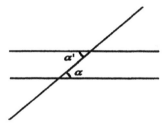

FIG. 4.6. A line transverse to two parallel lines.

Two symmetries are needed to see the truth of the proposition, but no further arguments are required, as in Fig. 4.7 (dashed lines are the axes of symmetry).

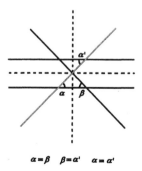

$\alpha = \beta \quad \beta = \alpha' \quad \alpha = \alpha'$

FIG. 4.7. Proof of Thales's fifth theorem.

Consider now the first two results (1, 2). In order to convince oneself that either one of these two propositions is a valid proposition, the introduction of auxiliary elements not present in the original problem or in the associated figure is required. One must use results of the type 3–5 or other symmetries, or the splitting of figures into congruent parts, as long as the results invoked are recognized as valid propositions. Furthermore, one must proceed by logical reasoning. This ad hoc setting of a proposition within a collection of other propositions accepted as evident or valid and then justifying the validity of the proposition in question through logical argument is called a *deductive mosaic*. (This term belongs to mathematical folklore. René Thom used it in private conversations held in Mexico about teaching geometry at elementary school; R. Thom, personal communication, 1985.)

Now, let us show how these mosaics work in the first two propositions above.

Example 1. The sum of the inner angles of a triangle equals two right angles, $2r$ (Fig. 4.8).

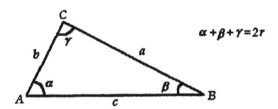

FIG. 4.8. The sum of the inner angles of a triangle.

Proof: Draw a parallel line to c, which goes through C (Fig. 4.9).

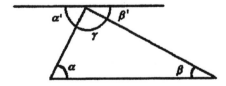

FIG. 4.9. Proof of Example 1.

We know, from (5), that $\alpha = \alpha'$ and $\beta = \beta'$. Moreover, $\alpha' + \gamma + \beta' = 2r$, therefore, $\alpha + \beta + \gamma = 2r$.

Example 2. All angles inscribed in a semicircumference are right angles (Fig. 4.10).

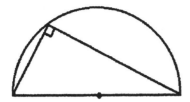

FIG. 4.10. Angles inscribed in a semicircle.

In order to prove this, we need three ad hoc assumptions: (a) All radii in a circle are of equal length, (b) statement$_3$, and (c) the result just proved (Example 1).

Proof: Draw a line from the center of the semicircumference to the vertex of the triangle (Fig. 4.11). By (a), we know that the line drawn is equal in length to the two lines composing the diameter of the semicircumference. We have two triangles and, for each, we have two sides of equal length; applying (b), we have that $\alpha = \alpha'$ and $\beta = \beta'$. Now, we apply (c) to measure the third angle for each triangle, which is $2r - 2\alpha$ in the first triangle and $2r - 2\beta$ in the second. But clearly, $(2r - 2\alpha) + (2r - 2\beta) = 2r$, and we conclude that $\alpha + \beta = r$.

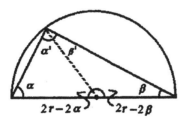

FIG. 4.11. Proof of Example 2.

Notice that the argument for Example 2 uses Example 1. This shows how several deductive mosaics are combined and how one can, in this way, construct, organize, and present one theory or another.

To conclude this section, let us make some observations concerning deductive mosaics that will prove important in the next section. These concern the notion of truth within deductive mosaic mathematics. To begin with, in deductive mosaic thought, the truth of a geometric proposition was regarded as given in the geometric object. A proposition within a deductive mosaic was shown to be true, people were led to see the truth of the proposition, or a concealed truth was brought to the foreground, the evidence being the logical chain formed with evident properties or with properties formerly shown to be true. In this mathematics, the truth of geometric properties was regarded as independent from their proof, so that the argument leading pre-Euclidean mathematicians to see the truth of a geometric proposition does not partake in this truth. For them, the deduction does not confer truth to the proposition: It was true even in the absence of a proof, which was only a way of realizing the fact stated. It seems that a naive realism underlies this conception of the mathematical truth.

Furthermore, there is no axiomatization (which is a completely different story, as we will see later) in deductive mosaic thinking. Even so, we contend that this form of mathematical thought can be regarded as a science, not only because of the depth of its results and its deductive character, but also because of the organization of its results in the form of theories. In ancient China, geometry was deductively developed, but not axiomatized, and arithmetic itself in Greece was also far from being axiomatized, even in Euclid's *Elements*.

EUCLID'S AXIOMATIC GEOMETRY AND THE EUCLIDEAN NOTION OF TRUTH

In this section, we show the radical changes in the mathematical thought introduced by Euclid in his *Elements* (Heath, 1956). As we have just seen, in the deductive mosaic thinking, pre-Euclideans started with a result considered to be true and built a set of assumptions and an organization of them addressed to justify the original result, which happened to be a property inherent to the object. The truth of a proposition lies in the proposition itself and the mosaic is just a path (a deductive argument) to make that result part of our knowledge. Different mosaics are possible for one proposition. On the other hand, in the axiomatic method, we start with a limited set of assumptions considered to be true and deduct a set of results whose validity is justified precisely because it is deductively derived from true premises. We may say that in mosaics we start up with one result and move down to the basis; in the axiomatic method we start down with a set of assumptions (the axioms) that we believe faithfully portrays the object under study and move up to produce a lot of results. To show how Euclid proceeded, we present his assumptions (axioms and postulates) and some examples of propositions. We pay particular attention to the postulate of parallels, which plays a critical role in what follows.

As is well known, Euclid's *Elements* are divided into 13 books. Except for books VII, VIII, and IX, which deal with the theory of numbers, the *Elements* deal with the geometry of the plane and of space. Book I begins by defining the basic objects of geometry. Since antiquity, different editions of the *Elements* add or suppress definitions, postulates, and axioms. In one edition,

Postulate 5 is an axiom. We have followed the English edition by Sir Thomas L. Heath (1956). There are 23 definitions, which are supplemented with more definitions in the other books. Some definitions in book I, literally taken from Heath (1956, pp. 153–154), are:

Def. 1: A *point* is that which has no part.

Def. 2: A *line* is a breadthless length.

Def. 4: A *straight line* is a line which lies evenly with the points on itself.

Def. 15: A *circle* is a plane figure contained by one line such that all the straight lines falling upon it from one point among those lying within the figure are equal to one another.

Def. 16: And the point is called the *center* of the circle.

Def. 23: *Parallel* straight lines are straight lines which, being in the same plane and being produced indefinitely in both directions, do not meet one another in either direction.

Given this, Euclid believed that five postulates are needed (again, taken textually from Heath, 1956, pp. 154–155). They involve:

Postulate 1: Drawing a straight line from any point to any point.

Postulate 2: Producing a finite straight line continuously in a straight line.

Postulate 3: Describing a circle with any center and distance.

Postulate 4: Recognizing that all right angles are equal to one another.

Postulate 5: Recognizing that if a straight line falling on two straight lines make the interior angles on the same side less than two right angles, the two straight lines, if produced indefinitely, meet on that side on which the angles are less than the two right angles.

This last postulate is known as the axiom of parallels. It is equivalent to Playfair's axiom, better known to us in the form (Heath, 1956, p. 220):

Postulate 5': Through a given point, one and only one parallel can be drawn to a given straight line.

Postulates 1, 2, and 3 can be regarded as a description of the use of ruler and compass in geometric constructions, but this does not dispel the Aristotelian overtones inherent in the choice of precisely straight lines and circles as the elements of geometry. Euclid continued with the axioms or common notions (Heath, 1956, p. 155):

1. Things that are equal to the same thing are also equal to one another.

2. If equals be added to equals, the remainders are equal.

3. If equals be subtracted from equals, the remainders are equal.

4. Things that coincide with one another are equal to one another.

5. The whole is greater than the part.

Euclid proves 48 propositions in Book I. Postulate 5 is used for the first time in the proof of Proposition 29 (Heath, 1956, p. 311):

Proposition 29. A straight line falling on parallel straight lines makes the alternate angles equal to one another, the exterior angle equal to the interior and opposite angle, and the interior angles on the same side equal to two right angles. This is illustrated in Fig. 4.12.

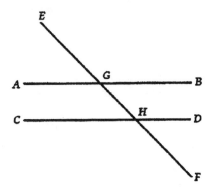

FIG. 4.12. A straight line falling on parallel lines makes alternate angles equal.

The first part of Proposition 29 was stated in the preceding section (see Proposition 5) and used as a matter of course in the proof that the internal angles of a triangle taken together are equal to two right angles. The realization that the proposition under Postulate 5 is a postulate was one of Euclid's greatest merits. Furthermore, using this postulate exactly at the point at which it is first needed gives the *Elements* the form of a precise logical analysis of the geometric plane. One can also think that Euclid did this because he thought that the proposition under Postulate 5 could be deduced from the other postulates. In fact, the proof of the axiom of parallels was attempted over and over again during the following 20 centuries. In any case, this is a milestone in Euclid's opera and has played a significant role in the later development of geometry and the whole of mathematics. But the main point, which cannot be overstated, is that this postulate unveils a shift in the object of geometry. Before Euclid, geometry was the study of figures by themselves; in Euclidean geometry, in some sense, the object is the space and what happens to the figures is simply a consequence of them living in the space. This statement about the space transcends our experience. No drawing whatsoever can illustrate the fifth postulate, because the proposition speaks about what happens beyond the drawing. Figure 4.13 illustrates this point.

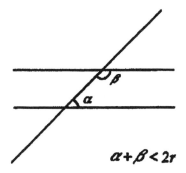

$$\alpha + \beta < 2r$$

FIG. 4.13. What happens beyond the drawing.

Many authors (Heath, 1956; Knorr, 1975, 1981; Tannery, 1912–1934, vols. 1–2; van der Waerden, 1961) have analyzed the contents and structure of the *Elements* and Aristotle's influence upon them. It is not our purpose to take part in this discussion. Our purpose is to show that the form given by Euclid to geometry entails a reductionist program. We begin by examining the relation of Euclidean geometry to the preceding deductive mosaics.

EUCLID AND THE PROBLEM OF DEDUCTIVE MOSAICS

Euclid proceeded from the standpoint that all geometric properties concerning the elements of plane geometry (circles, straight lines, triangles, polygons, etc.) can be deduced from axioms and postulates, in particular, from properties established in the deductive mosaic mathematics that preceded his theory. From Euclid's point of view and very much in contrast with the deductive mosaic thinking that preceded him, it was not necessary to introduce ad hoc principles for the proof of new propositions, even though the axioms and postulates given by Euclid are incomplete. As Leibniz (Gerhart, cited in Brunschvicg, 1945, pp. 115–116) pointed out very early on, Euclid still used extra properties implicit in figures in the proof of the first proposition in Book I:

Proposition I–To construct an equilateral triangle on a given finite straight line (Fig. 4.14):

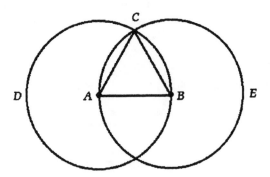

FIG. 4.14. Constructing an equilateral triangle on a given finite straight line.

As Leibniz pointed out, it does not follow from the postulates that the two circles intersect at all. This situation was a matter of concern for geometers across many centuries. The solution to this problem required the development of modern axiomatic theory in the 19th century and was finally given by Hilbert in 1899 (Hilbert, 1902). However, this does not alter the central idea of axiomatic geometry: The axioms and postulates of geometry are characteristic of the plane (or of space) in the sense that they produce a fair picture of its geometric objects and their properties. According to this, any proposition, no matter how simple and immediate, will be a logical consequence of the axioms and postulates. In this way, theorem 4 in the preceding section appears as Proposition 15 in the *Elements*. That opposite angles are equal is proved as follows (Fig. 4.15):

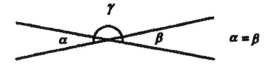

FIG. 4.15. Result 4 and Proposition 15.

We know that $\alpha + \gamma = 2r$, where r stands for right angle, but $\gamma + \beta = 2r$, hence $\alpha = \beta$. It is easy to check, but it is not an axiom, therefore it has to be proved. The point is that, in Euclidean geometry, the truth of the postulates extends to the propositions through logical inference; it is not an evident property of the figures or, if it is, that does not suffice to accept it as part of the theory. Any and all propositions whatsoever, no matter how simple, can and must be reconstructed starting from the postulates and axioms. This has the remarkable effect of duplicating the notion of geometric truth. On the one hand, truth continues to be given in the geometric object, as in deductive mosaics; on the other hand, truth is given to the object by the proof that starts from the axioms. For us, the meaning of this shift in the notion of truth of geometric propositions entails a reduction of geometric objects and their properties to the elements central to Euclidean geometry.

This can be clarified by the reduction of symmetry to congruence. For this, let us consider Proposition 5 in Book I of the *Elements* (Heath, 1956, p. 251). This is the theorem on the equality of the base angles of the isosceles triangle attributed to Thales (theorem 3, which was justified through a symmetry argument).

Proposition 5. In isosceles triangles, the angles at the base are equal to one another and, if the equal straight lines be produced further, the angles under the base will be equal to one another (Fig. 4.16).

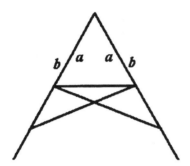

FIG. 4.16. The side-angle-side theorem of congruence.

As we already remarked, this proposition is not proved by symmetry; instead, Euclid used Proposition 4 (Heath, 1956, p. 247), known as the side-angle-side theorem of congruence of triangles.

Proposition 4. If two triangles have the two sides equal to two sides respectively and the two angles contained by the equal straight lines equal, they will also have the base equal to the base, the triangle will be equal to the triangle, and the remaining angles will be equal to the remaining angles respectively, namely those which the equal sides subtend.

This is one of the two propositions in Book I that Euclid proved using superposition of figures. In *The Foundations of the Geometry*, Hilbert (1902) used a simplified version of the proposition as an axiom of congruence. Along this line of thought, the self-evidence of bilateral symmetry has been reconstructed in terms of congruence properties of space applied to triangles. Reduced in this way, the notion of symmetry is no longer elementary; it has been reduced to the concept of congruence. We remark that symmetry in the mosaics was conceived of as a property of the figure, whereas congruence in the Euclidean setting follows from properties of the space, though not yet in the modern sense. We hold this to be a case of material reduction.

After Euclid, symmetry was no longer a central topic in Greek geometry. In the 19th century, Felix Klein, in his Erlanger Programm (Klein, 1974), defined different geometries in terms of their symmetry groups. This new concept of symmetry, however, is a property of the space, not of the figures as in mosaic thinking.

THE EUCLIDEAN REDUCTIONIST PROGRAM

The last two propositions in Book I of the *Elements*, Propositions 47 and 48, are Pythagoras' theorem and its converse. The proof not only succeeds in integrating the results of deductive mosaics into axiomatic geometry, but also deepens the significance of the theorems themselves. This reduction of important deductive mosaics to Euclidean principles led to attempts to reduce all geometric properties of circles, straight lines, polygons, and angles to axioms. That vast undertaking is what we call the Euclidean reductionist program. We speak of reduction when the *reduction* has been successful, of *reductionism*, when the reduction becomes a program or project. Presently, we shall see that the Euclidean reductionist program was bound to fail, but this is a present-day perspective. It was not until the 19th century that its mathematical impossibility could be demonstrated.

There is, however, another side of this coin to be considered. This concerns the fact that the Euclidean reduction, from its very beginning, was paradigmatic. By this, we mean that the kind of geometry that Euclid introduced in the *Elements* was carried over to domains whose objects were not contemplated in Euclid's great work. Consider, in this respect, Apollonius' conics (Heath, 1961). Furthermore, as is well known, Euclidean geometry remained an approach, an example to be followed in science and in the search for truth, even with the advent of mathematical physics and the experimental sciences up until the 19th century, when mathematical analysis produced an epistemological shift toward empiricism.

It is important to point out that the Euclidean reductionist program has a characteristic difficulty. Even if the formulation of a problem refers exclusively to circles, straight lines, angles, and so forth, it is not possible to know in advance whether its analysis will or will not require the introduction of ad hoc elements, as in deductive mosaics. This difficulty produced, in the Euclidean tradition, the three classical problems of geometry: the duplication of the cube, the trisection of the angle, and the quadrature of the circle.

These three problems had been solved in several different ways before the advent of Euclidean geometry. It will suffice to consider only the duplication of the cube to illustrate our point. The problem is as follows: Given a cube, give a construction of a double cube. It was shown a century before Euclid that this problem was equivalent to the problem of constructing a compound mean proportional. Menaechmus solved the problem (Knorr, 1975) using the intersection of two parabolas or a parabola and a hyperbola. The problem recurred in Euclidean geometry because Menaechmus' solution used elements beyond the scope of Euclid's system. It took mathematicians 2000 more years to prove the impossibility of constructing a compound mean proportional using only a ruler and compass, the tools implicitly allowed by the postulates.

In a similar vein, it can be shown that proving the impossibility of the three classical problems of Euclidean geometry was one of the great achievements of 19th-century mathematics. The attempts to solve the classical problems led, across many centuries, to important and deep results in mathematics. The tool used in these impossibility proofs belongs to algebraic field theory; its relation to Euclidean geometry is obtained through Cartesian geometry. (An excellent exposition of these results is found in Courant & Robbins, 1977, pp. 117–139).

In view of this, it makes sense to say that the virtue of the kind of reductionism under discussion here is not to solve problems, but to create them. The 19th century proved that the Euclidean reductionist program was an impossible program. The properties of the elements of Euclidean geometry, some properties of circles, straight lines, and angles, lie beyond the reach of the Euclidean axioms and postulates. If reduction is to occur at all, another partition must be sought.

NON-EUCLIDEAN GEOMETRY AS A CRITIQUE OF THE EUCLIDEAN NOTION OF TRUTH

We have remarked throughout our analysis on the changes in the notion of truth in going from mosaic to axiomatic geometry, basically, the shift from the geometric object itself to the properties of the figures inherited from those of the space. Nevertheless, in both conceptions the truth lies in the object. The advent of non-Euclidean geometry produced a dramatic change in this conception of geometric truth, which no longer lies in the object, but becomes part of the formal structure of the theory. In fact, some geometers stopped talking about truth and started referring simply to proof. This shift is possible because of the axiomatic approach and shows both virtues and constraints of the axiomatic method and thus of Euclid's reductionist program.

Attempts to find a proof of the fifth postulate, in terms of the other four, led to the advent of non-Euclidean geometry, discovered independently by Gauss, Bolyai, and Lobachewsky (Bonola, 1955). The fifth postulate, in the form of Playfair's axiom, demands the existence and *uniqueness* of a line passing through a given point parallel to a given line. In non-Euclidean geometry, there is an infinity of parallel lines passing through the given point. This new axiom of parallels seems to contradict our perception of space. Nevertheless, it was proved that the axioms of Euclidean geometry do not lead to a logical contradiction if and only if the axioms of non-Euclidean geometry do not lead to a logical contradiction. Therefore, Euclidean geometry is as consistent as non-Euclidean geometry, that is, both geometries have the same logical status.

This brings to the foreground the fact that the two already mentioned notions of truth underlying Euclidean geometry, the one that asserts a property belonging to the object and the one that confers truth through proof, do not imply each other. Both geometries could have equal logical status, but, it was thought, only one would reflect the truth as given in the geometric object. Therefore, as the following remarks of Lobachewsky (Bonola, 1955) show, the only way to determine which geometry was realized in nature was through empirical evidence:

"The fruitlessness of the attempts [to prove the axiom of parallels] made, since Euclid's time, for the space of 2000 years, aroused in me the suspicion that the truth, which it was desired to prove, was not contained in the data themselves; that to establish it the aid of experiment would be needed, for example, of astronomical observations, as in the case of other laws of nature." (Bonola, 1955, p. 92)

Lobachewsky's attempts to establish which was the "real" geometry, by means of the measurement of the parallax of distant stars, failed. This left the way open for the alternative notion of geometric truth, in modern terms. This truth would be not the truth given by the "geometry of nature," but, rather, the truth given by the logical consistency of axioms. As is well known, this led to the problem of the foundations of axiomatic mathematics and to new reductionist programs, in particular that of Hilbert (1902). From there, it also led to the contributions of Gödel (1931), demonstrating the impossibility of Hilbert's program. Discussion of these issues is, however, beyond the scope of this chapter. Nevertheless, even to mention the fallout of the Euclidean program clearly indicates the role that reductionism continues to play in the development of mathematics.

To the best of our knowledge, the analysis of reductionism in mathematics has been neglected in the literature. If we have made clear, through our analysis of deductive and axiomatic geometry, that reductionism not only is present in mathematics, but also has been a conception underlying many of its fundamental changes along its history, we have achieved our purpose. Our goal was simply to point out a new direction in the study of what constitutes reductionism in mathematics and what might be its virtues, limitations, and failures.

AUTHOR NOTE

Jaime Oscar Falcón Vega, UNAM–Facultad de Ciencias, Departamento de Matemáticas, Circuito Exterior, Ciudad Universitaria, Planta Baja, Delegación Coyoacán, 04510 México DF; e-mail: jofv@hp.fciencias.unam.mx.

Gerardo Hernández, Sección de Metodología y Teoría de la Ciencia, Cinvestav, San Borja 938, Col Del Valle, Delegación Benito Juarez, 03100 México DF; e-mail: ghernand@mail.cinvestav.mx.

Juan José Rivaud, Sección de Metodología y Teoría de la Ciencia, Cinvestav, San Borja 938, Col Del Valle, Delegación Benito Juarez, 03100 México DF; e-mail: jrivaud@mail.cinvestav.mx.

We are grateful to the editors for their critical comments and suggestions, which greatly improved the original manuscript.

REFERENCES

Barnes, J. (Ed.). (1985). *The complete works of Aristotle: The revised edition* (Vol. 1). Princeton, NJ: Princeton University Press.

Bechtel, W., & Richardson, R. C. (1993). *Discovering complexity: Decomposition and localization as strategies in scientific research*. Princeton, NJ: Princeton University Press.

Bertalanffy, L. von. (1975). *Perspectives in general systems theory: Scientific-philosophical studies*. New York: G. Braziller.

Bonola, R. (1955). Non-Euclidean geometry. In H. S. Carslaw (Ed.), *Non-Euclidian geometry* (pp.). New York: Dover.

Boyer, C. A. (1968). *History of mathematics*. New York: John Wiley & Sons.

Brunschvicg, L. (1945). *Las etapas de la filosofía matemática* [The stages of mathematical philosophy]. Buenos Aires, Argentina: Lautaro.

Coulston-Gillispie, C. (Ed.). (1981). *Dictionary of scientific biography* (Vol. 4). New York: Scribners Sons.

Courant, R., & Robbins, H. (1977). *What is mathematics? An elementary approach to ideas and methods* (6th ed.). Oxford, England: Oxford University Press.

Dawkins, R. (1987). *The blind watchmaker: Why the evidence of evolution reveals a universe without design*. New York: W. W. Norton.

Gödel, K. (1931). *Über formal unentscheidbare Sätzeder Principia mathematica und verwandter Systeme*. Monatshefte für Mathematik und Physik 1931 pgs. 173–198.

Hankins, T. L. (1985). *Science and the enlightenment.* Cambridge, England: Cambridge University Press.

Heath, T. L. (1956). *The thirteen books of Euclid's Elements.* New York: Dover.

Heath, T. L. (1961). *Apollonius of Perga: Treatise on conic sections.* New York: Barnes & Noble.

Heath, T. L. (1981). *A history of Greek mathematics.* New York: Dover.

Hilbert, D. (1902). *The foundations of geometry* (Trans. unknown). La Salle, IL: Open Court.

Klein, F. (1974). *Le programme d'Erlangen: Considérations comparatives sur les recherches géométriques modernes* [The Erlangen program: Comparative considerations on modern geometric research] (M. H. Pade, Trans.). Paris: Jacques Gabay. (Original work published 1872)

Knorr, W. R. (1975). *The evolution of the Euclidean elements.* Dordrecht: D. Reidel.

Knorr, W. R. (1981). On the early history of axiomatics: The interaction of mathematics and philosophy in Greek antiquity. In J. Hintikka, D. Gruender, & E. Agazzi (Eds.), *Pisa conference proceedings* (Vol. 1, pp. 145–186). Dordrecht: D. Reidel.

Piaget, J. (1979). *Tratado de lógica y conocimiento científico* [On logic and scientific knowledge] (Trans., Vol. 7). Buenos Aires, Argentina: Paidós. (Original work published Logique et connaissance scientifique, Gallimard, Paris 1967)

Szabó, Á. (1978). *The beginnings of Greek mathematics.* Dordrecht: D. Reidel.

Tannery, P. (1912–1934). *Mémoires scientifiques* (Vols. 1–13). Paris: Gauthier-Villars.

van der Waerden, B. L. (1961). *Science awakening.* Oxford, England: Oxford University Press.

II

REPRESENTATION

5

The Biological Emergence
of Representation

Mark H. Bickhard
Lehigh University

NATURALISM AND EMERGENCE

Emergence is a difficult and sometimes contentious issue. What is at stake? On one side, what is at stake is the success of naturalism, of understanding our world as being constituted of integrated natural phenomena. Many kinds of phenomena have, at various points in history, been considered to be exceptions to a naturalistic framework, and to instead require specific substances to be postulated that interacted with the rest of the world, but had no deeper relationships. That is, they have been thought to require a dualism, or higher multiplicity, of fundamental ontological kinds. Fire, life, magnetism, heat, and so on were all once thought, at least by some, to be due to their own dedicated substances—phlogiston, vital fluid, magnetic fluid, caloric, and so on—but are now understood as emergent phenomena of particular kinds of natural processes. Naturalism is now a basic assumption of the scientific enterprise, though it is much easier to espouse naturalism than it is to develop models that are consistent with naturalism.[1] I argue, in fact, that con-

---

[1]Naturalism is often and all too easily equated with some kind of physicalism or scientism. I use the term to refer to a kind of regulative ideal that presupposes an integrated world in which further questioning is always appropriate. Empedoclean earth, air, fire, and water, for example, constituted an advance over simpler categorizations, but also blocked inquiry: One cannot ask about the origin of such basic substances, for an explanation of their properties, and so on. The same can be said for the many modern equivalents of such substance assumptions (Bickhard, in preparation; Bickhard & Christopher, 1994).

temporary models of function and representation fail the standards of naturalism and I offer alternatives that meet those standards.

Phenomena that remain unintegrated into the naturalistic world view today are primarily kinds of normative phenomena. Function, representation, rationality, and ethics are all examples of normative phenomena for which we have no consensual naturalistic models, and for which some would argue no such models are possible. The claim that normative phenomena cannot be addressed naturalistically is sometimes made with the slogan "You cannot derive ought from is," that is, the claim that one cannot derive norms from facts.[2] A failure of naturalism here would introduce some kind of dualism for mental phenomena and perhaps also for biological normative function as well.

On the other side, emergence is also deeply involved in contentious issues *within* the framework of naturalism. In particular, one could propose a naturalism in which emergence did not exist and everything that we take as seeming to be emergent would be proposed for some kind of eliminative reductionism. Such an eliminative reductionism has been proposed for much of the mind: Only brain processes are real and all appearances to the contrary are *merely* appearances (Churchland, 1986; Churchland, 1989).

More broadly, however, if naturalism holds, but emergence does not exist, then most of our familiar world—rocks, trees, other people, our own minds—is at best epiphenomenal, not really causally efficacious in the world, and at worst fictitious, simply illusions. The only reality is that of fundamental physical particles. It is difficult to take such a possibility seriously, especially for our own minds, but science has certainly made a case for strongly unobvious and counterintuitive results before, and there are powerful arguments to that effect for emergence.

A less personal but more directly scientific issue that is at stake is that many kinds of phenomena, whatever their status as *ontologically* emergent (or not), clearly once did not exist in any form (e.g., at the time of the Big Bang) and do now exist. Any model of such phenomena that makes such emergence, whether epiphenomenal or not, impossible thereby cannot account for the existence of the phenomena at all. This can serve as a strong critical consideration when evaluating models, such as those of representation, because many current models fail that test of the emergence of novel phenomena.

This point raises issues about what emergence is. Is it mere novelty, or is, for example, causal efficacy required? Again, there is no consensus. Emergence involves new properties or entities "emerging" at new levels of organization, but there have been many proposals concerning just exactly

---

[2]See Bickhard (1998, in press-b) for a reply to this argument against the emergence of normative phenomena.

what emerges (e.g., properties or entities, must they be causally efficacious, etc.), how such emergence can be understood, and what counts as a relevant "level." The British emergentists earlier in this century—Broad, for example—proposed that certain natural laws applied only when particular kinds of organization came into existence, but, in any instance in which those critical organizations did exist, the laws had full effect. These laws were thought to be natural, and therefore in that sense did not violate naturalism (though they did violate the anti-ad hoc spirit of naturalism), but were not derivable or predictable from any of the constitutive entities or processes that participated in the critical organizations. One of the primary examples of the British emergentists was chemical valence and, when quantum mechanics was able to explain valence without recourse to such ad hoc laws, British emergentism faded (Stephan, 1992).[3] Nevertheless, such a strong version of emergentism still serves as a backdrop for many contemporary discussions in the form of claims that anything that is derivable from lower level considerations cannot count as emergent.

The notion of emergence began as a reference to phenomena that could not be explained as *additive* consequences of underlying phenomena (Stephan, 1992). Non-additivity has remained an important consideration, but additivity versus non-additivity, or linearity versus nonlinearity, is not sufficient to address the basic issues of epiphenomenality or eliminative reduction. If, for example, all causality were resident in fundamental physical particles (as will be discussed later), then whether the causal dance of those particles was additive or non-additive, linear or nonlinear, would be irrelevant to the point that all causality would be resident in those particles, not in any higher level that was composed out of those particles. All apparent higher level 'causality' would be epiphenomenal.

Few would reject the claim that new causal regularities can occur in particular kinds of underlying system organization. The emergence issues turn on whether these regularities constitute emergence in any metaphysically important sense, in particular, whether mind can be understood as being more than just a (nonlinear) regularity of underlying nonmental processes, that is, if mind is merely epiphenomenal.

A deeply related issue is that of downward causation. If genuine non-epiphenomenal emergence does occur, then it ought to not only be manifested in causal consequences at the level of the emergence and at higher levels, but it also ought to have consequences at lower levels. That is, we should find downward causation from emergent phenomena (Campbell,

---

[3]Piaget rejected emergence (Kitchener, 1986), but his conception of emergence seems to have been that of the British emergentists and his grounds for rejection do not hold for other conceptions of emergence. In fact, Piaget's entire *oeuvre* can be seen as an attempt to model the biological emergence of cognition and rationality within a generally naturalistic framework (e.g., Piaget, 1971).

1974a, 1974b, 1990). A classic purported example is the downward causal influence on the molecules making up a soldier termite's jaw—which is too large for the termite to even feed itself, therefore requiring constant tending by nest mates—from the higher level social and evolutionary processes of the termite species and nest. A closer-to-home example would be whether or not mind makes any causal difference at all in the physical processes at lower levels that we associate with presumably mental organisms, such as ourselves.

KIM'S ARGUMENT

I do not attempt to address all of these issues here. I do address, however, one of the strongest arguments against causally efficacious emergence, that of Jaegwon Kim (1993a, 1993b, 1997, 1998). I choose Kim's arguments not only because they pose one of the strongest challenges to any concept of emergence and any model of purported emergent phenomena, but also because Kim, in my judgement, has discovered in his argument a *reductio ad absurdum* of important standard assumptions. That is, I argue that Kim's argument does not ultimately hold, but that avoiding it requires important shifts in other common assumptions. In particular, it requires abandoning the substance and structure assumptions that are ubiquitous in contemporary psychology (Bickhard, in press-d; Bickhard & Christopher, 1994).

Kim points out that we seem to be faced with a dilemma: Either all causality resides in the fundamental physical particles and all higher level phenomena are just the working out of the causal interactions at this basic particle level, or something that is not part of fundamental physics has causal influence. In the first case, everything above the fundamental physical particles is causally epiphenomenal. In the second case, the universe is not physically closed, and naturalism is false.

The crucial move in this argument is that, whereas emergence is intuitively a product of higher level organizations of lower level processes and particles, Kim's argument points out that such organization is merely the framework within which the particles engage in their causal dance. Such organization cannot contribute any causal power itself—all causal power is resident in the particles. But, since organization cannot be a legitimate locus of causal power, there is no way in which any higher level emergence can have any causal power. The only properties in the higher level that are novel are the organizational properties, but if organization has no possibility of causal power itself and is restricted to being just a stage for the working out of fundamental particle causality, then all higher level phenomena are at best causally epiphenomenal.

Particles themselves, on the other hand, have no organization. They can *participate* in organizations of processes of interacting with other particles, but no fundamental particle itself has organization—otherwise it would not be fundamental. This point is the flip side of the ineligibility of organization as a possible locus of causal power: Organization is the framework within which particles, which have no organization, can work out their interactive causal consequences. Therefore, organization cannot be the locus of causal power and no higher level organization can manifest more than causally epiphenomenal "emergence."

But particles and organization are all there is. In particular, if organization cannot constitute a locus of causal power, then causally efficacious emergence cannot occur *unless* causal power resides in more than basic particles. But then naturalism takes a serious blow because reality would not be physically closed; something not part of the physical realm of basic particles would influence physical processes.

I find this argument to be valid, but unsound. I have argued that the critical move is the diremption between organization and locus of causal power (Bickhard, 2000b; Campbell & Bickhard, in preparation). Particles have no organization but do have causal power, while organization must be merely the framework for working out particle causal consequences, or else naturalism fails. The incorrect assumption in this reasoning is the assumption that the physical realm is constituted by particles interacting in space and time.

In fact, our best current physics shows that there are no particles, none at all (Brown & Harré, 1998; Cao, 1999; Davies, 1984; Saunders & Brown, 1991; Weinberg, 1977, 1995–2000). All of physical reality is composed of quantum field processes and the appearance of particles is a manifestation of the quantum nature of the field processes. But that quantum nature, in turn, is no more a manifestation of individual particles than is the quantization of the number of wave lengths in a guitar string—there are no "guitar sound" particles. The number of manifest particle interactions is not even an invariant, but will vary from one observer to another.

This shift to a field framework is of fundamental importance for the issues at hand. Field models are process models, not particle models. The crucial characteristic of process models, including (quantum) field models, is that there is *nothing* that does not possess organization. Everything has organization; it is not just that everything *participates* in organization, but that everything *has* organization. In particular, all quantum field processes are inherently organized. They cannot exist without organization; they cannot exist at a single point.

But if everything is inherently organized, if process organization is constitutive at all levels, then it is not legitimate to delegitimate organization as a possible locus of causal power. If everything has organization, then anything that has causal power will have organization. Furthermore, the causal properties will vary depending on such organization: Organization has causal potency. Conversely, if organization is rejected as a legitimate locus of causal power, then *nothing* has causal power.

Moreover, this point holds at all scales. Quantum phenomena such as superconductivity, for example, can occur at any scale, so it is not possible to specify a scale below which organization might have causal power, but above which organization would be merely a framework for working out lower level causal powers.

Finally, if organization cannot be precluded from carrying causal power, then higher level organization cannot be precluded from manifesting new, nonlinear, emergent causal power. After all, all higher level organization is "just" a potentially very complex quantum field organization, and quantum field organizations are all there is. So, if something, X, is ontologically constituted as a kind of organization of (quantum) processes, then whatever the causal properties are of that organization, they are the causal properties of what that organization constitutes. They are the causal properties of X, nonepiphenomenally.

The move from a particle metaphysics to a process metaphysics, then, undercuts Kim's arguments. In effect, Kim has discovered a *reductio ad absurdum* of particle metaphysics. Such a metaphysics makes emergence impossible (or forces a violation of naturalism). Conversely, any naturalistic theoretical framework that is committed to a particle metaphysics cannot account for emergence, and is thereby committed to an eliminative reductionism.

Of what relevance is this for issues in psychology? It is deeply relevant. Much of psychology is still committed to various kinds of atomisms or substance models. That is, much of psychology is still not developed within a process metaphysics and, therefore, cannot account for the emergence of basic psychological phenomena. But, if such models cannot account for the *emergence* of psychological phenomena, then they are likely to be poor models of the *nature* of such phenomena. Phlogiston could account for some properties of fire, but failed miserably to account for its basic nature and could not address many properties of fire that emerged naturally within a model of fire as a process of combustion.

PRAGMATISM AND PIAGET

Failures to be consistent with naturalism can be subtle, not perspicuous at all, and are therefore an easily committed error even for those who espouse naturalism. This is also true for failures to account for emergence. The first caution for both issues is to proceed within a process metaphysics. Otherwise, one is committed either to a nonnaturalism or to a strong reductivism.

Pragmatism is a philosophical orientation that is deeply committed to a process metaphysics and, therefore, is a candidate for naturalistic investigation, especially for studies of mental phenomena. Pragmatism introduced novel ways of conceptualizing representation and mind that offer possibilities of avoiding millennia-long aporia in standard approaches (Joas, 1993). Piaget worked within a generally pragmatist framework—the influence included the line from Peirce and James through Baldwin to Piaget—and is therefore among the few psychologists to explore an orientation that might ultimately succeed in naturalizing the mind. Most of psychology is still dominated by traditions extending back to the ancient and classical Greeks, by what pragmatists have dubbed "spectator" models of representation, in which perception and cognition are matters of passive receipt of impressions from the world (Smith, 1987).

I will pursue the Piagetian programme of modeling the nature and emergence of representation within a process, a pragmatist, framework. With respect to mental phenomena, the most important manifestation of a process orientation is the shift from passively conceived perception as the metaphor for mind to an understanding of action as the proper framework for modeling mental phenomena (Joas, 1993). This commitment to action as the fundamental framework is one of the most important aspects of Piaget's work, but one whose importance is at times underappreciated even by Piagetians.

I approach the model of representation via the initial emergence of normative function, with representation constituting a further emergence for serving a particular kind of function. Along the way, I address some of the alternative models on offer, arguing that they fail the criterion of accounting for the naturalistic emergence of these phenomena.

FUNCTION

Some processes are fleeting, such as the fall of a leaf. Some patterns or organizations of process, however, can be stable, perhaps even for cosmological lengths of time. One major kind of such stable patterns of process is that of energy well stabilities. A pattern of process that is persistent due to an energy well stability is one in which the process is in some (local) energy well and would require an input of energy sufficient to raise its energy level above some threshold in order to change its pattern. Much of the basic furniture of the world is constituted by such energy well stable process patterns, such as atoms, molecules, rocks, and so on.

Another kind of stability of process is exhibited by certain far-from-thermodynamic equilibrium processes (Nicolis & Prigogine, 1977). Far-from-equilibrium processes require ongoing interactions and transactions with their environments in order to maintain their far-from-equilibrium conditions. In some cases, maintenance of these conditions depends entirely on external stabilities—a chemical bath maintained in far-from-equilibrium conditions will depend on the external conditions of the chemical containers remaining nonempty, the pumps continuing to work, the electricity for the pumps (and perhaps a stirrer) continuing, and so on.

Self-Maintaining Systems

There is a special kind of far-from-equilibrium process, however, that can make its own contributions to the maintenance of its own far-from-equilibrium conditions. One simple example is a candle flame: It maintains above combustion threshold temperature; in a standard atmosphere and gravitational field, it induces convection, which maintains a supply of oxygen and removes waste products, and so on. These are called *self-maintenant systems*. I propose to model the emergence of function in terms of self-maintenant far-from-equilibrium systems.

Serving a Function

The basic point is simple: The contributions that a self-maintenant system makes to its own stability constitute functions that are being served relative to that system. The property of being self-maintenant is a natural property and has causal efficacy in that the continuance (or lack thereof) of the far-from-equilibrium process makes a causal difference in the world. It is an emergent property in the sense that it emerges in particular organizations of process and cannot be reduced to properties of any of its parts. In fact, it may not have any stable parts: Far-from-equilibrium systems are necessarily open systems and the components of the process may completely change over time. Neither the fuel nor the oxygen nor the combustion products remain constant in a candle flame.

This notion of serving a function is relative to the system to which contributions are being made. The heart of a parasite, for example, may be functional to the parasite, but dysfunctional to the host.

Function is normative, in the sense that conditions of success and failure are involved.[4] A kidney may have the function of filtering blood by virtue of

---

[4]There is also a form of functional analysis, sometimes called *causal role analysis*, that focuses on the causal contributions made in a system to some outcome or property of interest to the observer doing the analysis (Cummins, 1975). There is no inherent normativity in this notion of function: All normativity is resident in or derivative from the purposes and interests of the individual doing the analysis. In both normative and nonnormative senses of function, some selection is being made among the actual or typical causal consequences as being causal consequences that are functionally relevant. A heart pumps blood, makes heartbeat sounds, and contributes to body weight, but only the pumping of blood is functional.

being an instance of a kind, a type, of a part of an organism that normally serves that function, even if this *particular* kidney fails to serve that function, even if it is dysfunctional.[5] Furthermore, serving a function is normatively asymmetrical to being dysfunctional precisely in the sense that serving a function tends to serve the stability of the system, whereas being dysfunctional debilitates that stability. That is, serving a function is normatively positive for the system at issue.

Etiological Approaches

The dominant models of function today are etiological (Godfrey-Smith, 1993; Neander, 1991). They attempt to model the nature and emergence of a part of a system having a function in terms of the history of predecessors to that part, the evolutionary history in particular. Kidneys have the function of filtering blood, in this view, because their evolutionary predecessors were selected for accomplishing that causal process. That is, this kidney is here, it exists, because of the evolutionary history of filtering blood of predecessor kidneys: Thus, the "etiological" model.

Etiological models have at least one counterintuitive consequence that I focus on because, I maintain, it reveals a deep problem: a failure of naturalism. Millikan (1984, 1993) points out that, in the science fiction case in which a lion suddenly popped into existence that was molecule for molecule identical to a lion in the zoo, the organs of the science fiction lion would not have any functions, whereas the organs of the zoo lion would have functions, in spite of the (by-assumption) molecular level identity between the two lions. The difference is that the science fiction lion and its organs would have no evolutionary history and, therefore, certainly no relevant evolutionary history, for its organs to have functions.

This example is just a particularly striking version of the more realistic point that, the first time some organ or process produces a useful consequence, that consequence is nevertheless not functional (at least not on the etiological account) and the organ or process has no function, because the evolutionary history is not present. If further generations retain that organ or process as selected for that useful consequence, then it will come to

---

[5]There are additional issues here involved in what constitutes being an element of a type. Is this tissue mass a kidney, having the function of filtering blood even though it is not doing so, or is it not? I do not focus on this issue here (see Bickhard, 1993, in press-a, in press-b). (Etiological approaches to function encounter the same issue of the metaphysics of kinds, but do not appreciate their complexity.) The central idea is that a functional process can presuppose outcomes and products, accessible in certain manners, of another process and, in so doing, *types* whatever is accessed for those outcomes and products. In other words, they are typed as having the functions that they are presupposed to be serving. The model of representation presented later in this chapter is a special anticipatory version of such process presupposition.

have that consequence as a function. Therefore, the first time (and for however many subsequent generations counts as sufficient), every useful evolutionary innovation is not functional and has no function.

These examples are counterintuitive, but that counterintuitiveness might well be a cost worth paying for the overall power and apparent naturalism of the etiological model. I contend, however, that these examples betray a fatal flaw: the epiphenomenality of etiological function.

Epiphenomenality

The etiological model holds that functionality is constituted in having the right kind of history. No history means no function, even for systems that are molecule-by-molecule identical. However, that is just a way of pointing out that history is not determinable in the current state of the system, and the etiological notion of function is, therefore, not definable in terms of the current state of the system. But only the current state of a system can be causally efficacious, so the etiological model of function commits to the consequence that function has no causal power.[6] Only the current state can have causal power, so etiological function has no causal power: It is causally epiphenomenal.

Because the etiological approach models representation and other normative phenomena in terms of the base-level model of function, not only is function causally epiphenomenal, but so are representation and all of the rest of mind. Etiology commits to an epiphenomenalism of mind (or else some alternative way of accounting for mental phenomena that does not depend on the etiological model of function).

This epiphenomenalist consequence of the etiological approach, in turn, constitutes a failure to naturalize function and mind—a failure with respect to one of the primary original motivations for the approach. I take these consequences to be a refutation of the etiological approach by its own standards—and certainly by the standards of causally efficacious naturalism. Function as a contribution to far-from-equilibrium system self-maintenance satisfies those standards.

REPRESENTATION

I turn now to representation. A self-maintenant system is a far-from-equilibrium system that contributes to the maintenance of its own conditions for

---

[6]The two lions are, by assumption, causally identical, but one has organs with functions and the other does not.

stability. Such a far-from-equilibrium stability is always relative to the environment in which the far-from-equilibrium conditions must be maintained: The candle flame will not survive a dousing with liquid oxygen because the heat-generating capacity is simply not powerful enough. Therefore, if there are changes in the environment, the self-maintenance of the system may be in jeopardy and a simple self-maintenant system will have no compensatory response possible.

Recursive Self-Maintenance

A *recursively* self-maintenant system, however, is a system that tends to maintain its own property of being self-maintenant against such changes in environment. This requires some contact with the environment that can detect such changes, more than one possible way in which to be self-maintenant, and processes for switching the self-maintenant strategies appropriately to the environmental detections.

Candle flames cannot do this, but one simple example of a far-from-equilibrium system that can is the bacterium that can tumble if it finds itself swimming *down* a sugar gradient, but can continue swimming if it finds itself swimming *up* a sugar gradient (Campbell, 1974b, 1990). Such adaptive adjustments are contributory to self-maintenance insofar as they are undertaken appropriately for the environmental relationships in which the system finds itself. There are two aspects to this recursively self-maintenant property: 1) the detections, and 2) the selection of a next (hopefully) self-maintenant process. Both are of fundamental importance, both to the organism and to the theory of representation. I address the selection, or guidance, of the self-maintenant process first.

Anticipative Selections

The critical property of such selections is that they are anticipative: they are anticipative in the sense that they are future oriented—they are selections of interactions for the immediate or near future and they constitute anticipations that the selected interactive processes will in fact be functional for the system. In other words, they anticipate that the environment will be, at the time of the interaction, appropriate for that kind of interaction to be functional. Such anticipation can be in error: The environment might not cooperate and the interaction may fail to be functional.

There is a very primitive emergence here that is nevertheless of central importance. Such an anticipation about the environment is an implicit predication about that environment—this is an environment of appropriate type for the selected interactive process—and that predication can be false. This is the most primitive version of representational truth value.[7]

Anticipative Indications

These implicit predications are indeed primitive, but additional steps of elaboration and sophistication are both possible and offer increasing adaptive power. The most important are concerned with additional sophistication of interaction selection. The selections illustrated previously are selections via simple triggering: When the appropriate detections occur, trigger the corresponding process. There is no selection process beyond the environmentally induced triggering. In more complex systems, however, environmental detections may indicate more than one possible next interactive process and some further selection of which process to engage in, among those indicated as possible or appropriate, must occur inside the system itself.

If indicated potential interactions are associated with indicated possible internal outcomes, this provides a sophisticated basis for further selection. In particular, the system can make selections on the basis of the indicated outcomes. It can select those interactions whose indicated outcomes best satisfy or heuristically approach current goals; that is, indications of potential interactions and their potential outcomes provide a basis for solving the general problem of action selection.

Simultaneously, such organizations of indications constitute even more sophisticated representations. An indication of potentiality is still an implicit predication and is capable of being false. In this organization, there is also the possibility that the system can itself discover such falsity, should the indicated interaction be undertaken. In particular, if the actual outcome is not among those indicated, then the indications were false. Such error can be useful for further selections of interactions or for invoking and guiding learning processes, should the system be capable of learning. At this point, we not only have representational error, we have system-detectable representational error.[8] Such a claim of the emergence of representation faces a number of possible challenges. I anticipate and address a few of them here.

---

[7]Note that this claim rejects any simple propositional model of representation, any model that holds propositions to be the only bearers of truth value.

[8]In simple systems, an indication of interactive potentiality will only occur in some particular environmental situation or condition, or with some particular conditional, and will have a corresponding truth value. In more complex systems that are capable of reflective consciousness, organizations of such indications can be separated from any particular conditions or "targets" that they are "about." In such cases, the organization of indications constitutes a representational content lifted out of a normal context of application. A full representation is an application of such a content to a "target," and truth emerges when the content is true of the target and false when the content is false of the "target." Abstracted content, however, can be useful in imagination, counterfactual thought, explorations of content per se, and so on (as well as subject to its own forms of abuse; Bickhard, 1993, in press-b; Bickhard & Terveen, 1995; Cummins, 1996).

Goals

First, if the goals that are involved in interaction selection are themselves representational, then representation has been explicated in terms of representation and the model commits a circularity. This is correct, but the form of goal directedness does not need to have explicitly represented goals. They need only be internal set points for a servomechanism process that selects one space of internal processes if the set point is not met and a different space of internal processes if the set point is met. Once representation is available, then, of course, goals can make use of representation without circularity.

Second, these representations are still quite primitive, perhaps appropriate for worms and maybe frogs, but do not look much like adult human representations of objects or abstractions. Such examples pose a challenge to the adequacy of the representational model: It might provide a model of the emergence of a primitive version of representational truth value, but can it account for more complex and more familiar kinds of representation?

Objects

I address the issue of object representation first. It is already clear that indications can branch out, with more than one possible further interaction indicated at a given time. It is also the case that they can iterate in the sense that the indicated outcomes of one interaction can themselves, if arrived at, serve to indicate still further potential interactions. Thus, indications of interaction potentialities can branch and iterate into potentially vast and complex webs of such potentialities.

A special organization within such webs of interactive potentiality has the following properties. First, all potentialities in the subweb are reachable from all other points in the subweb. In other words, if any part of the organization of potentialities is reachable by the system, perhaps with intermediate interactions with the environment, then all of the subweb is reachable in the same way. The subweb, then, is closed and reachable with respect to the interactions that make it up. Second, that subweb organization is itself invariant under a class of interactions, physical interactions in particular for the current example. I propose such closure, reachability, and invariance properties as characteristic of object representations.

Consider, for example, a toy block. A child can do many things with it, from visual scans to manipulations to chewing to throwing and so on. If any of these are possible, then all are possible, perhaps with intermediate interactions, such as a manipulation to bring a particular visual scan back into view. Furthermore, the entire web of interactive potentialities that the block affords remain invariant under a large class of physical interactions, such as hiding, leaving in the toy box, walking out of the room, and so on, though it is not invariant under such processes as burning or crushing. From an epistemological point of view, this *is* a small manipulable object. Obviously, this is essentially Piaget's model of object representation translated into the language of the interactive model (Piaget, 1954).[9]

Abstractions and Knowing Level Stages

The answer to the challenge of the representation of abstractions is similarly Piagetian. A system interacting with its environment and representing various properties and objects in it may itself, as an interactive system, have properties that would be useful for the system to represent. But the interactive representational relationship is asymmetric, so a system cannot directly represent itself. A higher level system, however, interacting with the first level similarly to the sense in which the first level interacts with the environment, can represent properties of that first level. Properties of the second level, in turn, could be represented by a third level and so on. There emerges a hierarchy of potential levels of representation.

Consider now a property that might be useful for a first-level interactive system. One heuristic strategy may involve doing something more than once in case the first time or two do not work. A control for that could iterate an activity, say, three times. If a second-level system developed a representation of this property of a control organization in the first-level system, that second-level representation would be a representation of the number 3. The second-level system will have abstracted a property of the first-level system.

The relationship here is much like Piaget's reflective abstraction (Piaget, 2001), and, like reflective abstraction, this induces a stage hierarchy of potential development. The reasoning is as follows: Interactive organization cannot be passively induced into a system by the environment. It must be constructed by the system, and tried out to determine if it is useful. Any action-based model of representation and cognition, then, forces a constructivism. If the constructions are not gifted with foresight, they may well be wrong and need to be modified or rejected. Action-based models, then,

---

[9]Piaget's constructivism is among his most important contributions, showing how an action-based model of representation and cognition could account for the full range of representational phenomena. But Piaget's focus was not most fundamentally on representation per se. He was concerned most centrally with providing a third way that transcended innatism and environmentalism and could account for the emergence of necessity, that classical battleground between empiricism and rationalism (Bickhard, 1992c). His model of representation, therefore, was relatively underdeveloped. It focused mostly on representations of kinds or categories of particulars, such as objects or universals. He did not focus, for example, on the emergence of representational truth value.

force a variation and selection constructivism, an evolutionary epistemology (Campbell, 1974b).[10]

If development occurs via such a constructive process, then it cannot skip over levels of representation in the hierarchy outlined previously. It is not possible for something at level $N+1$ to represent something at level N if that something at level N does not already exist. Therefore, development must climb the hierarchy one level at a time, at least in the sense that there must always be support at lower levels for the particular constructions at higher levels. This imposes a stage organization on possible development, though not necessarily an age-synchronous or domain-general stage constraint. Constructions could be quite variable with respect to which level has been reached among multiple domains of knowledge.[11]

I have argued that the anticipatory aspect of the solution to the problem of action selection is also the solution to the problem of the emergence of representation, and cognition more broadly, with multiple consequences, including a necessary constructivism and a stage constraint on development, thereby providing explanations of such constructivism and stage constraints. I now turn to the detection aspect of action selection.

Detections

In the most primitive model, interactions are simply *triggered* by environmental detections. In more complex versions, environmental detections are the grounds for *indicating* which further interactions might be appropriate in particular environments. Such detections are the means by which an organism is sensitive to the environment in ways that further its own ends

---

[10]Piaget rejected the power of variation and selection models to account for the exquisite accomplishments of development or even for the exquisite design of the eye (Bickhard, 1992c). In part, he was anticipating contemporary claims that self-organization plays a central role in evolution and development, along with variation and selection (Christensen & Hooker, 1999). In part, he was making an even stronger rejection of emergence, for example, in such claims as that reason evolves rationally or that reason does not change without reason, which, it should be noted, implies that reason can only come from reason: Reason or rationality cannot be the product of contingency (Kitchener, 1986). I reject this Humean claim (Bickhard, 1998, in press-b).

[11]Elsewhere, I have offered a model of the process of ascending such levels, the process of reflective abstraction (Campbell & Bickhard, 1986). It has among its consequences that the ascent to Level 2 should involve a neural maturation and, therefore, should be roughly age synchronous and domain general, whereas all higher levels can be reached in purely logical fashion, with no constraints on age or domain other than the basic sequential constraint outlined previously. This initial age-synchronous, domain-general, developmental shift, followed by non-synchronous, domain-specific development, seems to be, in fact, what is found empirically (Bickhard, 1992a). Note that there are no structures of the whole in this model, in fact, no structural characterizations of stages at all (Campbell & Bickhard, 1986).

and, in particular, in ways that tend to recursively maintain far-from-equilibrium conditions.

Such environmental detections can themselves be quite complex and can, for example, involve full environmental interactions. For my current purposes, however, their importance is more for their role in standard models of representation than for their dynamics in action selection and anticipatory representational emergence.

The reason is that standard models of representation take such detections to *be* representations, to constitute the emergence of representation. A detection is held to represent what it detects. This view is of ancient provenance, going back to the ancient Greeks, and is still dominant today. In strong contrast, the interactive model advanced here (or any action, pragmatist, model) sees detection as only part of a representation. A repertoire of actions and some way of selecting among them are also needed (Bickhard, 1993, 1999, in press-b; Bickhard & Terveen, 1995). It is worth noting that Piaget was one of the few prominent advocates of an action-based model of representation.

In proposing the interactive model, then, I have issued a promissory note to, among many other things, critique these standard models of representation. This critique is quite extensive, with many related arguments pointing out many related flaws in the approach to representation. Furthermore, additional flaws and arguments are discovered even today. I cannot provide an overview of all of these here, so I focus on a few central and illustrative critiques.

Encodingism

In standard models of representation, internal detections or differentiations of environmental properties (or events or objects) are taken to represent those properties by virtue of some sort of correspondence between the outcome of the detection and the property detected. The crucial sort of correspondence involved is variously claimed to be a causal correspondence, or a lawful correspondence, or an informational correspondence, or an isomorphic correspondence (Bickhard, 1993, 1999, in press-b; Bickhard & Terveen, 1995). The detection is taken to *encode* the property by virtue of that correspondence and representation in general is assumed to have this character of encoding. I have called such assumptions about the nature of representation *encodingism*.

It is clear that encodings do exist, Morse code being a paradigmatic example, so the critical question focuses on the assumption that all representation is constituted as encodings, especially mental representation. Clear cases of encodings, such as Morse code, are cases in which both ends of the encoding correspondence are known and the correspondence itself is known. In Morse code, "···" encodes "s" by virtue of the conventional knowledge of "···" and "s" and the correspondence that links them. Lest this seem to be merely a manifestation of the conventionality of Morse code, consider a usage such as "This neutrino flux encodes information about fusion processes in the sun." Again, vast amounts of knowledge are necessary in order for this to hold: knowledge about neutrino fluxes and how they are detected, knowledge about processes in the sun, and knowledge about the links, the correspondences, between them.

This point is just one perspective on the fact that encodings require interpreters. That is not a problem for genuine encodings, but, if we are attempting to model mental representation, this is unacceptable. Mental representation is (part of) what is involved in some epistemic agents *being* such an interpreter. Therefore, to invoke encodings—any version—as a model of mental representation is to invoke mental representation to account for mental representation, to invoke a regress of interpreters each interpreting the encodings produced by the previous interpretation. Mental representation, whatever it is, cannot require such interpretation on pain of circularity or infinite regress. Here we have the first of a great number of arguments against encodingism.

Piaget (1970) had a powerful version of this circularity and regress argument that focused on the genetic aspects of our representations: If our representations of the world are copies of the world, how do we know the world in the first place in order to be able to construct our copies of it? We would have to already have a copy from which we could construct our copy, which would, in turn, require a still prior copy for the construction of that one, and so on.

Another perspective on the problems of encodingism derives from the recognition that the correspondences of the sort that are supposed to constitute representation—causal, lawful, and so on—are ubiquitous in the universe. Every instance of any causal law, for example, creates a causal, a lawful, and an informational correspondence, while any two instances of any pattern—where what counts as an instance of a pattern is completely free—yields an isomorphism correspondence. Virtually none of these are representations, so the next problem, in the encodingist perspective, is to add conditions to narrow the field to just those correspondences that do constitute representations. If, however, the only kinds of genuine "representations by correspondence" are the genuine encodings, such as Morse code, then this approach to modeling representation is doomed: Mental representations cannot be encodings for the interpreter reasons already mentioned (as well as many additional reasons not mentioned).

The problem is that an element or event that happens to be in correspondence with something else does not announce in its nature either that it is in a correspondence nor what the correspondence might be with.

There is no information available that the element or event in question is supposed to be a representation at all, nor about what the purported representation is supposed to represent. There is no representational content.

Representational content is what specifies what a representation is *supposed* to represent. This is a normative issue: A particular representation is, perhaps, supposed to represent a cow, but is being used at this moment to represent a horse (on a dark night). That is, the representation is false in this instance, and it is the content that determines that this application is in error.

This point highlights still another problem. If a correspondence of the favored type exists, then the representation (supposedly) exists, and it is correct. But, if the favored type of correspondence does not exist, then the representation does not exist and, therefore, it cannot be incorrect. There are three cases that must be distinguished: The representation exists and is correct, the representation exists and is incorrect, and the representation does not exist. But there are only two possibilities available for making those distinctions: The correspondence exists, or the correspondence does not exist. The available resources are inadequate to be able to account for the possibility of representational error.

There has been a major industry in the philosophy of mind in the last two decades of attempts to provide a model of representation that can account for the possibility of representational error. I will not review the arguments here, but none of them work (Bickhard, 1993, 1999, in press-b). At best, they characterize error as some external observer on the system might be able to determine it. For example, an external observer, if it could determine that the representation was supposed to represent cows—that is, if it could determine the representational content—and could have independent access to the world to determine that the case in point was in fact a horse, could then announce that this deployment of the representation was in error. There are two kinds of problems with all of the available proposals: (a) No system is itself in a position to determine the contents of its own purported representations (the proposals can involve complex evolutionary or learning histories, or equally complex relations among various kinds of counterfactual conditions that might have happened, but did not or have not) and (b) even if it could, it would then have to compare the content to what is currently being represented to find out if the deployed content is correctly representing it, but that is the original problem of representation all over again. Circularity rears its head yet again.

The central problem here is that encodingist models provide no model of the emergence of representational content. Genuine encodings borrow their content from whatever defines them, but original mental representations cannot borrow them from anywhere. But there were no representations at the time of the Big Bang and there are now, so representation must have emerged. Any model that cannot account for such emergence is thereby falsified.

Rather than face this problem of emergence, however, major figures in the field develop arguments based on it. Fodor (1981), for example, argued that, because there are no models of learning that can account for the emergence of new content, all possible basic contents that humans are capable of must be innate, must be in the genes (Bickhard, 1991). The problem, however, is a logical one: How can the emergence of content be accounted for at all? If it is, according to some model, impossible, then evolution cannot do it either; conversely, if it is possible for representational content to emerge, then there is no reason available why organic evolution *could* avail itself of such emergence and mental development could *not*. Nevertheless, Fodor's claim has given aid and succor to a major industry in developmental psychology of disproving Piaget by showing that multiple realms of representation must have innate bases.[12]

Just to remind the reader, I point out that the interactive model has no problem whatsoever with the emergence of content in particular kinds of interactive system organization, with the possibility of representational error, or with the possibility of system-detectable representational error. The central problems that have vexed the encodingist approach, for not only decades, but millennia, are trivially solved and dissolved by the interactive approach.

This is just a sampling of the problems faced by encodingist approaches to representation (Bickhard, 1993, 1999, in press-b; Bickhard & Terveen, 1995), but it will suffice for now.[13] It is clear that these approaches suffer from deep flaws, which I argue are fatal flaws. Moreover, it is clear that the most central of them—content, emergence, error, system-detectable error—are trivially solved by the interactive model.

SO WHAT?

A legitimate question at this point, however, is: What difference does it make? How does the interactive model, or any pragmatist model, affect theory in psychology, particularly developmental psychology? The first answer, of course, is that these models of function and representation provide naturalistic accounts of the emergence of two fundamental normative phe-

---

[12]This is far from the only manifestation of the deep and fatal problems in Fodor's models, but it is one that has had a particularly unfortunate effect on developmental psychology. (For more detailed discussions of Fodor, see Bickhard, 1991, 1993, 1996, 1999, in press-b; Bickhard & Terveen, 1995; Levine & Bickhard, 1999.)

[13]See the references for detailed refutations of particular models, such as those of Cummins, Dretske, Fodor, Millikan, and Newell.

nomena, arguably the only such models. But the second question asks, does the interactive model leave everything else unchanged? Or, conversely, what would be different in this new perspective? There are two kinds of answers to this question: (a) new possibilities it opens up for different kinds of models in cognition and development and (b) changes that it forces in models in related domains. This is not the occasion for any developed response to this question—that would involve a full model of the person—but I briefly adumbrate some illustrative examples from each of these.

Functional Scaffolding and Self-Scaffolding

The first example is an expanded notion of scaffolding that is made possible by the explicit variation and selection model of developmental construction. Scaffolding is usually thought of as involving a Vygotskian notion of internalization (Bruner, 1975), although models of the actual process of internalization are difficult to find (Wertsch, 1985; Wertsch & Stone, 1985).[14] Consider the following as a possible model for what *internalization* is used to refer to, even though the metaphor of internalization works poorly here. If some framework of selection pressures exists external to the organism, then, insofar as the organism comes to be able to satisfy them, it will have constructed, via an evolutionary epistemological process, some means and coordinations of interaction that "fit" those pressures. This is not a straightforward internalization, because what fits or satisfies those pressures may not have any structural resemblance to those pressures at all—it need only be a control system that is interactively competent with respect to them.

In such a view, development will proceed, among other ways, via the construction of task competencies, which will then serve as the foundation for and framework within which further variation and selection constructions take place. It is crucial to notice that any task or selection criterion that requires a great deal of construction to minimally accomplish is not ever likely to be mastered. The chances of hitting on the right construction diminish rapidly as the necessary construction becomes more complex (Si-

---

[14]The theoretical notion of internalization has drawn increasing attention recently. One theme in this work has been to move internalization from the individual into the social realm (Cox & Lightfoot, 1997; Winegar, 1997). I have strong sympathies with this kind of move as a matter of balance in modeling many of the phenomena for which internalization has been invoked. But no such move can eliminate entirely the fact of changes in the individual and some degree of stability in those changes in the individual; those phenomena must be accounted for. They are the phenomena for which "internalization" has been a most attractive, but unfortunate, metaphor. Thus, the shift of emphasis toward the social cannot eliminate the theoretical problem with internalization and the model presented in this chapter is offered as an account of a part of the individual aspect of the process of what "internalization" might be.

mon, 1969). One way around this difficulty, for tasks that are inherently complex, is to block or bracket some of the relevant selection pressures. In this way, some easier constructions that are much more likely to be found may become successful in the reduced selection pressure environment. If such blocking of selection pressures is ultimately successful, it may become possible for the organism, the infant or toddler (or adult), to ascend a path of such "special environment" points of constructive stability to eventually reach a full task competence with respect to the full task selection pressures. At that point, of course, there is no longer any need for the blocking of selection pressures: The construction of the full task competence has been "scaffolded" by those blockages, and the scaffolding can be dismissed when the full construction is accomplished.

This functional notion of scaffolding provides a more general way of thinking about scaffolding and its possible functions and uses, but it also has a special consequence: Self-scaffolding becomes a possibility. If to scaffold is to provide a structure or organization that can then be internalized, then self-scaffolding makes no sense. If, however, to scaffold is to block selection pressures, then it is clear not only that an individual can do it for him- or herself, but also that we all do it all of the time. We break problems down into subproblems, we move to ideal cases, we seek resources that we can perhaps do without later on, and so on. Once the point is seen, in fact, it is clear that self-scaffolding skills are a major aspect of development, one almost universally overlooked.[15] Elsewhere, I offer a model of attachment as a form of self-scaffolding (Bickhard, 1992d).

Another possibility opened up by this functional notion of scaffolding is that of permanent scaffolds, scaffolds that are necessary to particular kinds of interactions and accomplishments and that are never discarded. I argue that the emergences of social reality, culture, and language have this character of permanent scaffolds (Bickhard, 1992b).

Cognitive Dynamics

A second example of a new theoretical possibility in thinking about cognition has to do with the dynamics of cognition. In standard models of representation, as previously mentioned, there is no model of the emergence of representational content. Because content cannot emerge, according to such models, it must always come from somewhere: It cannot just "emerge" into existence. With a focus on the organism, there are only two possible

---

[15]Self-scaffolding is likely to be an important aspect of what might often be simply categorized as scaffolding. If so, then scaffolding will (most) often be a coconstructive process, with a simultaneously active individual and active environment, with respect to the construction or utilization of blocks to selection pressures.

sources that it could come from: the environment (empiricism) and the mind or genes (rationalism). These are the alternatives that Piaget wanted to transcend with his "third way", and his efforts were quite well directed: They can be transcended by a model of emergent content, content that does not have to come from anywhere.

This assumption that content must always already be there (somewhere) is behind the Fodor argument mentioned earlier that all content must be innate and the flaw in that argument is apparent once it is recognized that content *has* to have emerged at some point. It is also deeply embedded in the computer-inspired models that so dominate the current scene. Symbol types are categories of symbols for which content is already known. Some hope that connectionist models will solve this problem or contend that they already do solve this problem, but trained connectionist nets provide *correspondences* between activation vectors and categories of inputs—they do not provide any content for the net itself about the fact that any such correspondence exists or what any such correspondence might be with. In other words, connectionist models do not address the problems of content; they only provide trainable correspondences. That is not trivial, but it is not representation either (Bickhard & Terveen, 1995).

Within the confines of such conceptual frameworks, cognition is thought of as the processing of such symbols or the flow and interactions among activation vectors, with content always presupposed to be in the background, somehow flowing along in parallel with the symbols or vectors and somehow making all these things into representations. If, however, content, thus representation, is freely emergent in certain kinds of system dynamics, then a very different kind of view opens up.

In particular, the creation of representation does not have to proceed via intermediary representation. Cognition does not have to "operate on" already-existing representation. Representation can be created and eliminated over and over again in a broader dynamic process. Representation can occur as a kind of organized froth on underlying cognitive dynamics, something like the froth of virtual particles in quantum field theory, at times simply disappearing and at other times having a major impact on the ensuing dynamics, again something like the emergence of conserved "particles" out of the froth of virtual particles in quantum field theory.

Such a view of cognitive dynamics makes very good sense of many results in cognitive psychology that are anomalous in standard views. These include evidence that categorizations are created anew for each new occasion and are in some ways unique for those occasions, that categorizations and judgments of similarity are highly context dependent and highly history dependent, that the constructive similarities of metaphor are central to cognition, not a secondary add-on, and so on (Bickhard, 2000a; Bickhard & Campbell, 1996; Dietrich & Markman, 2000; Freyd, 1987; Shanon, 1993;

Smith & Samuelson, 1997). These kinds of dynamics are handled either not at all or, at best, with very ad hoc additions, in standard models. A model of the dynamics of representational emergence, then, provides a very different view of the nature of cognition in general.

Related Domains

A pragmatic approach to representation not only opens new perspectives on its home ground, but also forces multiple changes in related domains. I do not provide an overview of any of these changes here—that is a vast programmatic project. I do, however, show how the pragmatic, interactive model and its associated critiques force several standard ways of thinking to be given up and opens up new avenues for exploration.

For one major example, if representation cannot fundamentally be a matter of encodings, then perception cannot be a matter of the transductive generation of encodings. A pragmatic, dynamic, interactive model of the nature of perception is required. I have argued that Gibson provides the core of such a model, though much overstatement must be peeled away and several important lacunae must be filled (Bickhard & Richie, 1983).

Equally, if representation cannot be a matter of encoding, then utterances cannot be the (transmissions of) encodings of mental contents. I have argued that social and functional models of language are steps in the right pragmatic direction, though here too there are deep vestiges of encodingist assumptions that are difficult to discern and difficult to remove. Language as a tool for interacting with social realities, not as a transmission of mental contents, is the kind of model ultimately arrived at (Bickhard, 1980, 1992b; Bickhard & Campbell, 1992; Bickhard & Terveen, 1995).

Finally, if persons are processing units operating on encoded information in their memory banks, then human sociality is nothing more than a storage of social information in those memory banks. Sociality is not constitutive of the person per se, but only of the information and skills available to that person. That is, human sociality is not a genuine emergent of development.

If, on the other hand, human beings are constituted in their interactive processing dynamics—if that is the basic ontology of persons—then the development of a social being in a particular family and culture is the emergence of a particular instance of a particular kind of being, formed in the context of and using the resources available in the social and cultural environment. It is only a pragmatic perspective on representation and persons more broadly that can account for the emergence of persons as social beings with a genuine social ontology, not just processors with a batch of social knowledge to be processed and used (Bickhard, 1995, in press-c).

CONCLUSIONS

Emergence, particularly normative emergence—particularly representational emergence—is at the heart of contemporary naturalism, and at the heart of contemporary psychology. It is the central issue in psychology becoming integrated into the naturalism of the sciences, of finally escaping the heritage of Cartesian dualism.[16] Issues of emergence come into sharp focus in developmental psychology: If psychological phenomena emerge somewhere other than in evolution, they do so in development. Piaget is among the few psychologists to address representational emergence and to do so within a framework that does not a priori preclude such emergence: pragmatism.

I have outlined a pragmatic, a dynamic, model of the emergence of normative function and of representation. These models carry forward the general programme of naturalism, without falling prey to the trap of eliminative reductionism, and provide a foundation for studies of the mind and person more generally. They do not, however, leave the remainder of the landscape unchanged. Illustrative new theoretical openings and forced changes are outlined with regard to scaffolding and self-scaffolding, cognitive dynamics, perception, language, and human sociality. Pragmatism provides a powerful alternative approach to understanding persons, but one that requires deep and sometimes difficult changes.

AUTHOR NOTE

Mark H. Bickhard, Department of Psychology, 17 Memorial Drive East, Lehigh University, Bethlehem, PA 18015; e-mail: *mhb0@lehigh.edu*; web site: *http://www.lehigh.edu/~mhb0/mhb0.html.*

Many thanks are due to Terry Brown and Les Smith for multiple comments, suggestions, and references.

REFERENCES

Bickhard, M. H. (1980). *Cognition, convention, and communication.* New York: Praeger.
Bickhard, M. H. (1991). The import of Fodor's anti-constructivist argument. In L. Steffe (Ed.), *Epistemological foundations of mathematical experience* (pp. 14–25). New York: Springer.
Bickhard, M. H. (1992a). Commentary on the age 4 transition. *Human Development, 35,* 182–192.

---

[16]It is frequently assumed that there is a dichotomy between dualism and reductionism, such that arguments against (Cartesian) dualism are taken to be arguments for reductionism. This is false and based on a false dichotomy; emergence is the third way that transcends both possibilities.

Bickhard, M. H. (1992b). How does the environment affect the person? In L. T. Winegar & J. Valsiner (Eds.), *Children's development within social contexts: Metatheory and theory* (pp. 63–92). Hillsdale, NJ: Lawrence Erlbaum Associates.

Bickhard, M. H. (1992c). Piaget on variation and selection models: Structuralism, logical necessity, and interactivism. In L. Smith (Ed.), *Jean Piaget: Critical assessments* (Rev. ed., pp. 388–434). London: Routledge.

Bickhard, M. H. (1992d). Scaffolding and self-scaffolding: Central aspects of development. In L. T. Winegar & J. Valsiner (Eds.), *Children's development within social contexts: Research and methodology* (pp. 33–52). Hillsdale, NJ: Lawrence Erlbaum Associates.

Bickhard, M. H. (1993). Representational content in humans and machines. *Journal of Experimental and Theoretical Artificial Intelligence, 5*, 285–333.

Bickhard, M. H. (1995). World mirroring versus world making: There's gotta be a better way. In L. Steffe & J. Gale (Eds.), *Constructivism in education* (pp. 229–267). Hillsdale, NJ: Lawrence Erlbaum Associates.

Bickhard, M. H. (1996). Troubles with computationalism. In W. O'Donohue & R. F. Kitchener (Eds.), *The philosophy of psychology* (pp. 173–183). London: Sage.

Bickhard, M. H. (1998). A process model of the emergence of representation. In G. L. Farre & T. Oksala (Eds.), *Emergence, complexity, hierarchy, organization* (pp. 263–270). Selected and Edited Papers from the *ECHO III Conference*. Acta Polytechnica Scandinavica, Mathematics, Computing and Management in Engineering Series No. 91. Espoo, Finland, August 3–7.

Bickhard, M. H. (1999). Interaction and representation. *Theory and Psychology, 9*, 435–458.

Bickhard, M. H. (2000a). Dynamic representing and representational dynamics. In E. Dietrich & A. Markman (Eds.), *Cognitive dynamics: Conceptual and representational change in humans and machines* (pp. 31–50). Mahwah, NJ: Lawrence Erlbaum Associates.

Bickhard, M. H. (2000b). Emergence. In P. B. Andersen, C. Emmeche, N. O. Finnemann & P. V. Christiansen (Eds.), *Downward causation* (pp. 322–348). Aarhus, Denmark: University of Aarhus Press.

Bickhard, M. H. (in press-a). Autonomy, function, and representation. *Communication and Cognition.*

Bickhard, M. H. (in press-b). The dynamic emergence of representation. In H. Clapin, P. Staines, & P. Slezak (Eds.), *Representation in mind: New approaches to mental representation.* New York: Praeger.

Bickhard, M. H. (in press-c). The social ontology of persons. In J. Carpendale & U. Mueller (Eds.), *Social interaction and the development of knowledge.* Mahwah, NJ: Lawrence Erlbaum Associates.

Bickhard, M. H. (in preparation). *The whole person: Toward a naturalism of persons. Contributions to an ontological psychology.*

Bickhard, M. H., & Campbell, R. L. (1992). Some foundational questions concerning language studies: With a focus on categorial grammars and model theoretic possible worlds semantics. *Journal of Pragmatics, 17*, 401–433.

Bickhard, M. H., & Campbell, R. L. (1996). Topologies of learning and development. *New Ideas in Psychology, 14*, 111–156.

Bickhard, M. H., & Christopher, J. C. (1994). The influence of early experience on personality development. *New Ideas in Psychology, 12*, 229–252.

Bickhard, M. H., & Richie, D. M. (1983). *On the nature of representation: A case study of James Gibson's theory of perception.* New York: Praeger.

Bickhard, M. H., & Terveen, L. (1995). *Foundational issues in artificial intelligence and cognitive science: Impasse and solution.* New York: Elsevier Scientific.

Brown, H. R., & Harré, R. (1988). *Philosophical foundations of quantum field theory.* Oxford, England: Oxford University Press.

Bruner, J. S. (1975). The ontogenesis of speech acts. *Journal of Child Language, 2*, 1–19.

Campbell, D. T. (1974a). "Downward causation" in hierarchically organized biological systems. In F. J. Ayala & T. Dobzhansky (Eds.), *Studies in the philosophy of biology* (pp. 179–186). Berkeley, CA: University of California Press.

Campbell, D. T. (1974b). Evolutionary epistemology. In P. A. Schlipp (Ed.), *The philosophy of Karl Popper* (pp. 413–463). LaSalle, IL: Open Court.

Campbell, D. T. (1990). Levels of organization, downward causation, and the selection-theory approach to evolutionary epistemology. In G. Greenberg & E. Tobach (Eds.), *Theories of the evolution of knowing* (pp. 1–17). Hillsdale, NJ: Lawrence Erlbaum Associates.

Campbell, R. J., & Bickhard, M. H. (in preparation). *Physicalism, emergence, and downward causation.*

Campbell, R. L., & Bickhard, M. H. (1986). Knowing levels and developmental stages [Monograph]. *Contributions to Human Development, 16.*

Cao, T. Y. (1999). Introduction: Conceptual issues in quantum field theory. In T. Y. Cao (Ed.), *Conceptual foundations of quantum field theory* (pp. 1–27). Cambridge, England: Cambridge University Press.

Christensen, W. D., & Hooker, C. A. (1999). The organization of knowledge: Beyond Campbell's evolutionary epistemology. *Philosophy of Science, 66* (Proceedings, PSA 1998), S237–249.

Churchland, P. M. (1989). *A neurocomputational perspective.* Cambridge, MA: MIT Press.

Churchland, P. S. (1986). *Neurophilosophy.* Cambridge, MA: MIT Press.

Cox, B. D., & Lightfoot, C. (1997). *Sociogenetic perspectives on internalization.* Mahwah, NJ: Lawrence Erlbaum Associates.

Cummins, R. (1975). Functional analysis. *Journal of Philosophy, 72,* 741–764.

Cummins, R. (1996). *Representations, targets, and attitudes.* Cambridge, MA: MIT Press.

Davies, P. C. W. (1984). Particles do not exist. In S. M. Christensen (Ed.), *Quantum theory of gravity* (pp. 66–77). Bristol, England: Adam Hilger.

Dietrich, E., & Markman, A. (2000). *Cognitive dynamics: Conceptual and representational change in humans and machines.* Mahwah, NJ: Lawrence Erlbaum Associates.

Fodor, J. A. (1981). The present status of the innateness controversy. In J. Fodor (Ed.), *Representations* (pp. 257–316). Cambridge, MA: MIT Press.

Freyd, J. J. (1987). Dynamic mental representations. *Psychological Review, 94,* 427–438.

Godfrey-Smith, P. (1993). Functions: Consensus without unity. *Pacific Philosophical Quarterly, 74,* 196–208.

Joas, H. (1993). American pragmatism and German thought: A history of misunderstandings. In H. Joas (Ed.), *Pragmatism and social theory* (pp. 94–121). Chicago: University of Chicago Press.

Kim, J. (1993a). The non-reductivist's troubles with mental causation. In J. Heil & A. Mele (Eds.), *Mental causation* (pp. 89–210). Oxford, England: Oxford University Press.

Kim, J. (1993b). *Supervenience and mind.* Cambridge, England: Cambridge University Press.

Kim, J. (1997). What is the problem of mental causation? In M. L. D. Chiara, K. Doets, D. Mundici, & J. van Benthem (Eds.), *Structures and norms in science* (pp. 319–329). Dordrecht: Kluwer.

Kim, J. (1998). *Mind in a physical world.* Cambridge, MA: MIT Press.

Kitchener, R. F. (1986). *Piaget's theory of knowledge.* New Haven, CT: Yale University Press.

Levine, A., & Bickhard, M. H. (1999). Concepts: Where Fodor went wrong. *Philosophical Psychology, 12,* 5–23.

Millikan, R. G. (1984). *Language, thought, and other biological categories.* Cambridge, MA: MIT Press.

Millikan, R. G. (1993). *White queen psychology and other essays for Alice.* Cambridge, MA: MIT Press.

Neander, K. (1991). Functions as selected effects: The conceptual analyst's defense. *Philosophy of Science, 58,* 168–184.

Nicolis, G., & Prigogine, I. (1977). *Self-organization in nonequilibrium systems.* New York: Wiley.

Piaget, J. (1954). *The construction of reality in the child* (M. Cook, Trans.). New York: Basic Books.

Piaget, J. (1970). *Genetic epistemology* (E. Duckworth, Trans.). New York: Columbia University Press.

Piaget, J. (1971). *Biology and knowledge* (B. Walsh, Trans.). Chicago: University of Chicago Press.

Piaget, J. (2001). *Studies in reflecting abstraction* (R. L. Campbell, Trans.). Hove, England: Psychology Press.

Saunders, S., & Brown, H. R. (1991). *The philosophy of vacuum*. Oxford, England: Oxford University Press.

Shanon, B. (1993). *The representational and the presentational*. Hertfordshire, England: Harvester Wheatsheaf.

Simon, H. A. (1969). *The sciences of the artificial*. Cambridge, MA: MIT Press.

Smith, J. E. (1987). The reconception of experience in Peirce, James, and Dewey. In R. S. Corrington, C. Hausman, & T. M. Seebohm (Eds.), *Pragmatism considers phenomenology* (pp. 73–91). Washington, DC: University Press.

Smith, L. B., & Samuelson, L. K. (1997). Perceiving and remembering: Category stability, variability, and development. In K. Lamberts & D. Shanks (Eds.), *Knowledge, concepts, and categories* (pp. 161–195). Cambridge, MA: MIT Press.

Stephan, A. (1992). Emergence: A systematic view on its historical facets. In A. Beckermann, H. Flohr, & J. Kim (Eds.), *Emergence or reduction? Essays on the prospects of nonreductive physicalism* (pp. 25–48). Berlin: de Gruyter.

Weinberg, S. (1977). The search for unity, notes for a history of quantum field theory. *Daedalus, 106*, 17–35.

Weinberg, S. (1995–2000). *The quantum theory of fields* (Vols. 1–3). Cambridge, England: Cambridge University Press.

Wertsch, J. V. (1985). *Vygotsky and the social formation of mind*. Cambridge, MA: Harvard University Press.

Wertsch, J. V., & Stone, C. A. (1985). The concept of internalization in Vygotsky's account of the genesis of higher mental functions. In J. V. Wertsch (Ed.), *Culture, communication, and cognition: Vygotskian perspectives* (pp. 162–179). New York: Cambridge University Press.

Winegar, L. T. (1997). Can internalization be more than a magical phrase? Notes toward the constructive negotiation of this process. In B. D. Cox & C. Lightfoot (Eds.), *Sociogenetic perspectives on internalization* (pp. 25–43). Hillsdale, NJ: Lawrence Erlbaum Associates.

6

The Role of Systems
of Signs in Reasoning

Terezinha Nunes
Oxford Brookes University

After several years during which Piaget's and Vygotsky's theories were pinned against each other as alternative explanations for children's cognitive development, it has now become clear that the two theories can be integrated into a more encompassing and satisfactory framework. This framework retains the essential role that Vygotsky attributed to social influences on development and simultaneously acknowledges the constructive nature of the processes involved in children's cognitive development emphasized in Piaget's theory. My aim in this chapter is twofold: first, to show that these two theories rely on the same metaphor of mind (Sternberg, 1990) while trying to solve complementary problems about the nature and development of human intelligence and second, to illustrate how the coordination of the two theories can describe one phenomenon in intellectual development that neither could do by itself.

The first part of this chapter considers the systems metaphor and its relation to Piaget's and Vygostsky's theories. The second part examines evidence on one schema of action, the correspondence schema, and how it can be used in the formation of reasoning systems that include progressively more powerful cultural tools. In discussing this evidence, I try to show that both theories are necessary to help us understand the results under analysis. Finally, I explore a new agenda for research into cognitive development formulated from a systems theory approach to intelligence.

THE FORMATION OF REASONING SYSTEMS

Although systems theory has been widely used in some domains of psychology, such as family studies (for an overview and historical account, see Anderson, 1993; Whitchurch & Constantine, 1993), and was central in the work of such eminent researchers as Bateson (1972), Bowlby (1991), and Gibson (1950), systems theory has not become a well-articulated metaphor in some areas of psychology. In the domain of intelligence, systems theory can be used to investigate how systems formed by persons and their tools function during problem-solving activities. An expressive and well-known example that illustrates how systems theory contributes to the analysis of higher order intellectual functioning is found in Bateson (1972):

> Suppose I am a blind man, and I use a stick. I go tap, tap, tap. Where do *I* start? Is my mental system bounded at the handle of the stick? Is it bounded by my skin? Does it start halfway up the stick? Does it start at the tip of the stick? . . . The way to delineate the system is to draw the limiting line in such a way that you do not cut any of these pathways [of information] in ways which leave things inexplicable. (p. 459, italics in original)

Sternberg (1990) considered systems theory to be the vaguest of the metaphors applied to intelligence, an attempt to bring together various other metaphors "by viewing intelligence in terms of a complex interaction of various cognitive and other systems" (p. 261). Thus I attempt to be more specific about the use of this metaphor in the study of intellectual development. I concentrate here on five basic aspects of systems theory, to be summarized later, and refer to them as I discuss how they were used in Vygotsgy's and Piaget's theories. I suggest that systems theory is not simply a framework compatible with Vygotsky's and Piaget's theories, but that it is actually more than that: Both theories rely on the systems theory paradigm. They use systems theory to solve one common problem—the relation between intelligence and the body—and arrive at the same solution: There is no specific organ for intelligence. They also use it to solve different, complementary problems. I consider each theory in turn, starting with Vygotsky and Luria.

Vygotsky and Luria

According to Luria (1973), the systems approach was introduced in Soviet physiology by Anokhin in 1935 through the concept of functional systems. A functional system is characterized by "the presence of a constant (invariant) task performed by variable (variative) mechanisms bringing the process to a constant (invariant) result" (Luria, 1973, p. 28). Functional systems were contrasted with functions: Whereas functions are defined as invariant tasks performed by an invariant tissue, functional systems are character-ized by their complexity and the mobility of their component parts.

Luria brought these ideas into the study of what he termed *higher mental functions*. The problem that Luria was trying to solve is how we carry out functions for which there are no specialized organs. I refer here to two ex-amples, the first one about memorizing and remembering and the second one about locomotion.

Luria pointed out that, if we want to remember something, we might at-tempt simply to commit it to memory by rehearsal, we might tie a knot in a rope to remind us of it, or we might write down what we would like to re-member. When writing, we may use a pencil or a pen, the right or the left hand, or even the foot—and I hasten to add both hands if we write with a computer. In any of these cases, there is one functional system, with the in-variant aim of recovering the information at a later point, one invariant re-sult, remembering, but a variety of mechanisms through which we can ac-complish our goal of remembering.

In his discussion of locomotion towards a goal, Luria drew on a well-known study by Evans (1936) that he mistakenly attributed to Hunter. In two experiments, Evans trained rats in a temporal maze problem with the maze flooded with water. The rats therefore had to swim. After the swim-ming habit was thoroughly established, the rats were placed in a dry maze. Although the pattern of movements that they had to execute was now rather different, running rather than swimming, their performance was rela-tively undisturbed. These studies (and others reviewed by Evans) led to the conclusion that what rats learn in a maze is not a particular series of move-ments that are recognized by proprioception and form a learned habit, but rather variable mechanisms that are means at the service of a functional system, locomotion. Locomotion to the goal can be accomplished by run-ning or swimming; the aim and the result are invariant, but the behavior or the component parts can be varied.

These examples show that Luria relied on the property of equifinality to define a functional system and drew directly on the systems metaphor in his analysis of mental functions. The parallel between the examples used by Luria and Bateson's (1972) blind man walking down the street are quite clear.

Luria (1973) relied on the language of systems theory when discussing higher mental functions, explicitly drawing on Vygotsky's ideas as he did so. To illustrate the point, I provide below two citations from Luria's book. The first stresses the role of actions in the formation of mental systems. Actions, not behavior, are the complex and mobile parts of functional systems:

The higher forms of mental processes have a particularly complex structure; they are laid down during ontogeny. Initially they consist of a complete, ex-

panded series of manipulative movements which gradually have become condensed and have acquired the character of inner mental actions (Vygotsky,
1956, 1960; Galperin, 1959). As a rule, they are based on a series of external
aids such as language, the digital system of counting, etc., all of which are
formed in the process of social history. [All mental actions] are mediated by
[such aids] and cannot in general be conceived without their participation. (p.
30)

This passage illustrates further characteristics of the systems approach
adopted in Luria's analysis—namely complexity, organization, and the idea
of development.

The second citation focuses on the essentially human nature of these
functional systems:

It is this principle of construction of functional systems of the human brain
that Vygotsky (1960) called the principle of "extracortical organization of complex mental functions," implying by this somewhat unusual term that all types
of human conscious activity are always formed with the support of external
auxiliary tools or aids. (Luria, 1973, p. 31)

This passage illustrates the open nature of the system proposed by
Vygotsky and Luria: External auxiliary tools can become integrated into the
system without loss of cohesion of the system. I also stress that, in defining
higher mental functions as open functional systems, Vygotsky did not fall
prey to the brand of Lamarckism criticized by Piaget (1963). Vygotsky
(1978) did not propose that all development is the result of external forces
or that this development is directly transmitted to the next generation. In
discussing actions that are mediated by external tools, he proposed that
mediated action is only possible after "a complex and prolonged process
subject to all the basic laws of psychological evolution" (p. 45). He further
noted that:

*This means that sign-using activity in children is neither simply invented nor
passed down by adults*; rather it arises from something that is originally not a
sign operation and becomes one only after a series of *qualitative* transformations. Each of these transformations provides the conditions for the next
stage and is itself conditioned by the preceding one; thus, transformations are
linked like stages of a single process, and are historical in nature. In this respect, the higher psychological functions are no exception to the general rule
that applies to the elementary processes; they, too, are subject to the fundamental law of development which knows no exceptions, and appear in the
general course of the child's psychological development as the outcome of
the same dialectical process, not as something introduced from without or
from within. (pp. 45–46, italics original)

This last passage shows that children and adults may be viewed as sub-systems within the broader system formed by people and their tools: Children's own development imposes constraints in the application of the principle of extracortical organization of complex mental functions. It also shows the constructive nature of developmental processes in Vygotsky's theory, as he argued that one stage provides the conditions for the next one and is itself conditioned by the previous one.

Piaget

The writings of Piaget are profoundly marked by his interest in the operations and the development of intelligence. Although he used a variety of philosophical sources in setting up his arguments, Piaget was always concerned with the connection between biology and knowledge, the adaptation of organisms and intelligence. He saw the origin of intelligence in adaptation and specifically connected his hypothesis about the origin of cognitive functions with a systems theory or cybernetic approach:

> The explanation of evolutionary mechanisms, for so long shackled to the inescapable alternatives offered by Lamarckism and classical neo-Darwinism, seems set in the direction of a third solution, which is cybernetics and is, in effect, biased toward the theory of autoregulation.... Now, the living being, for all it contains such mechanism, does not possess differentiated organs for regulation, unless we consider as such an organ the nervous system, which in another respect is the instrument of cognitive functions....
> *Cognitive processes seem, then, to be at one and the same time the outcome of organic autoregulation, reflecting its essential mechanism, and the most highly differentiated organs of this regulation at the core of interactions with the environment.* (Piaget, 1971, p. 26, italics original)

This passage suggests that Piaget was grappling with the same problem as Luria, namely how it is possible to carry out functions for which there is no specific organ. Piaget's focus on autoregulation as an invariant across all functions is at the core of his theory and of the systems metaphor.

The biological model used by Piaget was discussed in a number of his works, where he stressed the need for a model that draws on the "two most general biological functions: *organization* and *adaptation*" (Piaget, 1963, p. 5, italics original). These are, as indicated in Table 6.1, basic characteristics of systems.

In *The Psychology of Intelligence* (1967), Piaget proposed:

> Emphasizing the interaction of the organism and the environment leads to the operational theory of intelligence.... According to this point of view, intellectual operations, whose highest form is found in logic and mathematics, consti-

TABLE 6.1
Five Basic Assumptions in Systems Theory

1. A system involves a set (or sets) of elements standing in interrelation amongst themselves and with the environment.
2. Systems operate through feedback and control mechanisms to maintain their equilibrium.
3. Systems are organized and may be open or closed; this property affects how they achieve equilibrium and development.
4. Systems may contain subsystems in their organization.
5. Systems show equifinality (i.e., the same result may be achieved in different ways).

tute genuine actions, being at the same time something produced by the subject and a possible experiment on reality. The problem is therefore to understand how operations arise out of material action, and what laws of equilibrium govern their evolution; operations are thus systems . . . and round themselves off only when the limit of the individual and social genetic process that characterizes them is reached. (pp. 16–17)

In this passage, Piaget clearly defined operations as systems whose development is governed by the laws of equilibrium—all of these are concepts at the core of the systems metaphor. Elsewhere, Piaget (1971) accepts Bertalanfy's definition of organisms as open systems and proposes that cognitive regulations are attempts by the organisms to close the open systems:

If the first essential function of cognitive mechanisms is the progressive closure of the "open system" of the organism by means of an unlimited extension of the environment . . . , then this function entails a whole series of others.
    The second function to be borne in mind is of supreme importance because it appertains to the equilibration mechanisms of the system. The living organization is essentially an autoregulation. If what we have just observed is true, then the development of the cognitive functions does indeed seem, according to our main hypothesis, to be the setting up of specialized organs of regulation in the control of exchanges with the environment. (Piaget, 1971, p. 354)

These passages illustrate Piaget's use of the systems metaphor as he considered the hierarchical organization of the system by attributing to cognitive functions the role of regulating the organisms' exchanges with the environment.

If Vygotsky and Piaget used the same metaphor of mind, why did they develop such distinct theories? I believe that the difference between their theories results from their specific aims and emphases rather than their basic metaphor.

Piaget's theory focused on the *origin* and the *invariants* of intelligence. He hypothesized that the origin of cognitive operations was in children's schemas[1] of action, and gave particular importance to the differentiation between ends and means (essential for flexibility and equifinality) and the coordination of simpler schemas into complex ones. Collective signs, such as language, were viewed as helping and accelerating development, perhaps even a necessary, but certainly not a sufficient condition for the completion of these structures in their generalized forms. Amongst others, a major Piagetian argument was that "children assimilate the language they hear to their own semantic structures, which are a function of their level of development. Adult language may help to modify these, in the long run, yet at any given moment, it is always interpreted in terms of them" (Inhelder & Piaget, 1964, p. 3). As Piaget (1962) himself pointed out, there is much agreement here between this theory and Vygotsky's.[2] Vygotsky was also thoroughly interested in the development of the meaning of words and of children's classificatory ability and in the difference between spontaneous and scientific concepts. But there is not total agreement.

Piaget's focus on invariants resulted in his neglect of collective signs, which vary across history and cultures, as do scientific concepts and explanations. Piaget was interested in some variable structures, namely those that constitute forms of equilibrium of the cognitive operations and appear in children's development as they attempt to carry out the invariant functions necessary to adaptation:

> The organism adapts itself by materially constructing new forms to fit them into those of the universe, whereas intelligence extends this creation by constructing mentally structures which can be applied to those of the environment. . . .
>
> In fact there exist, in mental development, elements that are variable and others which are invariant. Hence stems the misunderstanding resulting from psychological terminology some of which lead to attributing higher qualities to the lower stages and others which lead to the annihilation of stages and operations. It is therefore fitting simultaneously to avoid both the preformism of intellectualistic psychology and the hypothesis of mental heterogeneities. . . .

---

[1]Following the Anglo-Saxon translation tradition, the author does not distinguish between the French words *schème* and *schéma*. Piaget (1969) clarified his use of these terms: "In our usage, these terms correspond to quite distinct realities, the one operative (a scheme of action in the sense of instrument of generalization) and the other figurative (a figural or topological schema)" (p. ix).

[2]Piaget's commentary is not included in Vygotsky (1962), in the MIT reprint (Vygotsky, 1986), or in Vygotsky (1987). It was retranslated by Smith in 1995 and is reprinted in Lloyd and Fernyhough (1999). In any event, most developmentalists seem to be quite unaware of Piaget's commentary.

The solution to this difficulty is precisely to be found in the distinction between variable structures and invariant functions. (Piaget, 1963, p. 4)

Piaget (1963) went on to discuss how the invariant functions (adaptation and organization) determine the categories of reason, that is, the principal categories "which intelligence uses to adapt to the external world—space and time, causality and substance, classification and number, etc." (p. 8). Each of these categories corresponds to an aspect of reality just as the sensory systems are related to special qualities of the environment. They are not generalized forms of perception: They are organized by the operations of thought that allow for the construction of particular cognitive structures, which are at first sensorimotor but later on involve systems of representation. It is here that the collective signs attain significance.

Children's understanding of number, for example, will develop in close connection with the acquisition of the numeration system used in their environment, but this understanding it is not a simple product of learning to count. Piaget's (1965) evidence is provided by his observations (and those of many researchers since) that children who know the counting sequence may be unable to use counting to solve simple numerical problems under many conditions. With understanding, they will become able to use the counting system available in their environment. Thus, the number words provided by the counting sequence are interpreted in terms of children's own ideas about number. Of course, the particulars of numerical problem solving vary across cultures because the numeration systems vary, but the basic category *number* does not. Thus, these variations are phenotypical variations, related to the adaptation of particular individuals to a particular social environment.

Piaget's (1965) argument seems very convincing and one can be tempted to stop here in the analysis of children's understanding of number. However, by focusing on the origin of children's understanding of number, he overlooked the consequences of knowing how to count when counting becomes coordinated with the cognitive operations involved in the understanding of number, and this left his analysis of cognitive systems incomplete. According to Vygotsky (1978), "*the most significant moment in the course of intellectual development, which gives birth to the purely human forms of practical and abstract intelligence, occurs when speech and practical activity, two previously completely independent lines of development, converge*" (p. 24, italics original). Vygotsky went on to state that this is the most essential feature of his theory and that his:

Analysis alters the traditional view that at the moment children assimilate the meaning of a word or master an operation such as addition or written language, their developmental processes are basically completed. In fact, they have only just begun at that moment. The major consequence of analyzing the educational process in this manner is to show that the initial mastery of, for example, the four arithmetic operations provides the basis for the subsequent development of a variety of highly complex internal processes in children's thinking. (Vygotsky, 1978, p. 90)

This amounts to saying that a child who has developed the understanding of numerical operations still cannot solve numerical problems without a numeration system. Numeration systems are historical constructions that only become accessible to children as tools when the children have developed the operations of thought necessary to use these signs. However, when the operations of thought have developed to the point that numeration systems can become tools for reasoning, children's reasoning systems change in new ways: They become able to quantify and calculate, not to simply understand quantitative operations.

The conclusion that Piaget and Vygotsky were solving complementary problems is inescapable. Piaget investigated the developmental processes that make learning possible, whereas Vygotsky investigated the consequences of learning for further development. The incompleteness of the theories has clear consequences for their explanatory power. Vygotsky's emphasis on collective signs and cultural variation led to the prediction of a "great cognitive divide" between those people who have and those who do not have some systems of signs (e.g., literacy), but this prediction turned out to be contradicted by the evidence (Scribner & Cole, 1981). Piaget's neglect of collective signs make it difficult for his theory to explain why some children may be very successful in solving some problems with one system of signs, but very unsuccessful when solving problems that require the same cognitive operations with a different system of signs. We (Carraher, Carraher, & Schliemann, 1985; Nunes, Schliemann, & Carraher, 1993) have shown this to be the case in the realm of number operations and other researchers (Abreu, 1993; Reed & Lave, 1981) have obtained the same results.[3]

In the next section, I will use this synthesis of the two theories to examine how one schema of action—the correspondence schema—can be identified as the invariant supporting problem solving in a variety of contexts, and how what can be accomplished with this reasoning schema differs as a consequence of learning to use different systems of signs.

---

[3]It is highly arguable that different representations of a problem represent different systems of signs, that is, different systems of representation. It is just as likely that, using a single representational system, people can arrive at easier or more difficult ways to go about things. In any case, Piaget (1972) acknowledged that success in problem solving varies considerably, depending on the way in which problems are presented and the material (concrete or representational) on which the subject is asked to work.

THE VARIABLE FORMS OF CORRESPONDENCE
REASONING

Background

Some aspects of Piaget's (1965) work on the correspondence schema had
more impact on the study of children's reasoning than others. His observation that young children were not very good about creating a one-to-one
correspondence between two sets of counters or understanding that numerical equivalence continued to apply after visual correspondence was de-
stroyed provoked much discussion concerning the relation between principles and skills in the development of numerical concepts. This debate
instigated the development of new methods for investigating children's reasoning and produced some interesting results, but I do not intend to review
these here because they do not relate to the aim of this analysis of the correspondence reasoning. My analysis focuses specifically on one-to-many
correspondence and its relation to multiplicative reasoning.

Piaget (1965) studied 5- to 7-year-old children's correspondence schema as
the origin of multiplicative reasoning. His procedure involved five steps: (1)
First, he asked the children to establish a one-to-one correspondence between a set of vases and a set of red flowers; (2) he then asked the children
to establish a correspondence between a set of blue flowers and the same
vases; (3) next, the children were asked whether the number of blue and red
flowers was the same; (4) subsequently, the children were asked how many
flowers would be in each vase if all the red and blue flowers were used; (5) finally, the flowers were put away and the children were asked to pick up the
number of tubes needed so that each flower could be placed in a tube by itself. Piaget observed that those children who could correctly infer that there
were as many blue and red flowers could also select the correct number of
tubes, by placing two tubes in correspondence with each vase. He concluded
that children's understanding of correspondence was the basis for both inferences and suggested that establishing correspondences is basic to children's
understanding of multiplicative reasoning.

In the last few years, some of my colleagues and I have been studying the
use of the correspondence schema to solve multiplicative problems. I use
the expression *multiplicative problems* rather than *multiplication problems*
because the term *multiplication* refers to a particular arithmetic operation
and the expression *multiplicative* refers to a particular type of relation between variables. Problems in which variables stand in a multiplicative relation may be solved by multiplication or division, but also by combinations
of operations. We have been able to document, in a variety of situations,
the use of the correspondence schema in problem solving from an early
age to adulthood. In the sections that follow, I present some of these results

in order to show that reasoning by correspondences is an early acquisition and remains important throughout life. I also argue that people can use diverse mechanisms to find the solution to multiplication problems and that the earliest solutions are observed in action. They are later mediated by counting and, even later, by arithmetic operations.

Young Children's Use of Correspondences to Solve Multiplication Problems

Kornilaki (1999) investigated young children's solutions to multiplication problems where the solution could be reached by means of actively setting things into correspondence. Children were shown two series of hutches (represented with colored paper cut in the shape of hutches) and were asked to imagine that the hutches contained rabbits. For example, in the problem presented in Fig. 6.1, they were asked to imagine that in each hutch in the row of blue hutches there were two rabbits and that in each hutch in the row of red hutches there were three rabbits. The rabbits in the blue hutches were going to be placed in a blue house at the end of the row and those from the red hutches would be placed in the red house at the end of the row. The children's task was to pick up one pellet of food for each rabbit and place the correct number of pellets on each of the houses at the end of each row.

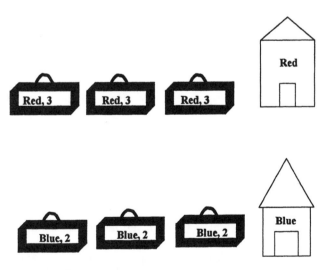

FIG. 6.1. An adaptation of Kornilaki's (1999) problem. There are three rabbits in each of the red hutches and two rabbits in each of the blue hutches. All rabbits go to the house of corresponding color to eat. Children are asked to place enough food pellets on each house so that all of the rabbits will have one pellet each.

Participants were 105 children in equal groups of 5-, 6-, and 7-year-olds attending a state-supported school in London; only the 7-year-olds had been taught the multiplication tables up to 5. Kornilaki observed that 67% of the 5-year-olds and all of the 6- and 7-year-olds were able to pick up the exact number of pellets needed to feed all the rabbits in each house. The 5- and 6-year-olds had two ways of solving the problems; neither depended on knowledge of multiplication facts. One solution may be named unmediated, in the sense that the children did not use signs but, instead, used actual objects—they established one-to-many correspondences between the pellets and the hutches by, for example, placing two pellets in front of each hutch. This would allow them to pick up the correct number of pellets, which would then be placed on the corresponding house. The second solution can be called mediated, in the sense that the children used symbols or signs instead of actual objects. For example, some children pointed two times to a hutch where they imagined there were two rabbits and counted as they pointed, thereby establishing the total number of rabbits in all the hutches; other children put out two fingers in front of the hutches and counted their fingers, or they counted in twos, if they knew this number sequence. Thus, instead of establishing a direct correspondence between the pellets and the hutches, they obtained the number of pellets through the mediation of counting. The 7-year-olds could either use these correspondence approaches or solve the problem through arithmetic, because they had learned multiplication tables. It is significant that the lack of knowledge of multiplication tables did not disadvantage the 6-year-olds in comparison with the 7-year-olds: All the children in both groups were successful. These results strongly suggest that the schema of correspondence can be used by children to solve multiplication problems before they learn about multiplication in school.

We (Watanabe, Nunes, Bryant, & van den Heuvel-Panhuizen, 2000) developed a paper-and-pencil version of this problem in which it was still possible for the children to use the same reasoning. In the paper-and-pencil version, the children could not place the food in correspondence with the hutches, but they could draw them in correspondence—and some of the children did so. Examples of children's productions are presented in Fig. 6.2.

In spite of the similarity between the problems presented with cut-out paper and the paper-and-pencil version, the latter was clearly more difficult. The 6- and 7-year-olds were not as successful in the paper-and-pencil version of the problem (no 5-year-olds were tested in this version). The percentages of correct responses in this problem were 52% for the 6-year-olds, 59% for the 7-year-olds, and 77% for the 8-year-olds (combined data from Nunes & Bryant, 1999; Watanabe et al., 1999). The difference in performance across the versions cannot be explained by counting errors being more fre-

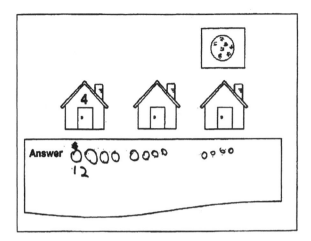

FIG. 6.2. A paper-and-pencil version of Kornilaki's (1999) problem, from Watanabe et al. (2000): Four rabbits live in each house. Look at the carrot biscuit in the top box. In the answer box, draw the right number of biscuits so that there is one for each rabbit (an actual protocol).

quent in the paper-and-pencil version, because only a small percentage of errors involved a number that differed from the correct answer by only one or two units. Thus, a problem that can be solved by the same correspondence procedures in principle becomes much more difficult if it is presented with paper and pencil. The use of paper and pencil seems to be taken as an indication that mediators—writing, counting, calculating—should be implicated in the solution. It is possible that the coordination between correspondence procedures and the use of written signs is not a simple matter. But it is also possible that children do not often encounter problems that they are expected to solve by means of correspondences in school and this leads them to stop considering the correspondence schema as important for solving mathematical problems. This form of socialization of mathematical reasoning, which I discussed elsewhere (Nunes, 1999), is of great importance, but its discussion is beyond the scope of this paper (see also Goodnow, 1990, for an analysis of this type of socialization of children's drawing performance). Suffice it to say here that our results suggest that correspondences can be used by children of about 6 years in order to solve multiplication problems and that they show different degrees of success in very similar problems when the medium of problem presentation implicitly brings to mind different mechanisms for solution.

Correspondence reasoning is not restricted to such simple examples and can be used to find the solution to problems that are typically viewed as proportions problems in school. The difference between the simple problem presented in Fig. 6.2 and typical proportion problems presented to children in school is straightforward: In the preceding problems, the unitary value is given, whereas in typical school proportion problems, the unitary value is not given. We presented typical proportions problems by means of drawings to the same 6-, 7-, and 8-year-old children. One example is presented in Fig. 6.3.

Proportions are not a topic included in mathematics lessons for 7- and 8-year-olds, but they receive instruction on various multiplication and division problems, including some that are quite similar to this one. The percentage of correct responses in our problem increased steadily with age level; the percentages were 31% for 6-year-olds, 36% for 7-year-olds, and 54% for 8-year-olds. Because of the nature of the test, a paper-and-pencil task, it is not clear how the children arrived at their solutions, although some did provide a hint, for example, the child whose response is displayed in Fig. 6.3. We know that children use the correspondence schema to solve problems of this type and expect that it was actually used by some children, but further research with individual testing is needed to reveal whether children in the 6- to 8-year age range do use correspondence reasoning to solve proportions problems or whether they use other forms of reasoning.

So far, I have suggested that correspondence is a basic cognitive schema and that young children can use it to solve multiplicative reasoning problems before they are taught about multiplication in school. If reasoning by correspondences is in fact developed independently of school, it should be possible to document its use in the solution of multiplicative problems among youngsters and adults with little or no school instruction. I present here three examples from work with unschooled groups, two from my own

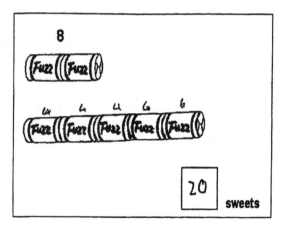

FIG. 6.3. A typical proportions problem, from Watanabe et al. (2000): The top roll of sweets has eight sweets altogether. How many sweets are there altogether in the bottom roll? This is an actual answer sheet, the fading 4s faithfully reproduced.

work in Brazil (in collaboration with Schliemann and Carraher) and one from a study done by Soto Cornejo (1992) in Chile. I first give a description of a typical solution and then quantitative information about the use of this operation.

The first example is taken from a study with street vendors (Nunes, Schliemann, & Carraher, 1993). MD, a 9-year-old girl attending a third-grade class in Brazil, was selling lemons for Cr$5 each (five *cruzeiros*, the Brazilian currency at the time). In the role of customer, I asked her how much I would have to pay for 12 lemons. MD separated two lemons at a time as she counted, 10, 20, 30, 40, 50, 60. MD was later asked to multiply 12 by 5 and her answer, 152, was obtained through an attempt to use the traditional multiplication algorithm (Nunes et al., 1993, p. 24). MD did not know how to use the computation algorithm to solve this problem, but was successful in solving problems by means of correspondence reasoning. The form of the correspondence reasoning that she used shows some interesting details. First, she did not have to work with the unit value (Cr$5 to one lemon). She worked instead with two lemons at a time, taking a shortcut to the solution through a route where she took advantage of the ease of counting in 10s. Second, her reasoning was by correspondence, although the arithmetic operation carried out was addition. When two lemons were added to the group of lemons that I was buying, the corresponding amount of money was added to my bill. We (Nunes & Bryant, 1996) used the term *replication* rather than *addition* to refer to these parallel transformations across variables. Third, whereas the lemons were manipulated directly, the money was represented through verbal symbols. This coordination between her activity and the verbal signs provided the means to obtain a numerical solution. I emphasize here the need to use both Piaget's and Vygotsky's theories to explain the process used in this solution. MD certainly used correspondences to solve the problem because she understood that correspondences allow for particular logicomathematical inferences in the situation, but in order to tell me how much I had to pay for the lemons, MD also had to coordinate the schema with a counting system. A schematic representation of her reasoning is offered in Fig. 6.4.

The schematic representation in Fig. 6.4 brings out the parallel transformations carried out in each variable, lemons and cost, which a verbal transcript on its own cannot show. This schematic representation also makes quite clear the similarity between MD's reasoning and the action of correspondences observed with real objects, as well as the children's drawings presented earlier. Finally, a conspicuous feature of the reasoning process is the straight connection between the numbers and the variables to which they refer. Although MD did not say the word *cruzeiros* as she moved the lemons, the only possible referents to the numbers she said are the *cruzeiros*. As it will be shown in subsequent examples, correspondence reasoning

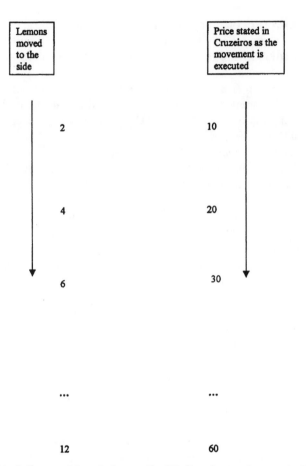

FIG. 6.4. A diagram of the solution used by MD. She takes two lemons at a time and verbally states the price of the total number of lemons moved to the pile, rather than the number of lemons moved, which she must be monitoring internally. If MD were simply counting lemons, she would not be saying "10," "20," and so on; these values represent the price, not the number, of the lemons.

consistently operates on numbers that refer to measures of variables in the problems.

The second example is taken from our work with fishermen. We (Nunes et al., 1993) asked fishermen to solve a series of problems about the relation between processed and unprocessed food, a relation that they understand well because it is central to their work. These fishermen catch a small fish called *whitebait* and sell it to a middleman, who processes the fish by salting and drying it in the sun. The middleman later sells the fish to the wholesale buyers, who bring the fish to be sold in markets away from the coast. To assess the fairness of the price they are paid, fishermen must have a good idea of how much fish the middleman will actually be selling, because the amount that he buys is actually larger than what he will sell. As the fish dry in the sun, water and thus also weight is lost.

Some of the problems that we presented to the fishermen (Nunes et al., 1993) were quite similar in structure to those presented to the children because they stated the unit value in one of the variables: for example, a farmer needs seven bags (an informal unit of weight) of cassava to produce one bag of cassava flour; how many bags of cassava does he need in order to produce five bags of cassava flour? These were easy problems for the fishermen, who showed an accuracy level of 91%. When such easy problems are presented, it is often difficult to obtain information on the method of solution because the solution is reached quite quickly. When more difficult problems are presented, in which the unit value is not part of the information given, the fishermen tend to calculate out loud and this makes it easier to record their reasoning. Two examples of problems are presented in Figs. 6.5 and 6.6.

Although the problem types illustrated in Figs. 6.5 and 6.6 might seem very similar to most educated people, our analysis (Nunes & Bryant, 1996) of how correspondence solutions are implemented leads to the prediction that they are quite different in level of difficulty. The prediction is that there is a straightforward solution to Type 1 problems through correspondence reasoning: By replicating the 3-to-10 correspondence four times, the participants can find out that 12 kg of shelled oyster can be obtained from 40 kg of unprocessed oyster. Solutions by replication are known as *scalar* solutions

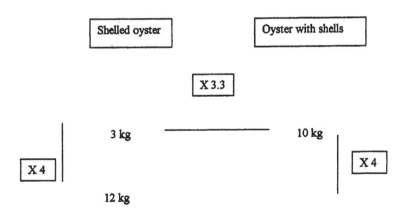

FIG. 6.5. Type 1 problem: There is a type of oyster in the South that yields 3 kg of shelled oyster for every 10 kg that you catch; how many kg would you have to catch for a customer who wants 12 kg of shelled oyster?

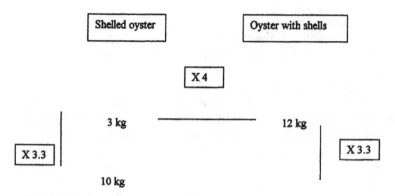

FIG. 6.6. Type 2 problem: There is a type of oyster in the south that yields 3 kg of shelled oyster for every 12 kg that you catch; how much do you have to catch if a customer asks you for 10 kg?

because the number of replications is the scalar factor that connects the amounts *within each variable* (see Vergnaud, 1983). In contrast, there is no straightforward scalar solution to Type 2 problems: Replicating the 3-to-12 correspondence does not lead directly to a pair where 10 is the amount of shelled oyster. Replication gives either the value of 9 kg of shelled oyster (three replications) or the value of 12 kg (four replications). A simple solution here would be to establish the functional value that *relates the values across the two variables*, but such functional solutions are not based on the action of replicating values in correspondence.

The Type 2 problems would actually be solved more easily through a different route. If the interviewee thought about the *relation* between processed and unprocessed food, rather than the amounts in each of these variables, there would be a simple solution: The amount of unprocessed oyster in this example is four times the amount of shelled oyster. Notice that the arithmetic is the same (3 times 4), but the concepts are different. Rather than thinking about the value in each variable, the second route to the solution depends on attempting to quantify the relation between the two variables and for this reason it is known as a *functional* solution (see Vergnaud, 1983). Despite the fact that a functional solution would require less computational effort, it is not connected to correspondence reasoning. It is thus expected to be less frequent in unschooled groups, who will resort more often to correspondence reasoning, which does not depend on social transmission.

Type 1 problems resulted in fewer errors than Type 2: The fishermen correctly solved 83% of the Type 1 problems, but only 70% of the Type 2 problems (Nunes et al., 1993). The majority of problems of both types was solved by means of correspondence reasoning. An example of a solution by replication (or correspondence) to a functional problem (Nunes et al., 1993, p. 112) is as follows:

Investigator: There is a kind of shrimp in the south that yields 3 kilos of
                shelled shrimp for every 18 kilos you catch. If a customer
                wanted the fisherman to get him 2 kilos of shelled shrimp,
                how much would he have to fish?

Fisherman: One and a half kilos [processed] would be nine [unproc-
                essed]. It has to be nine because half of eighteen is nine
                and half of three is one and a half. And a half-kilo [proc-
                essed] is three kilos [unprocessed]. Then it'd be nine plus
                three is twelve [unprocessed]; the twelve kilos would give
                you two kilos [processed].

Note that in both examples the reference is to corresponding amounts in
both variables throughout the solution.

The example shows quite clearly the characteristics of correspondence
reasoning: In this example, only symbols are set into correspondence. In
contrast to the solution offered by MD, there is no manipulation of objects.
The possibility of working exclusively with symbols promotes changes in
the reasoning system that make the system more powerful: If the fishermen
had to actually deal with the kilos of oyster about which they spoke, they
may not have been able to solve the problem. Yet there is no fundamental
difference in the organization of the reasoning system as such: The correspondence schema is the invariant here.

The third example is taken from the work of Soto Cornejo (1992). The
woodcutter interviewed by Soto Cornejo in Chile sells wood to be burned
as fuel. The price of wood is calculated by volume. The interviewer draws a
truck with a trailer in the back. The drawing of the trailer shows the dimensions 5 m (length), by 2 m (width), by 1.5 m (height). The question is how
much wood can be carried in this trailer. The example (Soto Cornejo, 1992,
p. 2, my translation) is as follows:

Woodcutter (makes marks on the drawing as he refers to the layers):
                First I make a layer one meter high and always five meters
                long. That gives you five cubic meters. And two times that
                [the width is 2 m], that makes ten cubic meters. Now I've
                got fifty centimetres two times. We fill in five centimetres
                [sic], this makes five times five, twenty-five, that is two and
                a half cubic meters, and this two times is five cubic meters.
                The total is ten plus five, fifteen cubic meters.

Three characteristics of the woodcutter's reasoning stand out. First, one
of the variables that the woodcutter worked with (a layer) is an imaginary
object created by the interviewee to solve the problem. Second, the same
reasoning by correspondences between the values of two variables is once

again clear: The woodcutter created correspondences between the imagined object, a layer, and its measure in cubic meters. This allowed him to solve a much more complicated problem than those presented earlier on, in which three variables (length, width, and height) are simultaneously proportional to a fourth one, volume. Finally, although the reasoning carried out was intrinsically dependent on the use of correspondences, the power of the reasoning system considered in this example is radically different from that in the examples observed among young children. The woodcutter did not depend on the manipulation of objects and could manipulate verbal signs whose referents most likely were constructed earlier on, during his everyday commercial activities. Volume problems are known to be very difficult, even for secondary school students after they have received instruction on this concept (Vergnaud, 1983), yet they could be solved by the unschooled woodcutter who reasons by correspondences. This highlights the power of the correspondence schema when this schema is part of the reasoning system of a problem solver who has constructed meaningful ways of representing the situation. Because the woodcutter could create a unit of volume, a layer, he could also set it in correspondence with the width and then the height, successively, and arrive at a solution.

The final example I will present here comes not from work with unschooled adults, but from work with school teachers. The aim of this example is to strengthen the argument that some problems that are difficult when their solution involves school-taught mechanisms can be solved in a logical way through correspondence reasoning. The problem, originally presented by Simon (1993) to prospective elementary school teachers in the United States, was: You need 3/8 cup flour to make one muffin. You have 35 cups of flour. If you make all the muffins you can make with this flour, how much flour will you have left?

This problem was designed by Simon (1993) as a difficult division problem. It has produced low percentages of correct responses among school teachers in the U.S., the United Kingdom, and Brazil (Campos, Magina, Da Cunha, & Canoas, 1996). There are many reasons for this difficulty, but two seem most important when the participants attempted to solve the problem through the school-prescribed mathematical solution. First, the route to solution involves division by a fraction: In order to find out how much flour will be used, we have to find out how many muffins can be made and then check what is left. This step is difficult because many people do not know that this division makes sense (dividing 35 by 3/8 means finding out how many 3/8 cups are contained in 35 cups) and many do not know how to implement the calculation. The second difficulty is in interpreting the result of this computation. If a calculator is used, the screen will show the following answer: 93.333. How does this number relate to the question "How much flour will be left?" The 93 refers to the number of muffins that can be made

Problem: You need 3/8 cup flour to make one muffine. You have 35 cups of flour. If you make all the muffins you can make with this flour, how much flour will you have left?

Diagram of an actual protocol showing a solution by correspondences:

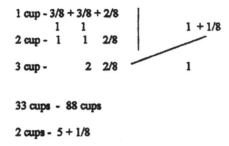

FIG. 6.7 Diagram of a solution obtained by correspondence reasoning.

with the 35 cups. The 0.33 is a fraction of muffin. To find out how much flour is left, it is necessary to convert the quantity back into 1/8 cups and this will give the correct answer: 1/8.[4] Simon did not explain how the successful teachers in their sample solved the problem. In the sample of Brazilian teachers in Campos, Magina, Da Cunha, and Canoas (1996), only 4 out of 20 university-trained teachers succeeded. Two of the four solved the problem by correspondence reasoning; one of these solutions is presented in Fig. 6.7.

- The respondent first wrote the two top lines, indicating the correspondence between 1 cup and the fractions that would allow for making muffins; 1 cup corresponds to 3/8, which makes 1 muffin (written underneath), plus another 3/8, which makes 1 muffin (also written underneath), plus 2/8, which will not be sufficient to make a third muffin.
- The third line repeats this analysis of the correspondences, this time between the second cup and muffins; the unused portion of this second cup is then connected to the unused portion of the first cup by a vertical stroke and the respondent writes down "1" (muffin) plus "1/8" (cup).

---

[4]If the division (35 divided by 3/8) is carried out with paper and pencil, the remainder is 1. The 1 here is the number of eighths of cups left. However, most of the teachers who carried out the division correctly did not interpret the result correctly. They probably realized that the 1 could not mean 1 cup because more muffins could still be made if there were a whole cup left. They interpreted the one to mean 1/3, perhaps because the last operation carried out was a division by 3. This illustrates the difficulty of functional reasoning, in which a value in one variable is divided by a value in another variable; the interpretation of results is not always straightforward. In this case, the quotient in the division (93) refers to the number of muffins that can be made and the remainder indicates unused portions (eighths) of cups of flour.

- Next, the respondent shortcuts the process, indicating that the third cup corresponds to 2 muffins plus 2/8 cup. She then draws an inclined line connecting the unused 2/8 from this cup with the unused 1/8 noted earlier and writes that this corresponds to one more muffin. She then counts the number of muffins obtained with 3 cups; as there are no unused portions, she establishes that 3 cups yield 8 muffins.
- Next, she uses scalar reasoning, multiplying 3 by 11 and 8 by 11, and writes the correspondence between 33 cups and 88 muffins.
- Finally, she writes down the correspondence between 2 cups (needed to reach the 35 cups in the problem) and 5 muffins plus the unused portion, 1/8 cup. The answer she gives is that there would be 1/8 cup of flour left.

Note that the correspondence solution involves keeping the number of cups of flour separate from the number of muffins. Each cup is analyzed into fractions that make up a muffin plus an unused portion; the unused portions are added to obtain sufficient flour for a new muffin. The solution does not involve computation across the two variables, only correspondences between different values in the two variables.

The similarity between this solution and those presented earlier on is remarkable. Cups are analyzed into corresponding groups of eighths—two groups of 3/8 plus one of 2/8—and the muffin-to-cups correspondence is analyzed until the teacher finds that 3 cups make exactly 8 muffins. The replication method was then applied using a shortcut to the value closest to 35, leading to the conclusion that 33 cups correspond exactly to 88 muffins. The teacher then considers the remaining 2 cups, which she had already analyzed in correspondence with the muffins, and the remainder, 1/8, is read from the previous analysis. This example illustrates once again the power of reasoning by correspondences with the support of signs and highlights the fact that the problem solvers using this reasoning are constantly referring to the quantities that are set in correspondence with each other.

In short, the evidence considered here shows that reasoning by correspondences is a powerful approach to the solution of many problems involving multiplicative relations. About two thirds of the 5-year-olds and all of the 6- and 7-year-olds interviewed by Kornilaki (1999) were able to use correspondences to solve simple multiplication problems in action. When the problems could not be solved through actions on concrete objects, the percentage of success declined significantly, but half of the children at age 6 and two thirds of those at age 7 were still successful. Even more difficult problems, in which the unit value is not part of the information given to the children, do not prove impossible at these age levels, with one third of the children at ages 6 and 7 and half of those at age 8 being successful, in spite of the unlikelihood that children at this age level had received instruction on such difficult problems. Reasoning by correspondences has been described in different situations and cultures when unschooled adults solve problems involving multiplicative relations. Although this form of reasoning does not seem to be directly taught in schools, it does not completely disappear in highly schooled groups and is a powerful way to solve complex problems that are often incorrectly solved when such groups apply school-learned procedures. The power of the reasoning by correspondences does not reside simply in the schema of action. It depends largely also on the coordination of the actions with signs, which at first may be simply the oral counting system, but later may involve other signs, such as diagrams and fractions.

A RESEARCH AGENDA FOR THE STUDY
OF THE DEVELOPMENT OF THINKING SYSTEMS

The integration of Piaget's and Vygotsky's ideas through a systems theory approach offers new possibilities for research on cognitive development. In particular, this analysis offers a new approach to the study of universals in cognitive development and educational applications. Working from the example of correspondence reasoning and its role in the understanding of multiplicative relations, it is possible to highlight the fact that the universals are, as Piaget (1963, 1971) suggested, grounded in schemas of action that can already be observed as part of children's reasoning from a relatively early age. This logic of action does not change in nature as the gestures of setting objects directly in correspondence are replaced with signs—which are themselves initially set into correspondence with objects, but later can be used in more condensed forms (i.e., one number word, say *eight*, can represent all eight objects in a display without the uttering of one word in correspondence with each object). The schema of correspondence can be viewed as a cognitive invariant that gives origin to a diversity of phenotypical variations when different systems of signs are integrated into a reasoning system operating with correspondences. It is then possible to analyze with more clarity whether, for example, functional reasoning is a refinement of correspondence reasoning, or whether a qualitative change is involved when subjects reason about the relation between two variables rather than about the pairs of values that are kept in correspondence.

The hypothesis that functional reasoning is a refinement of correspondence reasoning is certainly plausible. Vygotsky (1978) proposed that educators play a major role in children's development by inverting the figure-ground relations in a situation, that is, singling out something from the background for the learner's attention and making it into a figure. In correspondence reasoning, the subject's attention is focused on the quantities.

The teacher may be able to shift the learner's attention from the quantities to the relation between them and provoke the transformation of correspondence reasoning into functional reasoning. Functional reasoning would then be another phenotype of correspondence reasoning. Instruments that can be used to provoke this attentional shift are, for example, graphs and tables. Graphs depict the nature of the relations between two variables so clearly that functions are named according to the picture they produce in a graph (e.g., linear versus nonlinear functions). Tables also allow a subject to verify whether the connection between two values is constant across pairs and what the nature of this connection is.

Alternatively, it is possible that there is a true discontinuity between understanding correspondences and functional reasoning. In this case, Piagetian theory would suggest that the mechanism for change resides in the process of conflict and equilibration. If the progress required in going from reasoning by correspondences to functional reasoning is more radical than an attentional shift, attempts to accomplish this attentional shift are doomed to failure. Teaching children about graphs and their implications would be like teaching them to count when they do not understand the idea of number: They could master the drawing and the reading of graphs, assimilating this teaching to their understanding of coordinates on a plane. But without further cognitive development the learners would be unable to see the trends that the teacher sees in a graph. These are empirical questions: Only further research will result in a better understanding of the connections between correspondences and functional reasoning. Interestingly, this would not be a test of one theory against the other, because they are both compatible with whatever result such investigations might provide.

I am confident that a synthesis between Piaget's and Vygotsky's theories is not only possible, but also a move toward further progress. Neither of these two theories can be reconciled with behaviorism, because of the assumptions that behaviorism makes about the role of specific responses in development. In contrast, a synthesis between them might very well advance our capacity to analyze cognitive development at a new level.

AUTHOR NOTE

Terezinha Nunes, Department of Psychology, Oxford Brookes University, Oxford OX3 0BP, Great Britain; e-mail: tnunes@brookes.ac.uk.

REFERENCES

Abreu, G. de. (1993). *The relationship between home and school mathematics in a farming community in rural Brazil.* Unpublished doctoral dissertation, Cambridge University, Cambridge, England.

Anderson, E. A. (1993). The application of systems theory to the study of family policy. In P. G. Boss, W. J. Doherty, R. LaRossa, W. R. Schumm, & S. K. Steinmertz (Eds.), *Sourcebook of family theories and methods: A contextual approach* (pp. 353–355). New York: Plenum Press.

Bateson, G. (1972). *Steps to an ecology of the mind: A revolutionary approach to man's understanding of himself.* New York: Ballantine.

Bowlby, J. (1991). Postscript. In C. M. Parkes, J. Stevenson-Hinde, & P. Marris (Eds.), *Attachment across the life cycle* (pp. 293–297). London: Routledge.

Campos, T., Magina, S., Da Cunha, M. C., & Canoas, S. (1996). Referent transforming operations: Teachers' solutions. In X. Puig & A. Gutiérrez (Eds.), *Proceedings of the 20th annual meeting of the International Group for the Study of the Psychology of Mathematics Education (PME)* (Vol. 2, pp. 185–192). Valencia, Spain: PME.

Carraher, T. N., Carraher, D. W., & Schliemann, A. D. (1985). Mathematics in the streets and in school. *British Journal of Developmental Psychology, 3,* 21–29.

Evans, S. (1936). The role of kinesthesis in the establishment and control of the maze habit. *Journal of Genetic Psychology, 48,* 177–198.

Galperin, P. Y. (1959). The development of research into the formation of intellectual action. *Psychological Science in the USSR, Izd. Akad. Pedagog. Nauk RSFSR* (Moscow). In Luria, A. (1973). *The working brain.* Harmondsworth: Penguin.

Gibson, J. J. (1950). *The perception of the visual world.* Boston: Houghton Mifflin.

Goodnow, J. (1990). The socialization of cognition: What is involved? In J. W. Stigler, R. A. Shweder, & G. Herdt (Eds.), *Cultural psychology: Essays on comparative human development* (pp. 259–286). New York: Cambridge University Press.

Inhelder, B., & Piaget, J. (1964). *The early growth of logic in the child.* New York: Norton.

Kornilaki, K. (1999). *Young children's understanding of multiplication: A psychological approach.* Unpublished doctoral dissertation, Institute of Education, University of London.

Luria, A. (1973). *The working brain.* Harmondsworth, England: Penguin.

Nunes, T. (1999). Mathematics learning as the socialization of the mind. *Mind, Culture, and Activity, 6,* 33–52.

Nunes, T., & Bryant, P. E. (1996). *Children doing mathematics.* Oxford, England: Blackwell.

Nunes, T., & Bryant, P. (1999). How do the phonological and lexical routes in reading and spelling develop? Unpublished ESRC report, Oxford Brookes University.

Nunes, T., Schliemann, A. D., & Carraher, D. W. (1993). *Street mathematics, school mathematics.* New York: Cambridge University Press.

Piaget, J. (1962). Comments on Vygotsky's critical remarks concerning *The language and thought of the child* and *Judgment and reasoning in the child.* In L. Vygostky, *Thought and language.* Cambridge, MA: MIT Press.

Piaget, J. (1963). *The origins of intelligence in children.* New York: Norton. (Original work published 1952)

Piaget, J. (1965). *The child's conception of number.* New York: Norton.

Piaget, J. (1967). *The psychology of intelligence.* Totowa, NJ: Littlefield Adams. (Original work published 1947)

Piaget, J. (1969). *The mechanisms of perception* (G. N. Seagrim, Trans.). New York: Basic Books. (Original work published 1961)

Piaget, J. (1971). *Biology and knowledge: An essay on the relation between organic regulations and cognitive processes* (B. Walsh, Trans.). Chicago: Chicago University Press. (Original work published 1967)

Piaget, J. (1972). Intellectual evolution from adolescence to adulthood. *Human Development, 15,* 1–12.

Reed, H. J., & Lave, J. (1981). Arithmetic as a tool for investigating relations between culture and cognition. In R. W. Casson (Ed.), *Language, culture and cognition: Anthropological perspectives* (pp. 437–455). New York: MacMillan.

Scribner, S., & Cole, M. (1981). *The psychology of literacy.* Cambridge, MA: Harvard University Press.

Simon, M. (1993). Prospective elementary teachers' knowledge of division. *Journal for Research in Mathematics Education, 24,* 233–254.

Soto Cornejo, I. (1992). *Mathématiques dans la vie quotidienne de paysans chiliens* [Mathematics in the daily life of Chilean peasants] (Vol. 2). Louvain, Belgium: Louvain-la-Neuve.

Sternberg, R. (1990). *Metaphors of mind: Conceptions of the nature of intelligence.* New York: Cambridge University Press.

Vergnaud, G. (1983). Multiplicative structures. In R. Lesh & M. Landau (Eds.), *Acquisition of mathematics concepts and processes* (pp. 128–175). London: Academic Press.

Vygotsky, L. S. (1956). Selected psychological investigations. *Izd. Akad. Pedagog. Nauk RSFSR* (Moscow). In Luria, A. (1973). *The working brain.* Harmondsworth: Penguin.

Vygotsky, L. S. (1960). Development of the higher mental functions. *Izd., Akad. Pedago. Nauk RSFSR* (Moscow). In Luria, A. (1973). *The working brain.* Harmondsworth: Penguin.

Vygotsky, L. S. (1978). Mind in society. In M. Cole, V. John-Steiner, S. Scribner, & E. Souberman (Eds.), *The development of higher psychological processes* (pp. XX–XX). Cambridge, MA: Harvard University Press.

Watanabe, A., Nunes, T., Bryant, P., & van den Heuvel-Panhuizen, M. (2000). Assessing young children's multiplicative reasoning. *Newsletter of the Developmental Psychology Section of the British Psychological Society, 55,* 7–15.

Whitchurch, G. G., & Constantine, L. I. (1993). Systems theory. In P. G. Boss, W. J. Doherty, R. LaRossa, W. R. Schumm, & S. K. Steinmertz (Eds.), *Sourcebook of family theories and methods: A contextual approach* (pp. 325–352). New York: Plenum Press.

7

The Role of Representation in Piagetian Theory: Changes Over Time

Luisa Morgado
Coimbra University

The analysis of representation is undoubtedly one of the most important questions in psychology. It has been addressed by several authors, starting with Wallon, Claparède, and Freud and it is still a topical issue today, as can be seen from the polemic between the defenders of the image-schema approach (Mandler, 1983, 1992a, 1992b, 1992c, 1998) and those of the action-theoretical approach (Müller & Overton, 1998; Müller, Sokol, & Overton, 1998b). In spite of all these efforts, it remains an open problem to which different schools of thought provide their own meanings and solutions, depending on their particular theoretical and epistemological bent.

My aim in this chapter is to analyze Piaget's concept of representation in view of its continued use in recent research (Bickhard, 1999; Mandler, 1998; Müller & Overton, 1998; Nelson, 1999; Scholnick, 1999). I begin by examining his interpretation of the term and then try to demonstrate how he integrated it into his work. I also highlight the difficulties Piaget felt when approaching this subject. In my opinion, these difficulties explain not only a certain ambiguity in Piaget's thought, but also why he chose to go down different paths at different times in his career from the late 1920s to his later writings. These difficulties show, therefore, representation was always an important issue for Piaget, an issue requiring repeated reflection.

I divide my discussion along the following lines. From the 1920s to 1945, representation was studied by Piaget within the context of the construction of intelligence at the sensori-motor stage, based on longitudinal empirical observations of his children. In the 1960s, at the height of his structuralist period, Piaget repeatedly investigated representation: On the one hand, it was integrated into his explanations of operational structures of thought (Piaget, 1970); on the other, it was associated with his experimental work on the development of mental image, work he expanded in collaboration with Inhelder (Piaget & Inhelder, 1971). Finally, toward the end of his life, Piaget addressed this topic once more in open-ended fashion, through his analysis of the notions of success and understanding (1978), in his equilibration model, and through analyses of the constructions of possibility and necessity (1987), consciousness (1977), and meaningful implication (Piaget & Garcia, 1991). In short, I conclude that three moments or periods must be taken into consideration if we are to understand the various meanings Piaget gave to representation throughout his *œuvre*.

THE FIRST PERIOD (1920s–1945)

In his three books *The Origins of Intelligence in Children* (1963), *The Child's Construction of Reality* (1968), and *Play, Dreams, and Imitation in Childhood* (1951), as well as in articles written during the same period (Piaget, 1927, 1935a), Piaget argued that representation could be defined in two different but complementary ways. In a broad sense, representation was considered to be equivalent to thought, i.e. intelligence, but only when intelligence was organized in a system of concepts or mental schemes. In a narrow sense, representation amounted to the mental image, the memory-picture, i.e. it amounted to the symbolic evocation of an absent object. In this case, it was a form of imaged or (symbolic) representation with unique characteristics like figurativity and individuality (Vonèche, 2001). These characteristics were held to differentiate it from a system of arbitrary and conventional signs typical of language.[1] Thus, representation was intimately linked to the development of the semiotic function and to the distinction Piaget drew between symbols and signs.

According to Piaget (1951), imitation, which in its most primitive form is manifested by the infant's sensori-motor copies and by coordinations of sensori-motor schemes, is at the root of inner representation. While all the later manifestations of imitation, such as mental images, language, and deferred imitation, are indications of inner representation, they have been prepared by motor representations that are the representational aspect of

---

[1]According to Piaget (1951), inner representation (as opposed to motor representation) alone can be conceptual or imaged: "In order to make a clear distinction between the two notions, we will from now on call representation in the broad sense 'conceptual representation' and representation in the narrow sense 'symbolic or imaged representation,' or merely 'symbols' and 'images' " (p. 68).

intelligence at the sensori-motor stage.[2] The upshot of all of this is that, according to Piaget's thinking on representation during this period, all of a child's behavior patterns, including those that require the discovery of new means by active experimentation (e.g., support-use behavior, hidden-object behavior), could be explained by the coordination of sensori-motor schemes, by the prolongation of actions based on perceptive *tableaux* organized around *indices*, throughout this developmental stage.[3] Representation, in the sense of hidden-object evocations with mental scheme coordination, was therefore not considered necessary to explain infant success at this level of psychogenetic development.

However, when examining Piaget's writings on the above-mentioned behaviors in more detail, one realizes that his perspective is more subtle and complex than it appears at first glance. The two following excerpts provide helpful illustrations.

1. Support behavior

I now increase the distance between the object and the handkerchief. I place the bottle 10–15 cm to the side of the handkerchief. Lucienne then limits herself to trying to reach the object directly and no longer bothers with the handkerchief. When I bring the object nearer she looks alternately at the bottle and the handkerchief and finally, when I place the bottle on the handkerchief she at once grasps the latter. It therefore seems that she has grasped its signification. (Piaget, 1963, p. 286)

Piaget's explanation of Lucienne's behavior was formulated in terms of her trial-and-error learning processes, in which representation of means and ends and an anticipated choice of action schemes by mental coordination

---

[2]Piaget (1935b) wrote: "Incipient imitation is neither a tool servicing intelligence, nor a simple product of the latter: It is intelligence itself in its representative form. Motor representations prepare inner representations" (p. 6). Motor representation constitutes a form of representation in action that allowed Piaget to explain, for instance, the gestural correspondences established by the infant between the nonvisible parts of its body and the actions of other people.

[3]The decision not to translate into English the words *tableau* (variously translated as "tableau," "picture," "image," and "scene") and *indice* (variously transalated as "indicator" and "index") is due to the divergence among Anglo-Saxon authors with respect to their translations and interpretations of these words (Smith, 1987, 1998). Personally, I agree with Smith (1987) when he argued that "a *tableau* is for the young infant a thing which has meaning only through the action which [the infant] performs. . . . A *tableau* exists when and only when the infant acts in relation to [a particular situation] and, in consequence, a *tableau* does not exist when an action has been terminated" (p. 218). In relation to the word *indice*, Piaget always considered it to be an aspect of the object or situation, therefore not constituting a signifier differentiated from the signified. On the contrary, mental images are signifiers, despite being individual and figurative (symbolic). Finally, language is constituted by arbitrary signifiers (signs) that have become universal conventions within a given language community.

were both lacking. Yet one cannot help but notice that Piaget seemed to believe that Lucienne understood the meaning of the action *to place on*: It became clear for her that there was no point in pulling the handkerchief when the bottle was not placed on top of it. Thus, it seems that, according to Piaget, the child not only has established a causal link between the means and ends (pulling the handkerchief and grasping the bottle), but also understands the signification of that link: Lucienne now knows when to pull or not pull the handkerchief. How can the fact that she attributed signification to her action be interpreted without accepting that some kind of prior representation had been constructed in her mind?

Piaget probably did not think of this question in such clear terms at this point in his career. However, he could not have been very satisfied with this explanation, or else it would be difficult to understand why he would readdress the same behavior many years later and reinterpret it, in a very different way, within a new conceptual framework (Piaget & Garcia, 1991).

2. Hidden object behavior

At the first attempt Jacqueline searches and finds in A where I first put the watch. When I hide it in B Jacqueline does not succeed in finding it there, being unable to raise the cushion altogether. Then she turns around, unnerved, and touches different things including cushion A, but she does not try to turn it over; she knows that the watch is no longer under it. (Piaget, 1968, p. 67)[4]

The explanation provided by Piaget for this behavior suggests attentional continuity in the form of recognizing a perceptual *tableau* that has certain mnesique persistence. It simply involves a prolongation of the action Jacqueline observed earlier. The question that remains to be resolved is how she knows that the object is not under cushion A, because once it becomes totally invisible it can no longer be considered an *indice* according to Piagetian theory. Therefore, the construction of imaged representation remains, I believe, the only acceptable answer to this question.[5]

Piaget certainly realized the complexity of this issue and decided to focus his thoughts by defining representation in a very elaborate way (1968). He argued that a subject's symbolic evocations of an object or event were

---

[4]A and B are two cushions set on the left (A) and on the right (B) of Jacqueline.

[5]Another example that illustrates Piaget's (1968) apparent doubts regarding his explanation of fifth-stage behaviors linked to representation is the formation of spatial fields with the construction of objective, but not representational, displacement groups. According to him, children do not yet represent movements outside their direct perception. The following question arises: How can we explain, without referring to imaged representation, that babies direct their steps, choosing the right path among several, in order to reach an end, if these paths are not marked in their spatial field?

not sufficient to justify use of this term; to do so, the subject had to also mentally combine representations.[6]

In summary, I believe that the difficulties Piaget encountered when justifying the absence of mental representation in children at the fifth stage of the sensori-motor period are obvious when considering the examples previously proposed. His position was clearly ambiguous: Although he denied the appearance of representation at this level of psychogenetic development, he was nonetheless obliged to accept evocation as a representation of past events, which seems necessary for explaining infant success at that stage. However, Piaget continued to believe that no one could speak of inner representation when referring to the simple evocation of hidden objects or the anticipation of ends that are to be attained by constructing new means using trial-and-error methods. He believed that this term for describing behavior involving immediate mental scheme combination and the evocation of an object's trajectory, when it is not directly perceived by the child, must be maintained. In order to postpone the appearance of representation to the sixth stage of the sensori-motor period, Piaget had to make the concept of representation successively more complex and more elaborate to avoid being confronted with contradictions in his own thought. This did not prevent him from feeling his explanations were incomplete, which explains the fact that he addressed and modified these ideas so many years later.

Many authors have criticized Piaget's theory of representation based on the work he published before 1945. I distinguish two types of comments: those regarding the attributes and definitions of the concept itself and those focused on the timing of the appearance of this new achievement. Among the first group of comments, I can highlight Mounoud's famous critique (Mounoud, 1971; Mounoud & Vinter, 1981, 1985). He argues that Piaget's concept of representation ignores the recognition or identification of objects or events. He also discussed the selection of action schemes, which are triggered by *indices* and could not take place without imaged representation, given that these inform the previously mentioned selection. This

---

[6]When referring to the construction of temporal notions, Piaget (1968) wrote:

When the child remembers that the object has been placed in A and has been rediscovered and finally hidden in B is he not yielding, thanks to memory, to an evocation properly so called which constitutes representation? That is possible while memory still consists in clarifying acts (the act of having grasped the object in A and the potential act outlined by perception of the object's departure to B) and leads to an orderly arrangement of events without necessitating representation of these events. But even if there is evocation, that is, representation of past events, it is one thing merely to reproduce the past and another mentally to combine representation of displacements which have never been directly perceived. (pp. 342–343)

view allows us to realize immediately that the word *representation* does not have the same meaning for both authors. In fact, Mounoud gave it a general meaning, identifying representation with recognition. In contrast, Piaget (1963, 1968) did not identify recognition and representation: Although he acknowledged the importance of recognition, he simply called it *recognition*, thus establishing a difference between the two terms. Piaget also believed that, from the simplest coordination of action schemes onward, there is a recognition of objects by assimilation, thus giving them practical and functional meanings. But, insisted Piaget, the distinction between signifier and signified is not yet present in babies and it is precisely that property that is necessary for inner representation.

The same conceptual issue must be kept in mind when discussing Bruner's (1974) model, because only the symbolic representation he proposed matches Piaget's notion of inner representation. At the same time, it must be noted that Piaget's expression *motor representation* is similar to the two other types of representation Bruner described.

The second kind of criticism aimed at Piaget, which concerns the timing of the appearance of representation in babies, comes from researchers who have studied infant behavior more recently (Baillargeon, Graber, Devos, & Black, 1990; Clifton, Rochat, Litovsky, & Perris, 1991; Goubet & Clifton, 1998; Hespos & Rochat, 1997; Willatts, 1997). In general, they have been able to show, through very clever experiments (that are not, however, totally free from methodological problems, as several authors have pointed out; Meltzoff & Moore, 1999; Rivera, Wakeley, & Langer, 1999), that very young children are capable not only of representing hidden objects, but also of identifying the actions needed to retrieve them.

These data are not, in my opinion, a critique of Piaget's theory, because the timing of a new behavior's appearance has never been a criterion for the establishment of psychogenetic developmental levels. In this respect, five defining criteria of developmental levels (stages) were set out by Piaget (1972a) and chronological age was not included in this quintet. Age references can have a heuristic function in sample selection, but not a constitutive function in determining developmental level (Smith, 1993). I also add that the 50 years that have gone by between Piaget's work and the research just described may play a role in this precocity. Such time-shortening effects have been observed by other researchers with consequential problems about their interpretation (Case, 1999; Lourenço & Machado, 1996).

Before moving on to the analysis of Piaget's later writings concerning representation, I would like to make some comments on the two models cited at the beginning of this chapter, namely, the image-schema approach and the action-theoretical approach. The image-schema approach, put forward by Mandler, is based on an empirical and connectionist perspective. Her view is that infants, from the first few months of life onward, begin to form meanings from their perceptual activity through a mechanism of perceptual analysis, the latter of which is used to redescribe perceptual information in an image-schema format. This theoretical model, as well as experimental data that Mandler used to support it (Mandler, 1983, 1992b, 1992c, 1998; Mandler & McDonough, 1993, 1995), has been criticized by a number of authors (Müller & Overton, 1998; Müller et al., 1998a, 1998b) who, I believe, have demonstrated the explicative deficiencies of the image-schema model well, both on theoretical and empirical levels.

In keeping with the theme of this chapter, my aim is to discuss some of the observations made by Mandler on Piaget's theory of representation. The first issue that I would like to discuss relates to Mandler's belief that Piaget attributed a minor role to the concept of representation. This type of critique might be valid for the works of Piaget published in the 1930s and 1940s, but it is certainly not the case for those of the 1960s and 1970s, where important modifications on this issue were introduced. Mandler (1983, 1998) unfortunately does not take these modifications into account.

Another issue relates to the definition of Piaget's concept of representation, which poses problems not only for Mandler but for other authors as well (Mounoud, 1971; Mounoud & Vinter, 1981, 1985). In fact, Mandler made a number of conceptual misinterpretations due to the fact that she did not take into consideration the different meanings that Piaget (1951, 1963, 1968) attributed to this concept. For instance, she is of the opinion that Piaget believed that images constitute conceptual forms of representation (Mandler, 1992c, p. 588) or, further still, that imitation is at the root of conceptual knowledge (Mandler, 1998, p. 273). According to Piaget (1951), it is via the internalization of imitation that mental images, memory-pictures, or so-called imaged representation are constructed, but it is the overall coordination of schemes that gives rise to conceptual representation (see also Smith, 1998). However, these two forms of representation develop and organize themselves in such a way that they support each other mutually and therefore cannot be separated (Piaget, 1951, chap. 3, 1995).

Finally, Mandler (1992c, p. 588) argued that Piaget could not explain, from a theoretical point of view, how sensori-motor schemes are transformed into concepts. In the 1930s and 1940s, this issue might not have been well grasped given the too-general and insufficiently explanatory notion of internalization proposed by Piaget (1951, 1963). However, he later took up the theme again in his study of reflective abstraction, where he presented a new approach (Piaget, 2000; Vuyk, 1981). This functional mechanism, through the process of *réflexion-réfléchissement*, explains the transposition of knowledge from one structural or substructural level to the next, with integration of external data through assimilation. Reflective abstraction becomes the key mechanism in explaining the construction of novelties everywhere in psychogenetic development, including at the sensori-motor level.

As indicated, Müller and Overton (1998) proposed an alternative to the image-schema account of the problem of representation with their action-theoretical approach based on the successive and integrative construction of operations (of first and second order). They claimed that the appearance of representation depends on language, therefore shifting the construction of representations in the child to a developmental stage later than that proposed in Mandler's model. This constructivist and interactionist viewpoint fits better with Piaget's perspective. There are, however, two important observations that I would like to make.

The first has to do with the construction of the mental image. Müller et al. (1998a, p. 232) argued that Piaget derived mental images from the internalization of perceptual activity. In contrast, I contend that Piaget (1951) always claimed that mental images are rooted in imitation. According to Piaget (1951), during the sensori-motor stage, imitation is a kind of symbolization in action. This explains why, when mental images are constructed by internalization (images are defined as internalized imitations), they become differentiated signifiers (symbols). Perceptual activities have their roots in sensorial and gestural actions; they are not related to the development of the symbolic function. Therefore, mental images cannot derive from the internalization of perceptual activities because these activities are not pré-representational, as is the case for imitation. Although mental images and perceptions are both figurative aspects of thought, this characteristic is not relevant for the issue that is being discussed here. In short, what must be pointed out, in response to Müller et al.'s observations, is the fact that imitation, but not perception, was already considered by Piaget to be a presymbolic function during the sensori-motor stage. Thus, only imitation can prepare the appearance of mental images.[7]

Finally, I provide a last word on the critique made by Müller and Overton (1998, p. 84) in relation to the construction of representation: According to them, Piaget made representation depend essentially on the figurative as-

---

[7]Piaget (1995) argued:

The sensorimotor functions (including sensorimotor play and perception) are not symbolic inasmuch as they only use undifferentiated signifiers (indexes or signals). The symbolic function begins around $1\frac{1}{2}$–2 years of age with the appearance of differentiated signifiers (signs and symbols) and consists in representing various figurative and cognitive schemes by means of these signifiers. In other words, the symbolic signifiers are derived from imitation which, before becoming interiorized, is already a kind of symbolization in action. This fact, however, in no way implies that symbolic instruments should be confused with figurative aspects of thought. Perception is figurative but not symbolic, while language is symbolic (in the broad sense) but not figurative. Interiorized imitation and images are, on the contrary, both figurative and symbolic. Mental imagery, in particular, is the product of interiorized imitation and not the simple residue of perception as it was previously believed. (p. 516)

pects of thought (i.e., deferred imitation) without taking the operative aspects of thought into consideration. As already highlighted in this chapter, Piaget (1963) addressed representation from two different points of view: a broad sense and a narrow sense. If in imaged representation (narrow sense) the figurative aspects prevail over the operative ones, without being exclusive, something different occurs with representation in the broad sense, which is constructed by mental coordination of the sensori-motor schemes, i.e. by an operatory transformation. In this way, to be able to say that the representative system is constructed in the child, it is necessary for both of these forms of representation to be present because, if I may use a metaphor, they are two sides of the same coin (Piaget, 1995).

In conclusion, the critiques of Piaget's theory of representation emphasized here stem, first, from a certain conceptual misunderstanding of the different meanings that Piaget attributed to this word as well as the holistic and integrative character that this concept presents and, second, from a majority of critical authors focusing exclusively on the writings of Piaget published before the 1960s, without taking into account his later work, where important theoretical attention was given to this issue.

THE SECOND PERIOD (1950s AND 1960s)

Piaget did not continue research on the sensori-motor stage after his work carried out between the 1920s and 1940s, but this did not prevent him from addressing the concept of representation in both a broad and a narrow sense. In a broad sense, representation continued to be identified with thought, but Piaget (1972b) then specified his idea in more detail. He associated representative structures and thought in children and tried to distinguish these concepts from the idea of intelligence.[8] What he came up with was the idea that intelligence is already present at the sensori-motor level in the form of nonrepresentational, but intentional, sensori-motor schemes. This terminology allowed him, in a certain sense, to move away from the issue of intelligence *versus* thought, by regarding intelligence as preceding

---

[8]Piaget (1972b) argued:

> If we divide behavior into three main systems, organic hereditary structures (instinct), sensori-motor structures (which may be learned), and symbolic structures (which constitute thought), we may place the group of sensori-motor displacements at the apex of the second of these systems, while operational groups and groupings of a formal nature are at the top of the third. (p. 119)

(Please note that the expression used by Piaget in French for "symbolic structures" is *structures représentatives*.)

thought and by using the notion of representation to distinguish between the two. In corollary, he continued to hold that representation, at the sensori-motor level, was dispensable for the explanation of behavior at the fifth stage.

During this period, however, Piaget focused rather intensively on the concept of representation in a narrow sense. Experimental research in collaboration with Inhelder (Piaget & Inhelder, 1971) regarding children's mental images would allow him to frame this question within the more general issue of figurativity *versus* operativity.[9] Imaged representation would therefore be considered one of the figurative aspects of semiotic-operational development and deemed to be essential to the construction of operations, even though empirical research seems to show that operational development directs and precedes the construction of imaged representation. However, this does not imply that Piaget and Inhelder only attributed a secondary role to this notion. On the contrary, imaged representation is considered, if not structurally then at least functionally, necessary for the construction of certain types of operations.[10] On the other hand, with regard to the psychological behavior of a subject, the role of image is indispensable in the sense that certain structures only function if they use this kind of representation. Therefore, one can observe that imaged representation is expressed very differently according to the psychogenetic development and level of expertise of each subject and also according to the context of the task and its area of application (physical or logico-mathematical).[11]

Although, during this second period, the theme of representation was assigned a lesser role in relation to actions and operations of thought, this does not mean that it was absent. It could not be, in view of the equivalence

---

[9]Today, much research in the area of mathematical problem solving highlights the importance of imaged representation in question wording for the discovery of correct solution procedures. This attempts to establish the importance of figurative aspects in the construction and generalization of discovery strategies (Nunes, 1997; Verschaffel & De Corte, 1997; Von Glasersfeld, 1991).

[10]Piaget and Inhelder (1971) argued that "the image then constitutes an auxiliary that is not only useful to but in many instances necessary for the functioning of operations. After having structured and fashioned it in their own likeness, the operations in fact come to depend on the image" (p. 378).

[11]Without going into details that are not relevant to this chapter, I must add, for example, that the imaged representation of a physical object, in the sense of some concrete entity, remains linked to the object, whereas the imaged representation of logicomathematical entities becomes increasingly arbitrary. Thus, from a certain moment in psychogenetic development onward, signs that form a conceptual system are those best adapted to represent logico-mathematical objects, even if mental images retain an auxiliary role as an individual and personal representation of the formal entities in question (Tall & Vinner, 1981; Vinner & Dreyfus, 1989).

of representation and thought in line with Piaget's own definition, previously quoted. In brief, I would like to point out that Piaget did not carry out any empirical research on children in the sensori-motor stage, nor did he theoretically discuss the issue of the appearance of representation; he only maintained his prior position on the topic (Piaget, 1972b). However, he seriously looked into the analysis of imaged representation and allotted a considerable role to this concept in psychogenetic development, for both the construction of operations (auxiliary role) from an epistemic point of view as well as for the functionality of such operations in the psychological subject (necessary role).

THE THIRD PERIOD (1970s)

Toward the end of his career, Piaget studied, albeit indirectly, the timing of the appearance of representation and its role in psychogenetic development. As I pointed out at the beginning of this chapter, he tackled this issue anew and intimately linked it with his research on the notions of success and understanding, possibility and necessity, meaningful implication, and grasp of consciousness.

Regarding the development of consciousness, Piaget (1963, 1968, 1969) seemed to have accepted, from the 1920s onward, that there were probably states of consciousness with varying degrees of organization, but without representative integration, that formed an integral part of the infant's activity from the earliest stages of sensori-motor development (Bringuier, 1977). He held that such states were necessary, not only to explain the intentionality of actions whose purpose is an invisible end (e.g., hidden-object behavior), but also to understand how implications between the meaning of actions in relation to an end are established in order for tasks to be accomplished. Without consciousness, how could one explain the lifting of an arm, reaching behind a screen to find an object, or picking up a scarf in order to find what lies beneath it? Clearly, consciousness was the source of meanings of this sort and of the implications among them (Piaget, 1977).[12] Furthermore, Piaget argued that, when success was no longer based on trial-and-error, but became systematic, the transformation implied an understanding of success itself and that understanding included a search for

---

[12]With respect to the expression *grasp of consciousness*, it seems that Piaget restricted its use from his earliest writings (Piaget, 1969) to his later ones (Piaget, 1977) to expressing conceptual reconstruction. This, he held, proceeds from the periphery to the center and is carried out via a process of reflection. On his view, the construction of consciousness is concomitant with that of inner representation (Morgado, 1998; Piaget, 1976; Pinard, 1986).

reasons. In other words, it constituted the moment when infants want to know why the action or actions they perform lead to a desired end, whereas others that were used earlier had to be abandoned.[13]

It seems, therefore, that toward the end of his career Piaget considered the double role of representation to be decisive when understanding is added to succeeding. On the one hand, it allowed subjects to construct plans of action that led to success and, on the other, it allowed them to seek reasons by reconstructing procedures. The specific connection between procedural and presentative schemes in a proactive then retroactive movement leads the subject (baby, child, or adult) to elaborate plans by choosing means to an end, but also to try to understand why certain procedures are valid and sometimes necessary, whereas others are not. Piaget postulated that representation reinforced such predictive abilities and made possible the organization of plans of action when the subject was confronted with a problem (Inhelder et al., 1992; Piaget, 1976, 1986, 1987; Vuyk, 1981).

Thus, representation acquires a fundamental role in Piagetian theory. To begin with, it is essential for the elaboration of anticipated action plans in view of success, which implies re-presentation of the data, of means and ends, and of the connections between them established by meaningful implications. Secondly, it is also necessary for the inverse reconstruction of procedures, the only way to seek reasons, even though these remain local at early psychogenetic levels and are not adequate for generalization.

The notions of success and understanding, meaningful implication, and retroactive and proactive movements are decisive in this new analysis. In the earlier analysis (1930–1940), representation had been portrayed more or less as surplus baggage added to sensori-motor action, although theoretically, Piaget explained it in terms of the development of imitation and the coordination of sensori-motor schemes. In the 1960s, Piaget hinted at the analysis to come, but it was only during this third period that he gave the topic new impetus by reframing it within a more functional framework focused on the subject's discovery procedures.

This fresh perspective would allow Piaget to return to the question of when representation first appeared in psychogenetic development. As I have shown throughout this chapter, the issue of the presence or absence of representation at the fifth stage of the sensori-motor period (that had remained ambiguous since the 1930s) was not forgotten. In the 1970s, Piaget returned to it and provided an innovative answer: He proposed that the behavior associated with the fifth stage leads infants to extract the meaning of

---

[13]In fact, Piaget (1978) argued that "the system of signifying implications supplies an element not included in either the goals or in the means, namely the determination of the reasons without which successes remain mere facts without [meaning]" (pp. 221–222). Thus, Piaget believed that it was the determination of reasons that established the difference between success and understanding.

reasons, that is, to understand why success occurs. Piaget also displayed his great qualities as a researcher always ready to reformulate his thought when, addressing the famous example of support in his last book, *Towards a Logic of Meanings* (Piaget & Garcia, 1991), he removed any doubts on his interpretation of this topic:

> For example, an object X might be laid on a support Y which the subject could use to draw it back, or else it might be placed next to the support. Observing either situation brings out implications between meanings, as long as the subject understands that in the latter case it is useless to pull the support: the relation or action "laying down upon" has acquired the meaning of a "reason." (p. 5)[14]

Piaget claimed that infants at the fifth sensori-motor stage seek reasons that, as I have just highlighted, would imply that a certain form of representation must be present alongside the beginnings of inference (Inhelder, 1991). I feel that this is the case, although the child at this stage is not yet able to express either representations or inferences verbally due to the lack of an appropriate linguistic system. Clearly, such seeking is impossible to accomplish without constructing the representations that are necessary for the retroactive presentation (e.g., re-presentation) of successful procedures. In addition, one can see that Piaget did not return to the hypothesis, formulated in 1936, that representation would necessarily imply immediate mental coordination of action schemes, because, under that conception, representation would be excluded when learning occurs through trial-and-error (even if this leads to success). At this point, I think that such learning is considered a simple discovery procedure for reaching some end and does not have the same dividing role as was earlier claimed.

---

[14]Piaget (1986) used the same kind of illustration when discussing the issue of the relation between the construction of necessities and the search for reasons:

> For example, at the sensori-motor level, a 10 to 12 month old infant will discover that in pulling a strip of cardboard at the end of which is placed an object . . . too far away to be grasped directly, the infant is able to draw the object nearer and succeeds in gaining possession of it. If the object is subsequently placed just beyond the cardboard . . . the infant still pulls . . . because the meaning of the relation "placed upon" is . . . not yet "understood." When by contrast, the infant uses the cardboard wittingly, we can say that for the infant the situation "placed upon" a support implies the possibility of being drawn along but if (and only if) it is placed "on" the cardboard and not [beside it]. We will designate, therefore, such relations [the word *apports* in the French edition means "contributions," which makes no sense; the French word *rapports*, meaning "relations," has therefore been substituted] by the term "meaningful implication" due to the fact that in this case one meaning, such as spatial position, entails another (in this case, its kinematic use). These relations determine a specific necessity to the extent that the subject understands their reasons. (p. 306)

In summary, two complementary and concomitant aspects of representation may be highlighted in Piaget's later work. The first is the interpretation of the role of representation in Piaget's entire theory, which gained in strength and depth from his more recent analyses developed within the framework of his equilibration model. The second aspect is the old issue of the timing of the appearance of representation in psychogenetic development, which Piaget was able to reformulate and reframe in admirable fashion, thus finally providing a solution to this problem for which we had waited a very long time. Although, to quote Inhelder (Inhelder et al., 1992, p. 47) in reference to representation, "the final word for designating this reality at the sensori-motor level may always be lacking," Piaget's contribution can be considered essential to this research and even to the broader understanding of this issue as a whole.

AUTHOR NOTE

Luisa Morgado, Faculty of Pyschology and Sciences of Education, Universidade de Coimbra, Rua de Colégio Novo, 3000 Coimbra, Portugal.

Thanks to my colleagues Magali Bovet, Terrance Brown, and Leslie Smith for helpful comments on an earlier draft of this chapter. Its preparation was supported in part by a grant from the Calouste Gulbenkian Foundation. I am also grateful to the Archives Jean Piaget for the facilities it provided in my search for bibliography.

REFERENCES

Baillargeon, R., Graber, M., Devos, J., & Black, J. (1990). Why do young infants fail to search for hidden objects? *Cognition, 36*, 255–284.

Bickhard, M. H. (1999). Interaction and representation. *Theory & Psychology, 9*, 435–458.

Bringuier, J. C. (1977). *Conversations libres avec Jean Piaget* [Free conversations with Jean Piaget]. Paris: Robert Laffont.

Bruner, J. S. (1974). The growth of representational processes in childhood. In J. M. Anglin (Ed.), *Beyond the information given: Studies in the psychology of knowing* (pp. 313–324). London: G. Allen & Union Ltd.

Case, R. (1999). Conceptual development in the child and in the field: A personal view of the Piagetian legacy. In E. Scholnick, K. Nelson, S. Gelman, & P. Miller (Eds.), *Conceptual development: Piaget's legacy* (pp. 23–51). Mahwah, NJ: Lawrence Erlbaum Associates.

Clifton, R. K., Rochat, P., Litovsky, R. Y., & Perris, E. E. (1991). Object representation guides infant's reaching in the dark. *Journal of Experimental Psychology: Human Perception and Performance, 17*, 323–329.

Goubet, N., & Clifton, R. (1998). Object and event representation in 6½-month-old infants. *Developmental Psychology, 34*, 63–76.

Hespos, S. J., & Rochat, P. (1997). Dynamic mental representation in infancy. *Cognition, 64*, 153–188.

Inhelder, B. (1991). Preface. In J. Piaget & R. Garcia, *Towards a logic of meanings* (pp. vii–ix). Hillsdale, NJ: Lawrence Erlbaum Associates.

Inhelder, B., Cellérier, G., Ackermann, E., Blanchet, A., Boder, A., De Caprona, D., Ducret, J.-J., & Saada-Robert, M. (1992). *Le cheminement des découvertes de l'enfant* [Children's journeys to discovery]. Neuchâtel: Delachaux et Niestlé.

Lourenço, O., & Machado, A. (1996). In defense of Piaget's theory: A reply to 10 common criticisms. *Psychological Review, 103,* 143–164.

Mandler, J. (1983). Representation. In J. H. Flavell & E. M. Markman (Eds.), *Handbook of child psychology* (Vol. 3, pp. 420–494). New York: Wiley.

Mandler, J. (1992a). Commentary. *Human Development, 35,* 246–253.

Mandler, J. (1992b). The foundations of conceptual thought in infancy. *Cognitive Development, 7,* 273–285.

Mandler, J. (1992c). How to build a baby: II. Conceptual primitives. *Psychological Review, 99,* 587–604.

Mandler, J. (1998). Representation. In W. Damon, D. Kuhn, & R. Siegler (Eds.), *Handbook of child psychology* (Vol. 2, pp. 255–308). New York: Wiley.

Mandler, J., & McDonough, L. (1993). Concept formation in infancy. *Cognitive Development, 8,* 291–318.

Mandler, J., & McDonough, L. (1995). Long-term recall of event sequences in infancy. *Journal of Experimental Child Psychology, 59,* 457–474.

Meltzoff, A., & Moore, M. (1999). A new foundation for cognitive development in infancy: The birth of the representational infant. In E. Scholnick, K. Nelson, S. Gelman, & P. Miller (Eds.), *Conceptual development: Piaget's legacy* (pp. 53–78). Mahwah, NJ: Lawrence Erlbaum Associates.

Morgado, L. (1998). La notion de prise de conscience dans l'oeuvre de Jean Piaget [The notion of grasp of consciousness in the work of Jean Piaget]. *Bulletin de Psychologie, 435,* 389–394.

Mounoud, P. (1971). Développement des systèmes de représentation et de traitement chez l'enfant [Development of systems of representation and processing in children]. *Bulletin de Psychologie, 296,* 261–272.

Mounoud, P., & Vinter, A. (1981). Representation and sensorimotor development. In G. Butterworth (Ed.), *Infancy and epistemology: An evaluation of Piaget's theory* (pp. 200–235). Brighton, England: Harvester Press.

Mounoud, P., & Vinter, A. (1985). La notion de représentation en psychologie génétique [The notion of grasp of consciousness in the work of Jean Piaget]. *Psychologie Française, 30,* 253–259.

Müller, U., & Overton, W. (1998). How to grow a baby: A reevaluation of image-schema and Piagetian action approaches to representation. *Human Development, 41,* 71–111.

Müller, U., Sokol, B., & Overton, W. (1998a). Constructivism and development: Reply to Smith's commentary. *Developmental Review, 18,* 228–236.

Müller, U., Sokol, B., & Overton, W. (1998b). Reframing a constructivist model of the development of mental representation: The role of higher-order operations. *Developmental Review, 18,* 155–201.

Nelson, K. (1999). Levels and modes of representation: Issues for the theory of conceptual change and development. In E. Scholnick, K. Nelson, S. Gelman, & P. Miller (Eds.), *Conceptual development: Piaget's legacy* (pp. 256–291). Mahwah, NJ: Lawrence Erlbaum Associates.

Nunes, T. (1997). Systems of signs and mathematical reasoning. In T. Nunes & P. Bryant (Eds.), *Learning and teaching mathematics: An international perspective* (pp. 29–44). Hove, England: Psychology Press.

Piaget, J. (1927). La première année de l'enfant [The first year of the child]. *The British Journal of Psychology, 18,* 97–120.

Piaget, J. (1935a). La naissance de l'intelligence chez le petit enfant [The origins of intelligence in the infant]. *Revue de Pédagogie, 11,* 56–64.

Piaget, J. (1935b). Les théories de l'imitation [Theories of imitation]. *Cahiers de Pédagogie Expéri-mentale et de Psychologie de l'Enfant, 6,* 1–13.

Piaget, J. (1951). *Play, dreams and imitation in childhood* (C. Gattegno, F. M. Hodgson, Trans.). New York: Norton. (Original work published 1945)

Piaget, J. (1963). *The origins of intelligence in children* (M. Cook, Trans.). New York: Norton. (Original work published 1936)

Piaget, J. (1968). *The child's construction of reality* (M. Cook, Trans.). London: Routledge & Kegan Paul. (Original work published 1937)

Piaget, J. (1969). *Judgment and reasoning in the child* (M. Warden, Trans.). Totowa, NJ: Littlefield, Adams, & Co. (Original work published 1924)

Piaget, J. (1970). *Structuralism* (C. Maschler, Trans.). New York: Basic Books.

Piaget, J. (1972a). *Problèmes de psychologie génétique* [Problems in genetic psychology]. Paris: Denöel-Gonthier.

Piaget, J. (1972b). *Psychology of intelligence* (M. Pierce, D. E. Berlyne, Trans.). Totowa, NJ: Little-field, Adams, & Co. (Original work published 1967)

Piaget, J. (1976). Le possible, l'impossible et le nécessaire [The possible, the impossible, and the necessary]. *Archives de Psychologie, 44,* 281–299.

Piaget, J. (1977). *The grasp of consciousness* (S. Wedgwood, Trans.). London: Routledge & Kegan Paul. (Original work published 1974)

Piaget, J. (1978). *Success and understanding* (A. J. Pomerans, Trans.). London: Routledge & Kegan Paul. (Original work published 1974)

Piaget, J. (1986). Essay on necessity (L. Smith, F. Steel, Trans.). *Human Development, 29,* 301–314. (Original work published 1977)

Piaget, J. (1987). *Possibility and necessity: The role of necessity in cognitive development* (H. Feider, Trans.). Minneapolis: University of Minnesota Press. (Original work published 1981 and 1983)

Piaget, J. (1995). The role of imitation in the development of representational thought (G. Voyat, B. Birns, Trans.). In H. Gruber & J. Vonèche (Eds.), *The essential Piaget: An interpretative refer-ence and guide* (pp. 508–514). Northvale, NJ: Aronson. (Original work published 1962)

Piaget, J. (2000). *Studies in reflective abstraction* (R. Campbell, Trans.). Hove, England: Psychology Press. (Original work published 1977)

Piaget, J., & Garcia, R. (1991). *Towards a logic of meanings* (D. de Caprona, P. M. Davidson, Trans.). Hillsdale, NJ: Lawrence Erlbaum Associates. (Original work published 1987)

Piaget, J., & Inhelder, B. (1971). *Mental imagery in the child* (P. A. Chilton, Trans.). London: Routledge & Kegan Paul. (Original work published 1966)

Pinard, A. (1986). *Prise de conscience* and taking charge of one's own cognitive functioning. *Hu-man Development, 29,* 341–354.

Rivera, S., Wakeley, A., & Langer, J. (1999). The drawbridge phenomenon: Representational rea-soning or perceptual preference? *Developmental Psychology, 35,* 427–435.

Scholnick, E. K. (1999). Piaget's legacy: Heirs to the house that Jean built. In E. Scholnick, K. Nel-son, S. Gelman, & P. Miller (Eds.), *Conceptual development: Piaget's legacy* (pp. 1–20). Mah-wah, NJ: Lawrence Erlbaum Associates.

Smith, L. (1987). The infant's Copernican revolution. *Human Development, 30,* 210–224.

Smith, L. (1993). *Necessary knowledge: Piagetian perspectives on constructivism.* Hove, England: Lawrence Erlbaum Associates.

Smith, L. (1998). On the development of mental representation. *Developmental Review, 18,* 202–227.

Tall, D., & Vinner, S. (1981). Concept image and concept definition in mathematics with particu-lar reference to limits and continuity. *Educational Studies in Mathematics, 12,* 151–169.

Verschaffel, L., & De Corte, E. (1997). World problems: A vehicle for promoting authentic mathe-matical understanding and problem solving in the primary school? In T. Nunes & P. Bryant (Eds.), *Learning and teaching mathematics: An international perspective* (pp. 69–97). Hove, Eng-land: Psychology Press.

Vinner, S., & Dreyfus, T. (1989). Images and definitions for the concept of function. *Journal for Research in Mathematics Education, 20,* 356–366.

Vonèche, J. (2001). Mental imagery: From Inhelder's ideas to neuro-cognitive models. In A. Tryphon & J. Vonèche (Eds.), *Working with Piaget: Essays in honour of Bärbel Inhelder* (pp. 123–128). Hove, England: Psychology Press.

Von Glasersfeld, E. (1991). Abstraction, re-presentation and reflection: An interpretation of experience and Piaget's approach. In L. P. Steffe (Ed.), *Epistemological foundations of mathematical experience* (pp. 45–67). New York: Springer.

Vuyk, R. (1981). *Overview and critique of Piaget's genetic epistemology 1965–1980* (Vol. 1). London: Academic Press.

Willatts, P. (1997). Beyond the "couch potato" infant: How infants use their knowledge to regulate action, solve problems and achieve goals. In G. Bremuer, A. Slater, & G. Butterworth (Eds.), *Infant development: Recent advances* (pp. 109–135). Hove, England: Psychology Press.

8

Breathing Lessons:
Self as Genre and Aesthetic

Cynthia Lightfoot
Pennsylvania State University

Count Monaldo Leopardi, father of the great 19th-century poet Giacomo Leopardi, said of his son that his adolescent self-consciousness was so well developed that, "thinking about breathing," he would have difficulty getting his breath and, "reflecting on the subtleties of urination," he would be unable to pass water (Parks, 2000). We may be amused by the Count's observation, but we are certainly not baffled by it. Adolescence is widely regarded as a significant developmental period in the capacity to look inward. Self-reflection, self-consciousness, and the search for self are all considered signposts of the age.

Erikson (1950) was among the first to devote considerable energy to the topic of the adolescent self. The crisis of adolescence, he argued, is to develop a fidelity to self, to integrate across roles and experiences some lasting and perdurable *I*. Inherent to his discussion is the assumption that there is something to be true to, something to hold in regard, to look for, discover, or confront and that to lay one's hands on it is to clasp maturity. Some such notion as this continues to drive contemporary scholarship on adolescent identity development (Blasi & Glodis, 1995; Chandler, 2000; Moshman, 1999) as well as theorizing about the ontological and epistemological status of self (Habermas, 1989; Taylor, 1989). It also lies at the heart of conceptions of adolescents as seekers of self and self-transforming experience and ideas about why all of us in general, and adolescents in particular, pursue what has been variously called a *felt* or *examined* life (Lightfoot, 1997a, 1997b).

In the following pages I undertake an exploration of changing conceptions of self within two distinct time frames—the sociocultural and the psychogenetic. In the main, I focus on self and identity issues expressed in narrative forms, written texts in particular. In the case of the sociocultural time frame, changing conceptions of self are explored within specific literary genres: the novel, the autobiography, and fantasy. In the psychogenetic frame, fictional stories written by younger and older adolescents provide material for examining changing conceptions of self. In the course of demonstrating parallel transitions across the two systems, I aim to illustrate and defend the importance of a historical approach to self as a means of gaining insight into the processes of development. There is thus some shared purpose with Piaget and Garcia's (1989) studies of the parallelism between the history of science and the emergence of mathematical knowledge in ontogeny. However, the analysis presented here lacks both the ambition and scope of their seminal project. Although the broad, sweeping changes of cultural history are used to provide important context and support for arguments regarding the nature of changing conceptions of self in literary genres, the sociocultural analysis provided here is, for theoretical as well as pragmatic reasons, a more circumscribed study. As you might suppose, there is a rich and conflicted literature on genre theory. Rosmarin (1985) notes that the question of genre has multiple phrasings: "Does genre constitute the particular or do particulars constitute the genre? Are genres found in texts, in the reader's mind, in the author's, or in some combination thereof? Or are they not 'found' at all but, rather, devised and used? Are they 'theoretical' or 'historical'? Are they 'prescriptive' or 'descriptive'?" (p. 7). Interwoven in all of this are questions of transformation: Just how do texts, minds, theories, or histories become configured or refigured in such a way as to achieve the status of a *genre*? At what point do new configurations assert a distinctiveness that merits a name?

Our own familiarity in psychology with questions of this type is both a comfort and a frustration. My strategy for present purposes is to focus on explicating general historical trends within what are typically purported to be coherent, identifiable, well-defined literary types, or genres. In other words, I will be less concerned with the exact timing of particular changes than with their sequence and direction. As I hope to make clear, evidence suggests that changing conceptions of self in both the sociocultural and psychogenetic systems can be analytically described in terms of two axes, one of which is spatial, the other temporal. One concerns the individuation of self, its differentiation and distancing from the world, and the transforming self-awareness, reflection, and critique that come of it. The other concerns a sense of temporality, an increasing and deeper infusion of self in historical and biographical time. The conjunction of these dimensions ultimately defines a fully generic conception of ourselves as historical, integral, and self-consciously and self-referentially aware of our own categorical status: a conception of self, that is, into which is written the problem of the self conceived.

THE SOCIOCULTURAL FRAME

There is substantial agreement among historians of Western culture that our conceptions of self underwent a radical revision between ancient and modern times. They have remarked on the emergence of new forms of speech used to describe the self, new types of relationships understood to hold between the self and others, and new qualities of feeling ascribed to the self. For example, Lock (2000) argues that the emotion of embarrassment requires a level of self-monitoring that was likely inaccessible to Western individuals prior to the 12th or 13th century. Likewise, there is scant evidence for the existence of expectations for self-control, civility, and good manners during the premodern era (Elias, 1978, 1982). There are certainly good methodological grounds for challenging the strong position that, in the absence of evidence to the contrary, premodern people were incapable of *minding* themselves. Less disputable, however, is the claim that minding the self, with its twin notion of self as fractured—as multiple, duplicitous, sincere or insincere, authentic or inauthentic—did not become remarkable, did not become a pervasive subject of art, discourse, study, and counsel until fairly late in the history of Western culture.

The transformation of the cultural conception of self went in hand with the transformation of understanding personal relationships. Like selves, loves could be true or false, public or private. Love poetry, for example, became something to lock away in secret places usually reserved for valuables. And it was replete with references to its own artifice, its inability to genuinely convey felt emotion, and the inadequacies of words to speak directly on matters of the heart. From "Astrophil and Stella" (Fumerton, 1991):

> Sweetner of musicke, wisedome's beautifier:
> Breather of life, and fastner of desire,
> Where Beautie's blush in Honour's graine is dide.
> Thus much my heart compeld my mouth to say,
> But now spite of my heart my mouth will stay,
> Loathing all lies, doubting this Flatterie is:
> And no spurre can his resty race renew,
> Without how farre this praise is short of you,
> Sweet lip, you teach my mouth with one sweet kisse.
> (p. 98)

The sociocultural reconstruction of self is also apparent in a variety of new objects devised to reflect the individual and monitor its changes

(Hannerz, 1983). Mirrors became larger and more plentiful. Portraiture began to depict individual characteristics rather than social role attributes alone. We privatized our physical spaces. Benches were replaced by chairs; more walls were built in our homes. By the late 16th century, all gardens of consequence had banquet houses, usually detached, that were designed for private repose (Fumerton, 1991). Analyses of architectural changes of the period find evidence of continual adjustments toward an impenetrable, unreachable interior. So great was the desire for privacy that closets had closets and retreats had retreats. All of this suggests an overarching process of withdrawal, detachment, and segmentation.

During the transition to the period that we now call *modern*, the cultural conception of self was remade into something fundamentally more individuated, self-conscious, and self-determining. Some controversy exists regarding the exact timing of the reconstruction. The conventional view marks the Italian Renaissance of the 15th century as the turning point between medieval and modern notions. A fringe of contemporary historians (Morris, 1972; Vance, 1987), on the other hand, is gaining ground and reputation with claims of greater continuity between the Middle Ages and the Renaissance, suggesting that a strong element of self-awareness made its appearance as early as the 12th century. The greater social and economic context of 12th-century Europe certainly favored such a development. It was during this time that Western Europe experienced an unprecedented growth of its cities. New social groups and classes created conflict and choices. One could be a monk, a knight, or a clerk. Increasing literacy, specifically the transition from a culture of the oral to one of the written, is also considered a factor that spurred a movement toward the individual as a principal object of attention (Godzich, 1987). Nevertheless, it is fairly well agreed that the confrontation between tradition and individual opinion was limited until the 17th century. It is thus not surprising to learn that although the 12th century witnessed the birth of a passionate interest in history, there was nothing that even approached the critical historical sense typically associated with the Romantic period. Likewise, although isolated instances of particular literary forms can be found early on (e.g., Bakhtin, 1986; McKeon, 2000), they appeared as precursors to, rather than examples of, the genre.

Self and Time in Text: The Novel

Although the language used thus far is rife with spatial metaphors and suggests a general trend toward increasing interiority and privacy, a constituting temporal dimension also became manifest in the transition to the modern self. The significance of self and time as conjunctive and interdependent has become a watershed of contemporary thought (Lightfoot & Lyra, 2000). It is central to the theorizing of Hegel, Cassirer, Marx, Bergson, Whitehead and Freud. Meyerhoff (1960) argues that the conceptual unity of self and time not only is definitive of modern literary works, but also constitutes the unity of the work of art itself. Be that as it may, many scholarly disciplines—certainly any of those concerned with the psychological and cultural development of self—have taken up the temporalized self as a consuming theme. Much has been made of the notion of time as a medium of life and narration and of our sense of time as fundamental to justifying such principal conceptions as continuity, relatedness, and identity.

Historians of written texts have been particularly attentive to the infusion of time in selves. Bakhtin's (1986) study of the novel provides a case in point (Lightfoot, 1997b). Focusing largely on the temporal embeddedness of the principle character, Bakhtin identified a variety of novelistic types. One of the earliest is the *novel of ordeal*, in which the world is an arena for testing an idealized, complete, and unchanging hero. The form does not recognize development and transformation because real time, that is, limited, unique, and irreversible time, is written out of it. Instead, action and events are packaged within a fairy time, disconnected from life and historical processes. The *biographical novel* departs from the novel of ordeal in several interconnected ways. In particular, embedding the individual in biographical time has the effect of placing him or her in the world of quotidian events and experiences: birth, school, work, marriage, and death. Although one's life is now subject to being incomplete, Bakhtin notes that it was not until the second half of the 18th century that literature provides an image of the self as an individual in progress. The previous novelistic categories laid the groundwork for the synthetic *Bildungsroman*, a form of the novel that details the psychological development of the principal character. In contrast to the static, isolated, and ready-made hero of the other novel forms, the central character of the *Bildungsroman* constitutes a dynamic unity engaged in a process of becoming.

More recently, McKeon (2000) has undertaken a historical examination of the novel, which he describes as a quintessentially modern genre. He makes much of its early association with issues of privacy, individuality, and domesticity and, particularly in the 19th century, with interiority, subjectivity, and the treatment of character as personality, and plot as the progressive development of individuals. Especially telling as a modern genre, however, is the crystallization of its own genre-ness into its form.

Interpretations of changing novelistic forms are consistent with a host of other evidence that supports the conclusions, in content and implication, regarding a radical revision of cultural conceptions of self. During the 17th century, recognizable differences emerged between history and story, between a past and a narrated present. Early stories were narratives of authority, often drawn from sacred sources. Their telling, a performance in oral societies, was commemorative: The aim was to animate the collective memories, the *memoria*, that gave meaning and purpose to life. As Godzich (1985) writes, "There are no individuals here. . . . Rather than being individuals with inherently endowed rights and privileges, they are persons in the etymological sense of the term, that is, material purports of roles which they do not write but accept, in the form of fate, from the power that resides in *memoria*" (p. xv). Homer chronicles the conquests of Achilles; Virgil relates Aeneas' encounter with the dead. The texts are impersonal histories. There is no allegory here. Even the story of Gilgamesh, one of the most beautifully wrought tellings of a hero's awareness of death, presents the experience "as a real, absolutely real, fact" (Paz, 1991, p. 11). With Dante the *I* appears; the author is himself a hero. However, the author as interpretive subject is not cast until the Romantic period. The Romantics introduced a double consciousness, one intent on its own mode of discourse. The Romantics were the first who were concerned to record not just the event, but the "I think" behind the event (Wolf, 1982). In hand was criticism and cultural revision. This is the point at which doubt crept in.

A History of Life Writing

Because the genre is, by definition, about the author's own life, autobiography presents a particularly natural study of changing cultural conceptions of self and self-transformation. Interestingly, in its earliest form, there is little evidence of a self embedded in time or subject to transformation. Early examples of the genre are but chronicles of exterior events, often professional accomplishments, that were met in larger-than-life, heroic fashion. A dramatic element is played out in an exaggeration of proportion; the author "creates a heroics of life in an epic-like battle against mankind" (Nalbantian, 1994, p. 8). A later arriving, but largely sympathetic, pattern is the story of the exemplary life, in which the author makes of himself a model, as did Ben Franklin. The narrative is meant to instruct. Notwithstanding the moral and public end in view, the character remains something of a mystery, one-dimensional and single-minded. Scant insight is provided into his development.

Jean-Jacques Rousseau (1762) is credited with authoring the first modern autobiography. It is in every sense a celebration of the individual, and takes up matters of sincerity (the self as true), authenticity (the self as real), and truth claims (the self as objective). In the era of modernity, autobiography details experiences of psychological relevance and formative significance. Indeed, a new use of time frames a succession of interior awakenings and emotional events that stand in stark contrast to the old way of describing a life path paved with objective results—works, deeds, feats, and so forth. Rousseau's autobiography was also significant because it was the first to reflect an historical self-consciousness of the genre itself. He writes: "I may omit or transpose facts, or make mistakes in dates; but I cannot go wrong about what I have felt, or about what my feelings have led me to do; and these are the chief subjects of my story. . . . It is the history of my soul that I have promised to recount" (cited in Nalbantian, 1994, p. 14).

We have in Rousseau's confessions an undisputed transmutation of the genre. There are, nevertheless, certain vestiges of the predecessor, including the claim to biographical veridicality: the insistence on telling nothing but the truth, albeit an inner, symbolic truth.

The elaboration of psychic facts and formative experiences continued into 20th-century autobiography. However, there has been a loosening of the hold of the truth claim, at least as far as *truth* is taken to mean the straight-talking reportage of experiences brought to light in the course of careful self-observation. The latter part of the 20th century has seen an incursion of fiction into autobiography. Nalbantian (1994) has dubbed this hybrid of fact and fiction *aesthetic autobiography*, arguing that it arises in a climate in which it is not unreasonable to claim, as does Sarte, that the truth about ourselves might be more fully revealed in fiction or that, as Gide insists, the complexities of our lives outdistance our best efforts to commit them to a chronological narrative form:

> The most annoying thing is to have to present as successive steps states that occurred in confusing simultaneity. I am dialogical; everything in me fights and contradicts itself. Memoirs are only half sincere, no matter how great the concern is to tell the truth: Everything is always more complicated than one supposes. Perhaps we even get closer to the truth in the novel. (translated in Nalbantian, 1994, p. 18)

Responding to a generalized concern over the issue of succession versus simultaneity, there is a compression of time in the emergent autobiographical form. They read more often like slices of life; epiphany figures prominently.

In her seminal study of the emergence of aesthetic autobiography, Suzanne Nalbantian (1994) shows the form to be dominated by "interior visions that use exterior events as accessories" (p. 25). "Such interior visions," she writes, "were projected onto the fictional narrative and a hybrid genre was created coalescing life fact and artifact in a movement away from the gauge of extrinsic verification. The only standard in this avatar of life writing is art" (p. 25).

The Rise of the Imagination and Literary Fantasy

The coupling of self and aesthetic imagination has received attention from other quarters. Irving Howe (1992) has remarked upon their coincident discovery and argues that the two—self and imagination—are in fact one and the same. They both presuppose an element of interiority, of separation of self from others, as well as from the corporeal world. Self and imagination go together in exactly the way that mind and body do not.

There emerged during the Romantic period an intense interest in the imagination. It was, for example, very much at the center of theoretical embryology and teratology debates. Eminent physicians, surgeons, and midwives of the period believed that the mother's imagination, appropriately fixed, could directly affect the course and outcome of fetal development. When the pregnant woman's imagination was occupied with objects of beauty, she bore a beautiful child. If, on the other hand, her imagination was excited by some loathsome object or possessed of unsatisfied desire, prolonged affection, or repugnance, there was no end to the fetal monstrosities that might ensue. There was thus a storm of public reaction when it was reported that "sometime in October 1726, Mary Toft, the illiterate wife of a poor journeyman cloth-worker, gave birth, in Godalming, Surrey, to her first rabbit, and that she went on to deliver sixteen more" (Todd, 1995, p. 1). The event is rendered in Fig. 8.1 by William Hogarth, an 18th-century artist who, interestingly, is credited with popularizing physionomics, the science of interpreting human character and intelligence in terms of physical appearances.

Mary Toft's story, although subsequently revealed as a hoax, was the talk of London because it was believable. Indeed, there is a fairly substantial literature from the period cataloguing a multitude of monstrous births—of frogs, worms, snakes, even fictitious beasts like harpies and tailless, ratlike things. The existence of such fantastic creatures provided both entertainment and livelihood throughout Europe for hundreds of years, but during the 18th century, exhibitors of monsters conducted an especially "brisk and profitable trade" (Todd, 1995, p. 5). In addition to flocking to see the pedestrian collection of midgets, giants, bearded ladies, and Siamese twins, audiences paid good money to see a boneless girl, a mermaid, a mother and daughter with three breasts each, a man with one head and two bodies, a woman with one body and two heads, and a boy with a live bear growing out of his back. Each monstrosity stands as an example of the distinctiveness of mind and body and the "mysterious intercourse" between them.

According to Todd's (1995) analysis, orthodox thinkers of the time, influenced by a century of Cartesian thought, came to count on the mind–body distinction as a means of preserving a coherent self. To locate the self in the body was to damn it to the fleeting, material vicissitudes of appetitive desire, waste, and decay. Such a conception, according to Joseph Butler, an early 19th-century philosopher, "when traced and examined to the bottom, amounts, I think, to this: that personality is not permanent, but a transient thing: that it lives and dies, begins and ends continually: that no one can

FIG. 8.1. William Hogarth's depiction of Mary Toft giving birth to rabbits. From Todd, D. (1995). *Imagining Monsters: Miscreations of the self in eighteenth-century England*, p. 296. Chicago: University of Chicago Press. Reprinted with permission of the British Museum.

any more remain one and the same person two moments together, than two successive moments can be one and the same moment: that our substance is indeed continually changing" (cited in Todd, 1995, p. 122).

Identity was assumed to be incapable of persisting in the face of unconstrained diversity and multiplicity. To locate it in the body was to annihilate it. The alternative, although not without its own problems, was to fix identity in the unchanging, persistent, immaterial substance of mind and soul. From there it could persist, indivisible and unchanging, across time and circumstance. Moreover, it could govern the body, set it in motion, and, in a moment of weakness, even cause it to give birth to rabbits.

It is no coincidence that the beginning of the 19th century also bore witness to the birth of literary fantasy—the fantastic tale yet another child of Romanticism. Calvino (1977) notes the family resemblance to philosophic speculation, which emerged at the same time. This doctrine is founded on the coherence theory of truth and understands reality to be composed according to principles of self or mind. The declared intention of literary fantasy, by Calvino's analysis, is to represent the reality of the interior, subjective world of the imagination, and confer upon that world a credulity to the degree that it partakes of emotional truth and fidelity to human experience that outdistance its fantastic content (p. ix). The new sense of interiority is felt in the construction of imaginative spaces populated by visionary apparitions—ghosts, ghouls, and other such beings and figures that play central roles in early 19th-century fantasy. Over the course of the next 100 years, however, another dimension of the interior becomes manifest. By the dawn of the 20th century, narrative tension is no longer contained by encounters with supernatural figures. The mystery has moved within. The spooks are mental shadows, the conflicts of an abstract, psychological nature. In this transition, the pen—the instrument for creating the fiction—has been transferred from the author to the character. Or, more properly, the author has created characters who are themselves authors of their experiences.

THE PSYCHOGENETIC FRAME

In examining modern adolescents' conceptions of self, it is reasonable to ask why one would focus on their written texts. For the sociocultural analysis, a case can be reasonably made about the status of texts as artifacts that, rightly interpreted, illuminate a past not otherwise accessible. That the interpretations of self in literature offered here show remarkable consistency with evidence from other quarters—other aesthetic forms, in particular (e.g., art and architecture)—lends support to the claim that changing conceptions of self are deeply intertwined with the sweeping changes of modernity. The rationale for examining adolescents' written texts is not so different. It stands to reason that adolescents' written texts, fictional texts in particular, are a form of aesthetic expression and, as such, may present unique opportunities for exploring identity issues. Given adolescents' preoccupation with all manner of aesthetic expression—they write diaries, poems, and stories, play musical instruments, dance, sketch, and paint more than any other age group (Boëthius, 1995)—there has been surprisingly little scholarly attention paid to such activities. When we do encounter studies of children's and adolescents' artistic and aesthetic productions, they tend to focus on certain cognitive developmental underpinnings of the gifted and talented (e.g., Milbrath, 1998; Parsons, 1987; Winner, 1982), rather than issues of self and identity expressed by typical children.

Consider, however, the cover illustrations (Figs. 8.2, 8.3, and 8.4) made by some of the ninth-grade high school students who participated in the fiction-writing project. As a part of an English class assignment, they were instructed by their teachers to compose a fictional story and, if they wished, to provide an illustrated cover and dedication.

"The Basketball Game" is a story about a girl's dream to become a star player on a college team. Although not particularly artful, the author's cover includes a dedication: "To my teammates and my future coaches." "Life or Death" unfolds a narrative about a suicide; it is dedicated to "all those who decided life is worth it." Likewise, "In My Room" chronicles a girl's battle with drug addiction and suicide. On the cover is an illustration of a girl lying on a bed, surrounded by drug paraphernalia, pills, and alcohol bottles. The author dedicates the story to friends and family "because they taught me what not to do." These stories are expressive of their young authors' aspirations and concerns, if not their direct experiences. In some small measure at least, the fiction is autobiographical. This is in fact consis-

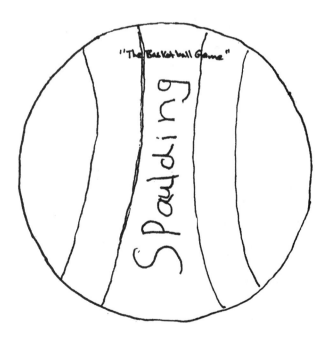

FIG. 8.2. "The Basketball Game."

FIG. 8.3. "Life or Death."

tent with the commentary in literary criticism, presented earlier, in which it was argued that fiction, although stripped of any pretense of referential truth, may be nevertheless just as relevant as autobiography to understanding the self (Auerbach, 1989; Calvino, 1977; Nalbantian, 1994).

There is also historical precedence for analyzing identity issues through written texts, although it has proceeded by fits and starts and tends to focus on texts written by adults. Freud and Erikson each made early and significant progress in psychological interpretations of texts, including those of an autobiographical nature. Allport (1942, 1965) championed intimate letters as material uniquely suited to revealing the inner narrative of a life. More recently, personal documents such as letters (e.g., Espin, Stewart, & Gomez, 1990; Haviland, 1983) and diaries (e.g., Crowther, 1999) have been mined for insights into psychological experience and identity development.

I dedicate my short story
to my parents, and my friends
for what they have taught me
not to do, also to my friends
because they have also taught
me what not to do.

Thank
You.

FIG. 8.4. "In My Room."

Nakkula and Ravitch (1998) and Newkirk (1997) considered written narratives as not only expressions of identity issues, but as tools of identity exploration, self-examination, and development.

What follows reflects the results of an initial effort to chronicle developmental changes in fiction writing across the adolescent years. I have argued elsewhere (Lightfoot, 1997a, 1997b) that adolescent identity development is an inherently aesthetic process and that to interpret it as such is to go some distance toward understanding adolescents' fascination with the dramatic and daring. Indebted to theoretical formulations regarding the place of play and art in human development and experience (see, e.g., the neglected third volume of Baldwin's early trilogy *Thought and Things*, 1911; Geertz, 1972; Winnicott, 1971), I reasoned that adolescent risk taking and subsequent storytelling of risk experiences, as well as the social construction of fantasies in peer groups, are all examples of the extent to which aesthetic considerations enter into identity-relevant activities. The work reported here is an extension of this broader view. The material is drawn from stories written by high school students (ninth graders; mean age = 14.7; 7 males and 7 females) and college students (mean age = 20.7; 7 males and 7 females) as a part of their normal English course requirements. For both age groups, the stories went through at least one round of peer and teacher review; they were considered to be major projects for the courses.

General Trends

The first level of analysis was aimed at discerning general age-group differences in the production of different forms of the self. Guided by insights from the sociocultural analysis presented previously, specific forms were distinguished on the basis of the self's relation to the events of the narrative, its embeddedness in time, and differences in the nature of the conflict that contributed to the narrative thrust of the story.

The stories sorted easily into three categories defining different forms of the self. One form is that of the *heroic self*, of which there were 10 examples in the sample. The central character is complete, noble, and initiated. The conception of self in time is undeveloped and there is no recognition of self-transformation. The dominant motif is the hero myth, in which the central character either overcomes or succumbs to events encountered by happenstance. All but two of the high school males, approximately 71%, produced stories of this ilk. Examples include encounters with ghosts, attacks by terrorists, and battles against disease. The form was much less popular with high school females (only two of seven) and college students (approximately 20% overall).

Another form is that of the *autobiographical self*. Eleven such stories were produced. Here, the self is conceived of as a culmination of particular events, a void to be filled over time. Thus, in contrast to the heroic self, it is subject to being incomplete. Events are construed in terms of their subjective relevance and meanings for the central character. There were no apparent age-group differences in instances of the form, although females were generally more likely than males to produce it (64% vs. 36%).

Finally, the *aesthetic self* was identified, of which there were seven examples, six of them from college students. There is a sense in these stories of self as perspective, that is, the self is understood to be composed of a history of experiences, but cannot then be divided back into them. Events are taken to interpret, represent, or challenge fundamental notions of truth, beauty, and morality. There is an emphasis on personal reconstruction and transformation.

In addition to examining forms of self, an effort was made to characterize the conflict inherent to the stories. Conflict is the source of dramatic tension in a narrative, and the stories differed systematically in terms of both the location of the conflict and what, or who, is threatened by it. Conflict can be located externally, in which case the dramatic tension exists between the central character and some outside force (e.g., battles of various sorts) or it can be located internally, in which case the character is at odds with him- or herself (e.g., mental and moral crises). Conceptually consistent with the age trends in the production of forms of the self, conflict of an external nature was most salient in the high school students' stories: Nearly 80% produced such stories. In contrast, a bit less than half (43%) of all college students composed narratives around external conflicts. Their stories, instead, involved a central conflict that is within characters, rather than between them.

In addition to having location, conflict also implies loss. For eight of the narratives, the conflict threatened the well-being of the central character's physical self. Usually, the threat was externally located, as in the case of being attacked or engaged in battle. However, the physical self could also be threatened by his or her own self, as in the case of drug abuse or suicide. The vast majority of these conflict types were produced by the high school students (six, i.e., 75%), mostly males. High school females tended to write about conflict that threatened the central character's well-being or relationship with some other person. The most common sort is the drama of a potboiler romance in which a third party threatens to undo a love relationship.

The college students produced stories of a very different nature. In their dramas, the character is torn between different moral choices or is challenged with respect to his or her world view. The conflict, in other words, threatens the integrity of the moral or epistemic self. More than half of the college students produced such narratives, whereas only two high school students did so.

Although the sample size is too small to make much of group differences, it is perhaps worthwhile to comment on the emerging story of gender differences in the high school and college samples. In particular, it appears that the narrative forms of the high school stories are especially mediated by gender. High school males were fairly consistent in producing versions of the classic hero myth, in which the main protagonist confronts and usually overcomes some formidable enemy. High school females, in contrast, were' more concerned with personal-relational conflicts. If this sounds predictably and stereotypically gendered, it may be but an example of the tight coupling of story and genre evidenced in the high school sample. That is, in addition to being gender typed in the extreme, high school students generally made greater use of classic, formulaic genres. Romances are cheap and all sorts of scary stories—ghost stories, murder mysteries, and so forth—although short on creativity, are long on cliché: Creaky doors, dark shadows, thunder and lightning, attic trunks, and mysterious strangers all figure prominently. Interestingly, in the college sample, not only are the stories more likely to be expressions of genre rather than the genre itself, but gender differences are much less salient. The college students seem less genre bound by their stories, more decoupled from and in control of the genre, and more agentive as authors.

In general, the high school stories are marked by a peculiar and radical affirmation of a self estranged. The circumstances and events of the narratives claim a certain presence, but lack history and future. Some of the events are survived by the characters; others are the characters' undoing. None of them, however, are, properly speaking, *experienced*. They are not strung along an interpretive axis of meaning that goes to point of view or broader context of significance and value. Rather, they are after the fashion of what Bakhtin (1986) describes as an adventure tale: the story of an event unfolded in a parallel world of fairy time. At the consummation of the adventure, the world and its characters simply resume their normal course.

Case Studies of Story Genres

The high school narratives are replete with examples of the adventure tale. In one, the narrator survives an attack by his deranged and crazy grandmother. After thwarting her effort to chop him into pieces with an axe, he gets in his car and drives off, muttering, "poor Grandma, poor Grandma." That was the end of his story.

Another narrator, with the help of his brother, kills his father, who has become the host body for an evil being released from an old, dusty chest in the attic. Borrowing directly from B-rated vampire movies, the author writes: "Timmy threw the stake, hitting our dad right in the heart! I hammered the stake with the mallet and Dad fell. The evil came out of Dad's lifeless body and disappeared leaving a pool of green ooze. That was it. Timmy and I now live with Grandma and Grandpa Griswald."

In yet another story, the narrator was himself possessed—by Superman. He writes:

> It all started on a Sunday morning, after a big delicious Sunday breakfast.... I felt a change coming from inside of me. I looked in the mirror and it wasn't me. It looked like Superman himself.... I heard a cry for help. My legs were moving in the direction of the cry of help, but my mind wasn't. I was changing

into something brave, intelligent, and strong looking. It felt like I didn't have any control of myself (like someone took over). Then I knew I was a different person now. I had a job to do: It was to defend my people.

Notwithstanding the young Cartesian Superman whose legs and mind move in opposite directions, there is no sense of personal transformation or reconstruction in consequence of these events. One complete identity has been simply exchanged for another.

One of the most distinctive features of the college stories is the internalization of conflict. References to mental states abound. Mind is very much at the center of the story, often in some state of epistemological or moral crisis. The narrator is typically at odds with him or herself. We find in these stories a preoccupation with genuineness, sincerity, and showing a true self, a moral self. "Playing games" is very much disparaged. Consider the following excerpt: "I sucked back my shot of tequila and stared at the fragmented likeness reflected before me. Half of my face was distorted [by the cracks of the bar mirror]." References to self-fragmentation, reflection, and distortion suggest a conflict between a real and a false self, and a concern with self-coherence. The story continues with the narrator commenting on the conversation of a couple at the end of the bar:

> She was going on and on about how one of her friends was seeing this guy who was "a player." I quit listening to the bitch's cream puff ramblings mid sentence and pretended to be genuinely interested in the [TV show]. . . . She was just spouting words . . . that suggest . . . pseudo knowledge. She sounded so painfully sincere and I'm sure that every morsel of bullshit that spilled out of her mouth was premeditated and deliberate.

The passage takes up the issue of authenticity. A "player" lacks authenticity; pretension, false knowledge, "bullshit," and premeditation are disparaged and set against spontaneity and genuineness.

At this point his girlfriend enters the bar. They had fought recently:

> [Her] mere presence quickened my sipping frequency. Lately, Jose [Cuervo], Jack [Daniels], and Pete [Wicked Ale] were the only people I seemed to be able to talk to. For the past week they've been my bros. They had the answers to my questions and never made me feel less than who I am.

Alcoholic beverages are personified as the "only people" with whom the narrator can "talk to," that is, they share matters of consequence and give proper weight and response to the narrator's "questions." The validation sought and apparently received is, of course, a self-validation. The passage exposes the narrator's solitude.

The narrator then questions the intentions of his girlfriend: "If she came down here just to perform her little act of desperate concern, I swear to holy Christ I'm gonna bury this pint glass in the bridge of her nose. Pathetically deliberate and with an air of rehearsal she squeaked out, 'I'm sorry . . . please, don't do this.'" The adjectives "little" and "desperate" are intended to mock the objects they modify; the girlfriend's actions—her "act," her "concern," are taken as contrived and "rehearsed."

She yells at him. He yells back. He hits her, much to his own surprise ("I couldn't believe I hit her."). A man at the end of the bar comes to her rescue. He throws the narrator through a glass door. The narrator stands, covered in blood and glass.

The entire story reflects an overarching preoccupation with self-fragmentation, distortion, multiplicity, and division into true and false, genuine and duplicitous, ending ultimately with the self literally torn to pieces. Nevertheless, the self as coherent, whole, and transcendent asserts itself in the end, a phantom self, a haunt, who breeches the boundary between the factual and the fictional selves: "I died right there on the bar floor. Don't cry now, I'm still around. . . . Every pool shot you botch I'll be that guy who bumped your stick. When your girl bends over, I'll be that phantom hand on her ass. . . . [W]hen a fight erupts, you'll know damn well who started it."

The issue of self as self, continuous and enduring, was also in evidence in the classic form of coming-of-age stories, of which there were several in the college student sample. The case presented here is about a young American woman who traveled to England because she "had an urge," as the author writes, to celebrate Christmas and the New Year somewhere else. It is noteworthy that she chose traditional holidays, usually associated with being or going home, as a time to leave. The narrative in fact overflows with allusions to self-discovery as a process of separation and individuation unfolding within a historical and cultural context:

> She felt pleased to be moving on and moving out. . . . She was visiting the dampish land from America. . . . She wanted to be alone, unnoticed, and solitarily swept up in something real and authentic. Scotland had a maturity of its own; she imagined red cheeks, and tartan plaid, whiskey and castles, songs and dance—all tightly bundled in a delightfully historic package. Mostly, she wanted to be away from her land, and away from familiar faces.

As in the previous story, authenticity and solitude are major issues. Here, however, is a greater emphasis on time, coherence, and progress. The main character, Sara, boards a bus to travel from England to Scotland. The driver engages her in conversation about her trip, noting to himself: "It was quite the trend these days to be alone. She was probably 'finding herself.'" The passage contains an explicit reference to an identity quest and the implication that it is a solitary endeavor. Importantly enclosed in quotation marks is a self-consciousness of the genre itself.

When Sara arrives in Scotland, she attends several folk celebrations of the holiday, one of which featured dancing:

> There was a closely knit bond between fiddler and dancer.... A certain warmth was concealed in the silent passing of music and dance from generation to generation.... There was a wholeness apparent here, a wholeness that Sara lacked. She felt detached and suffocated. Withdrawn and tired ... , she looked straight ahead for something new.

Whatever Sara sought was not found here. She was a witness to connections between fiddler and dancer, between generations, but not in any sense a part of them. The quest continues, and through it, Sara, "withdrawn and tired," resigned to her *Bildungsroman*.

CONCLUSIONS

For the last century, the self has been understood and depicted as a project under construction, engaged in a process of transformation. There is a new obsession with time and novelty: a compulsion to move on, a fear of boredom and lassitude. We observe it in our adolescents and in our literature. It has been argued that even our architecture has undergone a transmutation from a conventionally defined, three-dimensional, spatial art to one that includes a fourth dimension—an "aesthetic of experiences in time," of "responses dependent on the passage from one part of the building to another" (Huxtable, 1995, p. 19). The aesthetic of modernism is the aesthetic of movement and change (Paz, 1991). Whatever else this is, and whatever else it might reflect of the modern condition, it is our current, canonical genre of self.

In an interesting analysis of parallel processes of change in history and individuals, Habermas and his colleagues argue that individualism may be seen to constitute both a historic and a psychogenetic solution to a problem of self-fragmentation (Dobert, Habermas, & Nunner-Winker, 1987). In the historical case, self-fragmentation (or perhaps a mass attentiveness to self-fragmentation) was a response to the teeming multiplicity of roles made available by the division of labor associated with the rise of modernity. In the psychogenetic case, a sense of self as multiple or divided emerges in the context of a developing awareness of norms and conventions, of a role-bound identity. The own self as coherent, integral, unitary, and unique rises in defiance of an otherwise consuming plethora of social roles and expectations, occupational possibilities, and filial duties and obligations. It is the quintessential modern genre, displaying "both continuity of an integral identity and, within that continuity, the discontinuity that confirms its existence over time and space, its capacity to change without changing into something else" (McKeon, 2000, p. xiv). Something very close to this reasoning defines the theoretical space in which Sass (1997) explores the etiological connection between modernity and schizophrenia. Indeed, in light of the adolescents' narratives presented earlier, there is much to recommend in her discussion of the relationship between modernism's doublet—the simultaneous objectification and subjectivization of human experience—and certain contemporary symptoms of schizophrenia, particularly the pervasive sense of inauthenticity and of being a mere player of roles.

I will leave to others—or to another time—the important discussion regarding the relationship between the sociocultural and the psychogenetic. Some sense of it is suggested here. The work of Elias (1982), Lock (2000), and Sass (1997), for example, would seem to favor a sociogenetic or social constructionist perspective in which social structures and practices are internalized in the course of joint action. Piaget's (1995) constructivism, which emphasizes the generative function of social relations established through interaction, is also relevant (Lightfoot, 2000). However, the point I would like to make with the converging sociocultural and psychogenetic evidence is simply that genres are themselves projects of a sort, subject to change and transformation over the course of historic and ontogenetic time. They are, nevertheless, highly constrained and organized, in themselves and in their evolution. I take it as axiomatic that each and every story, every narrative, every instancing of the generic is unique and novel and, therefore, distinct from the generic form of which it is an instance. There are, however, developmental and cultural limits to the proprietary claims of the subject-author on the construction or interpretation of the story. Thus, although we can play with genres—see in them oppositions and similitude, order them, integrate them, outgrow them, juxtapose or even strike out against them—we cannot avoid being generic. It is no surprise that the dawn of this understanding took Leopardi's breath away.

AUTHOR NOTE

Cynthia Lightfoot, Human Development and Family Studies, Penn State Delaware County, 25 Yearsly Mill Road, Media, PA 19063-5596; e-mail: CGL3@psu.edu.

Portions of this paper were presented as a keynote address to the Brazilian Developmental Psychology Society, Rio de Janeiro, July 2000, and as a part of the symposium, "The Self and the Dynamics of Social Change" at the Society for Research in Child Development, Minneapolis, MN, April 2001.

The author is grateful to the editors, Terry Brown and Les Smith, and to Larry Nucci for their thoughtful comments on an earlier version.

REFERENCES

Allport, G. (1942). *The use of personal documents in psychological science.* New York: Social Science Research Council.

Allport, G. (1965). *Letters from Jenny.* New York: Harcourt Brace Jovanovich.

Auerbach, J. (1989). *The romance of failure: First-person fictions of Poe, Hawthorne, and James.* New York: Oxford University Press.

Bakhtin, M. (1986). *Speech genres and other late essays.* Austin: University of Texas Press.

Baldwin, J. (1911). *Thought and things: Vol. 3. Interest and art.* New York: Macmillan.

Blasi, A., & Glodis, K. (1995). The development of identity: A critical analysis from the perspective of the self as subject. *Developmental Review, 15,* 404–433.

Calvino, I. (1977). Introduction. In I. Calvino (Ed.), *Fantastic tales: Visionary and everyday.* New York: Pantheon.

Chandler, M. (2000). The persistence of identity in this culture and that. *Culture and Psychology, 6,* 209–231.

Crowther, B. (1999). Writing as performance: Young girls' diaries. In R. Josselson & A. Lieblich (Eds.), *The narrative study of lives* (pp.). Thousand Oaks, CA: Sage.

Dobert, R., Habermas, J., & Nunner-Winkler, G. (1987). The development of the self. In J. M. Broughton (Ed.), *Critical theories of psychological development* (pp.). New York: Plenum Press.

Elias, N. (1978). *The civilizing process: Vol. 1. The history of manners.* Oxford, England: Blackwell.

Elias, N. (1982). *The civilizing process: Vol. 2. Power and civility.* Oxford, England: Blackwell.

Erikson, E. (1950). *Childhood and society.* New York: Norton.

Espin, O., Stewart, A., & Gomez, C. (1990). Letters from V: Adolescent personality development in sociohistorical context. *Journal of Personality, 58,* 347–364.

Fumerton, P. (1991). *Cultural aesthetics: Renaissance literature and the practice of social ornament.* Chicago: University of Chicago Press.

Geertz, C. (1972). Deep play: Notes on the Balinese cockfight. *Daedalus, 101,* 1–37.

Habermas, J. (1989). *The structural transformation of the public sphere: An inquiry into a category of bourgeois society.* Cambridge, MA: MIT Press.

Hannerz, U. (1983). Tools of identity and imagination. In A. Jacobson-Widding (Ed.), *Identity: Personal and socio-cultural* (pp. 347–360). Atlantic Highlands, NJ: Humanities Press.

Haviland, J. (1983). Thinking and feeling in Woolf's writing: From childhood to adulthood. In C. Izard, J. Kagan, & R. Zajonc (Eds.), *Emotions, cognitions and behavior* (pp.). New York: Cambridge University Press.

Howe, I. (1992). The self in literature. In G. Levine (Ed.), *Constructions of the self* (pp. 249–267). New Brunswick, NJ: Rutgers University Press.

Lightfoot, C. (1997a). The clarity of perspective: Adolescent risk-taking, fantasy and the internalization of cultural identity. In B. Cox & C. Lightfoot (Eds.), *Sociogenetic perspectives on internalization* (pp. 135–156). Mahwah, NJ: Lawrence Erlbaum Associates.

Lightfoot, C. (1997b). *The culture of adolescent risk-taking.* New York: Guilford.

Lightfoot, C. (2000). On respect. *New Ideas in Psychology, 18,* 177–185.

Lightfoot, C., & Lyra, M. (2000). Culture, self and time: Prospects for the new millennium. *Culture and Psychology, 6,* 99–104.

Lock, A. (2000). Phylogenetic time and symbol creation: Where do Zopeds come from? *Culture and Psychology, 6,* 105–129.

Meyerhoff, H. (1960). *Time in literature.* Berkeley: University of California Press.

Moshman, D. (1999). *Adolescent psychological development: Rationality, morality, and identity.* Mahwah, NJ: Lawrence Erlbaum Associates.

Nakkula, M., & Ravitch, S. (Eds.). (1998). *Matters of interpretation: Reciprocal transformation in therapeutic and developmental relationships with youth.* San Francisco: Jossey-Bass.

Nalbantian, S. (1994). *Aesthetic autobiography.* New York: St. Martin's Press.

Newkirk, T. (1997). *The performance of self in student writing.* Portsmouth, NH: Boynton-Cook.

Parks, T. (2000). In love with Leopardi. *New York Review of Books, 47,* 38–41.

Parsons, M. (1987). *How we understand art: A cognitive developmental account of aesthetic experience.* Cambridge, England: Cambridge University Press.

Paz, O. (1991). *The other voice: Essays on modern poetry.* New York: Harcourt Brace Jovanovich.

Piaget, J. (1995). *Sociological studies* (2nd ed.) (L. Smith, et al., Trans.). London: Routledge. (Original work published 1977)

Piaget, J., & Garcia, R. (1989). *Psychogenesis and the history of science* (H. Feider, Trans.). New York: Columbia University Press. (Original work published 1983)

Rosmarin, A. (1985). *The power of genre.* Minneapolis: University of Minnesota Press.

Sass, L. (1997). The consciousness machine: Self and subjectivity in schizophrenia and modern culture. In U. Neisser & D. Jopling (Eds.), *The conceptual self in context: Culture, experience, self-understanding* (pp.). New York: Cambridge University Press.

Taylor, C. (1989). *Sources of the self: The making of the modern identity.* Cambridge, MA: Harvard University Press.

Vance, E. (1987). *From topic to tale: Logic and narrativity in the Middle Ages.* Minneapolis: University of Minnesota Press.

Winner, E. (1982). *Invented worlds: The psychology of the arts.* Cambridge, MA: Harvard University Press.

LOOKING TOWARD
THE FUTURE

9

From Epistemology to Psychology in the Development of Knowledge

Leslie Smith
Lancaster University

A foundational problem in psychology concerns its relations with other disciplines. Epistemology is a case in point. If psychology is the study of mind and epistemology is the study of knowledge, what is the relation between psychology and epistemology in an empirical investigation of human knowledge? This question arises for any psychological account of *cognitive development* which refers to two different things:

- children and the development of their minds
- knowledge and its development by children

The primary meaning of *cognitive development* for Flavell (1982) is the former; the primary meaning for Piaget (1985) is the latter. Children's minds have factual properties. Knowledge has normative properties. A unitary account that deals with both would have to provide an answer to the foundational question about the relations between psychology (directed on children's development) and epistemology (directed on the development of knowledge).

Reductionism arises here. Epistemology is traditionally regarded as a major branch of philosophy. As such, epistemology is a normative discipline. There is a temptation to reduce the normative problems that have historically been addressed in epistemology to psychological problems. This temptation is rarely explicit, but it surfaces all the same. Sometimes this is manifest as an argument from psychological authority: "I am not convinced, however, that modal knowledge is the quintessential feature of human cognition" (Karmiloff-Smith, 1994, p. 736). Sometimes it is manifest as an omnibus knock-down argument, as when a theoretical—and so normative—critique due to Müller and Overton (1998) was rejected because they "provide no new data to support their view; instead they cite[d] Piaget and various philosophical authorities" (Mandler, 1998, p. 125). If Western philosophy is a series of footnotes to Plato, it is fairly clear that some psychologists have missed the main plot.

My argument concerns this incipient collapse of epistemology into psychology. There is a *tertium quid*, or third alternative, here, a mediator that is neither (normative) epistemology nor psychology. It is the identification and characterization of this mediator that I want to elaborate. My nonreductionist argument is that some epistemological problems pose valid problems for psychology, even though these problems are not and could not be psychological problems and even though psychology makes an essential contribution to their explanation. Problems of knowledge and development are paradigm cases.

This argument is in four parts, one dealing with logic, psychology, and epistemology, another with developmental epistemology, a third with five epistemological values, and a final one with implications for developmental psychology. Psychologically minded readers who want to go straight to the four implications for developmental psychology in the final section of this chapter are welcome to do this. However, the other sections are the basis of these implications and are intended to be more than food for thought.

LOGIC, PSYCHOLOGY, AND EPISTEMOLOGY

The argument in this section is that an account of the development of knowledge during childhood requires some position to be taken about the relations between psychology and logic. Is there an exclusive relation here? If there is, is it also exhaustive? The answer to be presented in this section is "Yes" and "No" with developmental epistemology identified as a potential mediator.

Epistemology has traditionally been directed on the problem of knowledge. A standard version of this problem is: "What is knowledge?" This problem continues to be unresolved over two millennia. Its answer would set out normative (defining) conditions of knowledge in two respects. First, all cases of knowledge would have to satisfy these conditions, that is, the conditions would be sufficient in that their presence would guarantee a case of knowledge. Second, only cases of knowledge would have to satisfy these conditions, that is, such conditions would be necessary in that their absence would guarantee which cases could not be a case of knowledge.

There is currently no consensus as to the success conditions of knowledge (Chisholm, 1977; Goldman, 1986; Maffie, 1990; Moser, 1995). This unresolved problem is instructive in that two millennia is a long time. First, it could be argued that the problem "What is knowledge?" was due to a bad question: no agreed account is to hand because there could be no such account anyway. Notice that this is a skeptical argument and, as such, is itself normative. Second, psychologists could argue that a bad answer has been given to a good question. The question asked by epistemologists was given a normative answer when the answer is empirical and psychology is in the business of contributing an empirical answer.

Developmental psychologists may well reckon that their time has come to make progress in explaining cognition and development in place of epistemology. This proposal amounts to the reduction of epistemology to psychology in either of two ways. The stronger version is that epistemology has been superseded by psychology in much the same way that astrology has been superseded by astronomy. Common problems at the intersection can, on this view, be explained by psychology, whereas specifically epistemological problems drop out. In other words, so-called epistemological problems are pseudo-problems that are psychologically irrelevant. The weaker version is that specifically epistemological problems can be "bracketed off" because they are peripheral problems. In other words, they are not central to progress in psychology.

This reduction will not do at all. There is a specific reason as well as a general reason why it will not do. These are now taken in turn.

The specific reason is that at least one normative condition of knowledge is on hand. This means that an exclusively empirical answer could not be carried through. Although there is no complete account of the normative conditions of knowledge, there is partial agreement. There is a consensus as to one such condition, namely that knowledge entails the truth of what is known (Moser, 1995). This is a normative condition. As such, this conditions makes it a requirement that whatever is true is in principle knowable, whereas whatever is false can never in principle be known at all. Of course, anyone can believe a falsehood, such as "New York City is the capital of the United States," but belief is not knowledge. People make mistakes and may think that they know something when they do not. Following Moser (1995), there has never been a serious challenge to the normative condition of knowledge in terms of the truth of what is known. Leaving open other (normative) conditions (cf. Chisholm, 1977; Moser, 1995), the presence of one normative condition means that an exclusively empirical answer could not be given as a complete answer to the normative question "What is knowledge?"

The general reason is a nonreductionist argument. The starting point of this argument is a distinction due to Reichenbach (1961) between two contexts:

- the context of discovery, which is subjective and psychological
- the context of justification, which is objective and logical

His interpretation of this distinction ran thus. A context of justification is such that an objective test can be applied in demarcating scientific knowledge from pseudoscience, for example, in demarcating Newtonian mechanics from Newtonian mysticism. A context of discovery is such that the conditions under which scientific knowledge is generated are irrelevant to its truth, for example, the irrelevance of an apple hitting Newton on his head (discovery context) as a condition of the truth of his laws of motion (justification context). Philosophers set out to determine an objective criterion of justification. According to Carnap (1962), this was confirmation or verifiability related to inductive logic. According to Popper (1979), it was falsifiability related to deductive logic. What is common ground between Carnap and Popper is their argument that psychology is directed on the context of discovery, not the context of justification. This meant that psychology is simply irrelevant to an objective account of the growth of scientific knowledge. On this view, a psychological context of discovery is subjective, marked by individual differences compounded by cultural variability. This heterogeneity has been characterized as a source of foundational problems in psychology (Chandler, 1997; Hamlyn, 1978; Macnamara, 1994).

In short, Reichenbach's (1961) distinction had devastating consequences for psychology that, on this view, could not, in principle, have anything remotely interesting to say about the development of knowledge, one of the grand problems of philosophy. There would have to be a parting of the ways. Macnamara (1994) put this rather well, noting that the philosophers were already slamming the door just at the point when the psychologists were leaving anyway. No doubt Macnamara had in mind Gottlob Frege, who first stated a principle that had been adapted to fit Reichenbach's distinction.

Logic as we now know is due to Frege (1972). Kenny (1995) stated quite simply: "If Aristotle was the founder of logic, Frege refounded it, and logic has developed faster and further in the period between his time and the present day than it did in all the centuries which separated him from Aristotle" (p. 209). Comparable views about the extent of Frege's contribution to logic were expressed by his contemporaries (Russell, 1903) and successors (Kneale & Kneale, 1962, p. 511). One of Frege's pupils was Carnap, whose work influenced both Popper and Reichenbach (see also Smith, 1999d).

In re-founding logic as a formal science, Frege set out to demarcate logic from psychology in his major book published in 1884 (Frege, 1950, p. x):

Es ist das Psychologische von dem Logischen, das Subjective von dem Objectiven scharf zu trennen (Frege, 1884, p. x)

(To separate sharply the psychological from the logical, the subjective from the objective—my translation.)

This seems fair enough. Logic is standardly defined as the formal science of truth (Frege, 1979, p. 128). Thus, transitivity is a valid principle in propositional logic (Sainsbury, 1991): $(p \rightarrow q) \& (q \rightarrow r) \rightarrow (p \rightarrow r)$ in that if a proposition p is hypothetically related to another proposition q and q is hypothetically related to proposition r, then p is hypothetically related to r. Psychology, by contrast, is equally at home with false inference (cf. Markovits, 1995). This is not an isolated case, because psychology is also at home with the perception of visual illusion, the formation of pseudoconcepts, and the like. In fact, children and adults may well reason in terms of "if . . . then" conditionals without attesting the transitivity of propositions (cf. Johnson-Laird, 1999). Frege's (1979) point was that from this it follows that a psychological account of inference could not be explanatory of true knowledge. Psychology lapses into psychologism just in case a psychological explanation (which could be a sound explanation of false inference) is given for a logical truth (which could never be false). His further point was that a representation (*Vorstellung*), image (*Bild*), or human thinking (*Denken*) is subjective; it is the thinking of one person in a specific context in a particular culture. Quite different is objective thought (*Gedanke*), for example, the thought that is the Pythagorean theorem. This thought is a theorem that is both objectively true and intersubjectively open to us all, irrespective of any representation, image, or thinking that Pythagoras may have had in mind (Frege, 1979, p. 198).

Even so, Reichenbach's (1961) interpretation of Frege's (1979) distinction is another matter. His distinction in terms of two contexts is one interpretation of Frege's principle, in that the distinction between psychology and logic is exclusive and exhaustive. More generally, the distinction between an empirical science (psychology) and a formal science (logic) is exclusive and exhaustive, exclusive in that neither can be reduced to the other, and exhaustive in that there is no mediator between them. However, this interpretation is open to the objection that it is an overgeneralization that goes beyond Frege's principle. Interestingly, this overgeneralization is present in the standard translation of Frege's (1950) text due to the linguistic philosopher J. L. Austin. In the standard translation, the word *always* appears as the first word in the excerpt quoted earlier. It is one word, the first word, but it is a key word. This word *always* (German *immer*) was not used by Frege in the original passage. Its presence leads exactly to the overgeneralization of his principle.

There is an alternative interpretation of Frege's (1950) principle. Reichenbach's distinction led to antipsychologism in that the distinction between logic and psychology is both exclusive and exhaustive. According to nonpsychologism, the distinction is exclusive but not exhaustive (Smith, 1999b). Historically, there have been competing views about the relation between logic and psychology and currently there still are (Haack, 1978; Kusch, 1995; Macnamara, 1994). A natural reading of the title of Boole's (1958) *Laws of Thought* is that he regarded his laws of thought to be true of both logic and psychology. It follows from this identity that there is some common ground between psychology and logic. In other words, this exclusive distinction is not exhaustive. Kant (1963, quoted in Smith, 1993, p. 14) had a comparable view in that he regarded logical laws to be "necessary laws [of a] science of thought." Normative properties are necessary properties that, on this view, are applicable to human thought. Furthermore, Frege may have had a similar view on two counts (Smith, 1999a, 1999b, 1999d). First, a contribution from psychology is strictly required in an account of human thought:

> In the form in which thinking naturally develops the logical and the psychological are bound up together. The task in hand is precisely that of isolating what is logical. *This does not mean that we want to banish any trace of what is psychological from thinking as it naturally takes place, which would be impossible*; we only want to become aware of the logical justification for what we think. (Frege, 1979, p. 5, emphasis added)

This proposal is in line with the exclusivity of psychology and logic. Neither can be reduced to the other, even though each has a proper function to perform in an account of human thinking. The failure to draw this distinction amounts to committing the fallacy of psychologism, which is the reduction of the normative to the empirical. Human thinking has an essentially psychological element the explanation of which is the task of psychology. Furthermore, a contribution from psychology is not enough. Something else is required as well. Frege (1979) expressed this point in the following way:

> Causes that merely give rise to acts of judgment do so in accordance with psychological laws ... [and so objective knowledge requires there to be] judgments whose justification rests on something else, if they stand in need of justification at all. *And this is where epistemology comes in.* Logic is concerned only with those grounds of judgment that are truths ... There are laws governing this kind of justification, and to set up these laws of valid inference is the goal of logic. (p. 3, emphasis added)

According to this proposal, the distinction between an empirical science (psychology) and a formal science (logic) is not exhaustive, because there could be a mediator that has a foot in both, and Frege identified epistemology as a potential mediator in this regard.

There is an obvious objection here. Epistemology was earlier defined as a normative discipline and it was specifically argued in this section that one condition of knowledge (i.e., knowledge entails the truth of what is known) is normative. This means that epistemology could in principle be linked to the normative science of logic, but how could it be linked to the empirical science of psychology? The reply to this objection is that normative epistemology is only one type of epistemology. Developmental epistemology is another. This was Piaget's *tertium quid* or third alternative, namely his developmental (aka genetic) epistemology. This insight is elaborated in the next section.

DEVELOPMENTAL EPISTEMOLOGY

An instructive starting point for this discussion is Piaget's (1963) response to the interpretation of his work in Flavell's (1963) commentary. In his commentary, Flavell expressed a view that he regularly invoked in later works, notably, the inspirational qualities of Piaget's work along with its explanatory limitations in psychology (Flavell, 1982). According to Flavell, Miller, and Miller (1993), Piaget's work was a major but incomplete contribution to developmental psychology. This looks to be decisive. Piaget had made explicit claims about psychology in his own work (Piaget & Inhelder, 1969). If Piaget was right in his characterization of his work, then that work is apparently vulnerable to Flavell's verdict. However, things are not so clear cut. Piaget (1963) expressed five reservations about this psychological interpretation of his work. It is instructive to examine these:

(i) *Experiment-theory*

It seems clear that Professor Flavell is more interested in the experiments than in the theory. (p. viii)

According to Piaget, Flavell was interested in experimental tasks at the expense of theory. The implication is that this is a methodological mistake on the grounds that evidence due to experimental tasks can be interpreted only through theory. This is a Popperian implication (Lakatos, 1974; Popper, 1979). Piaget's point was that his theory had been disregarded in the interpretation of psychological evidence. Vonèche (2001) attested the Popperian commitment made by Inhelder, which by implication covers their joint work (Inhelder & Piaget, 1980; Piaget & Inhelder, 1969).

(ii) *Interpretation from without and within*

[This]) sometimes gives me the impression of having been understood on certain issues more from without than from within. (p. viii)

This contention is that Piaget's work was interpreted by Flavell "from without" at the expense of an interpretation "from within." The implication is that this is a key difference. This invites the question about what difference to psychology this (nonpsychological) difference could make. To re-state this question, what difference to psychology could an epistemological difference make? After all, Piaget (1950, 1972) also characterized his work as a contribution to developmental epistemology.

(iii) *Theory as spider web*

Professor Flavell argues that I have expended too much energy spinning an in-tricate theoretical spider web which does not catch enough of reality in it [but] I have the distinct impression that it is already catching more than flies. (p. viii)

In Piaget's view, Flavell regarded Piagetian theory as a spider web mak-ing an inadequate fit with reality through its explanation of both too few phenomena and too few major phenomena. Piaget's (1967) view was that the phenomena explained by his theory were important and fundamental.

(iv) *Structures as reifications*

Professor Flavell thinks that I have multiplied intellectual structures beyond necessity. (p. viii)

Piaget attributed to Flavell the view that such a web amounted to a breach of Occam's razor (*entia non multiplicanda praeter necessitatem* "things should not be multiplied beyond necessity") inasmuch as Piagetian structures were unnecessary reifications. Piaget declined to accept the im-plied instrumentalism behind this view (Inhelder & Piaget, 1980).

(v) *Developmental psychology and epistemology*

In Professor Flavell's opinion, there is too wide a gap between the facts that I describe and the theories I invoke—it could be argued that the differences be-tween us stem from the fact that his approach is perhaps too exclusively psy-chological and insufficiently epistemological, while the converse is true for me. (pp. viii–ix)

This final contention goes to the heart of the matter. If Flavell was more in-terested in developmental psychology than epistemology, the exact oppo-site was true of Piaget. Or so Piaget declared.

This difference in (v) merits discussion. It is undeniable that Piaget re-garded his work as a contribution to psychology. It is also clear that Piaget's work, so interpreted, is at best insufficient and at worst problem-atic. This is Flavell's point. However, this leaves epistemology out of account. If Piaget's work is regarded as a contribution to epistemology, what difference does this make to its explanatory power in psychology?

Recherche was Piaget's (1918) first book; it has never been translated into English, although it has attracted commentary in English (Chapman, 1988; Kitchener, 1986; Vidal, 1994; Vonèche, 1992). The word *recherche* has two meanings: "search" and "study"; both are relevant to its main problem. This problem is the search for a way to reconcile science and faith. At issue were not merely the competing demands of two disciplines, religion on the one hand and science on the other, both of which purport to generate truths about reality. Rather, what was fundamentally at issue was how any one study could combine fact and value. In addressing this fundamental problem, *Recherche* set out what Piaget (1918, p. 148) called his "research-program." Recall, in this respect, that a research program is not a scientific theory. Rather, it is a set of constructs and principles that define the problems to be addressed in specific theories along with ways to resolve them (Lakatos, 1974). Although Piaget (1970) rightly considered himself the chief revisionist of Piaget's theory, he should have added that his serial revisions remained within the research program set by *Recherche*.

Identification of the Problem

According to Piaget (1918): "The reconciliation of science and faith is the problem at the source of all current disequilibrium" (p. 21, translation). In making this claim, Piaget was in part alluding to the Great War in Europe. A comparable allusion to this significant event has recently been made by Searle (1999). Piaget's specific concern was religion's battle to defend itself against the advance of science. According to Piaget (p. 150), the demarcation problem arose because the physical sciences are studied quantitatively in the modern world. However, when the same model is applied in the life and social sciences, faith and value, being nonquantitative, must be sacrificed at the altar of science and truth. Therefore, some choice had to be made between them. Piaget expressed this forced choice by using the metaphor of two cults, which "exclude each other in the search for truth and the search for value" (p. 41). They exclude each other inasmuch as "faith and science are contradictories" (p. 109). Faced with a contradiction between two positions, one should be accepted at the expense of the other. This is because contradictories are mutually exclusive of each other, requiring a forced choice between them.

This contradiction was serious because its detection depended on a subtle argument. The case for each of the contradictories was independently persuasive. According to Piaget (1995), both truth and value are required in the life and social sciences, therefore, there is a persuasive case for retaining both, as long as each is independently considered. Indeed, Piaget pointed out a general problem here as well:

> Logicians are accustomed to speak of the principle of contradiction as if it were a legal law, which by itself could foresee its own meaning and the extent of its application. But it is clear that the principle of contradiction does not apply to itself, for in and of itself, it does not indicate whether something is contradictory or not. We know in advance that, if A and B are contradictories, we must choose between them, but we do not know at the outset if that is what they are. (p. 189)

This is an important point that strikes right at the core of human rationality. Contradictory thinking is hardly rational and Piaget is asking how any thinking intended to be rational can be insured against self-contradiction, which is nonrational. The lurking questions are twofold: What guarantees are there for rationality in the human mind at all? What guarantees are there for rationality in developing minds?

Significance of the Problem

According to Piaget (1918), the contradiction between science and faith is particularly acute within the life and social sciences, where both fact and value are required. In these sciences, the contradiction is serious, with no easy way out. Both contradictories appear as if they should each be inclusively retained, whereas contradictories are exclusive. Thus, the real problem is the apparently internal contradiction within the life and social sciences. The problem arises because action is the unit of analysis in these sciences and action has both factual and normative properties: "Action necessarily deforms the ideal in virtue of its mixture of fact and norm" (Piaget, 1918, p. 116). The tension here can be explained in this way: A fact is a fact and, therefore, is not a value. Any action is a fact in virtue of its performance, but if that action is also the right action to perform, then that action is also value laden. This is because whatever is right (just, fair, good, or, in general, something that should be done) thereby has a value. Therefore, an action on its performance combines both fact and value. The problem that Piaget was raising is how this could be so, how one and the same thing can have these exclusive properties. Take as an example the action performed in giving the right answer to the question "What is $7 + 5$?" Declaring the answer "12" is something that an agent does and this answer is also correct: It is true that $7 + 5 = 12$. As such, the currently prevailing view in science is that this response is causally conditioned by the circumstances in which that agent is placed. It is true that this view has still to be made good, but its outlines are such that contributions are expected from a range of disciplines that are set to include biology, neurophysiology, and psychology (Searle, 1999; Wachs, 2000). However, what should not be left out of account is the agent's recognition of this truth. Technically, this is a judgment (to be discussed later in this chapter). To be sure, this correct answer can—and usually is—given without a judgment, yet this is not always the case and, in writing this paragraph, I was making this very judgment. This is not an autobiographical remark. Can we not all do this some of the time? Piaget's problem is significant because the presence of exclusive properties has implications for which other disciplines should make a contribution. How great is the range? Does this include epistemology?

Three assumptions were being made here by Piaget (1918). Two of these are widely accepted. One is that religion is directed on values. The other is that science is directed on facts. It is the third assumption that generates the problem, because both religion and science are also accepted to be directed on truth. Yet truth is a value because its properties are normative, not empirical. Two points are important here and both can be explained by exploiting some parallels between the epistemologies of Frege and Piaget (Smith, 1999a, 1999b, 1999d). First, Frege (1979) defined logic as the formal science of truth: "The word *true* can be used to indicate a goal for logic, just as *good* for ethics and *beautiful* for aesthetics. . . . Logic can also be called a normative science. . . . Logic is the science of the most general laws of truth" (p. 128).

Frege's point continues to be accepted as the standard view in logic (von Wright, 1983). Logic is directed on truth in virtue of its concern with truth-preserving inference through which valid inference is defined. As Haack (1978) put it, a valid inference in logic is such that it not merely does not, but rather could not, lead from true premises to a false conclusion. Piaget (1949, p. 4; 1971, p. 35) had a comparable view. It is for this reason that Piaget used logic in the characterization of mental organization. His argument was that, if this organization is structured, there are two questions for an investigator to answer. One is what this structured organization is: Is there one structure or are there several structures of mental organization? The other is whether these are also structures of reality. Piaget's (1949) strategy was to characterize his structures as logical structures, logical in view of the definitional link between logic and truth. A logical structure "is only a system of possible substitutions [that is] axiomatized in formal logic" (Piaget, 1995, p. 94). From this, it follows that the use of a structure with a logical characterization would make possible the formation of true knowledge. Whether this possibility is actualized is another matter and Piaget (1985, pp. 6, 13) expressly denied that the mere use of a structure was sufficient in this regard. The structure may itself be wrong or incomplete or the right structure might be put to the wrong use. This is why the use of a structure is not enough.

And this leads to the second point. Frege (1979, p. 128) contended that any definition of truth, such as "an idea is true if it agrees with reality", is circular. His argument was that only true ideas could agree with reality and yet there is no way for proponents of this definition to ascertain what reality is like other than through ideas. However, in denying that "truth is agreement with reality" could serve as a definition of truth, Frege did not thereby challenge the basic insight in this remark, which continues to be accepted by many philosophers (Popper, 1979; Searle, 1999). Others have, however, challenged the very notion of truth as correspondence between human representation and external reality (Bickhard, chap. 5, this volume; Bickhard & Terveen, 1995). Piaget's (1971, p. 342) position was in line with this latter stance through his denial of an equality (identity) between any mental structure and the structure of reality.

In short, there is some basis for each of the three assumptions invoked by Piaget (1918), but this amounts to confirming that there is a problem in the life and social sciences directed on the joint presence of both fact and value.

Resolution

The third step was a resolution. Piaget (1918, p. 150) set out "to introduce a positive theory of quality, taking into account only relations of equilibrium and disequilibrium between those qualities. In this way may a science of life be founded on metaphysical ruins." The claim here needs to be unpacked (see also Smith, in press-a). The distinction between fact and value was recast by Piaget in terms of his equilibrium concepts. Piaget (1918, p. 151) cited the use of these in the physical sciences, mechanical equilibrium (cf. Piaget, 1985, sect. 14), as one basis for their use in the life sciences. Piaget (1918) did not envisage that equilibrium was unitary and thus he did not envisage that mechanical equilibrium and mental equilibrium were the same. There are three reasons why. One is that living systems are self-organizing:

> Life is definable as assimilation, source of all organization. The living being assimilates, that is, by the very fact that it is alive, it reproduces something identical to itself. It has therefore an independent and stable over-arching quality. On the other hand, in assimilating, it undergoes the influence of the substances that it assimilates, of the milieu. (Piaget, 1918, p. 155)

This definition of life entails that a living being has the problem of maintaining equilibrium that is ruptured by disequilibrium arising from its own activity. In assimilating, living beings generate identities that are ruptured by the differences arising from accommodation. On this view, ideal equilibrium is a value and initial disequilibrium is a fact whereby any equilibrium is generated from earlier disequilibria. However, the restoration or equilibrium has its origin in the self as agent. A second reason is that mental, but not mechanical, equilibrium is value laden and so normative. According to Piaget (1918): "Fact is a form of equilibrium—or disequilibrium—and the ideal is another equilibrium, as real in a sense as the first, but often invoked rather than realized: The ideal is a limiting case, as the mathematicians say, or rather the full equilibrium onto which false or unstable equilibria of reality converge" (Piaget, 1918, p. 46). The point that Piaget was making here is that, if a disequilibrium is a fact and an equilibrium is a value (norm, ideal), then a constructivist theory combines both fact and value. Such a position has the consequence that one and the same science of life would combine facts and values in one account. In that case, however, the relation between facts and values is inclusive, not exclusive. The third reason why mental equilibrium is different from its mechanical counterpart is that it includes both real and ideal elements. This emerges in Piaget's (1918) interpretation of the manner in which facts and values can be combined in one scientific study. In *Recherche*, Piaget (1918) qualified his statement of reconciliation by a requirement of their nonconflation that he secured in this way:

> Two realities contribute to life, real disequilibria and ideal equilibrium *towards which real disequilibria tend*. Truth is exactly this—biological truth, just as moral truth, just as aesthetic truth, just as religious truth. A thinker who wishes to know the truth must commit himself or herself to ideal equilibrium, never to reality. (p. 115; emphasis added)

This distinction between real and ideal applied to mental equilibrium would have no sense in application to mechanical equilibrium.

In other words, both in his first book and certainly in later texts, the demarcation of mental and mechanical equilibrium was required (Piaget, 1985; see also Brown, 2001; Chapman, 1992; Vonèche, 1992). The important point that Piaget was making turns on the word *reality*. In stating at the outset that there are two realities, Piaget was using this term in its metaphysical sense, which covers objects in the actual world and abstract objects as well. Numbers and logical classes are paradigm examples of abstract objects. Indeed, constructivism has been defined as an account of the "creation of new objects (*êtres*) such as classes, numbers, morphisms etc." (Inhelder & Piaget, 1980, p. 21). In this sense, Piaget was claiming that *real disequilibria* and *ideal equilibrium* are two realities, in much the way that Popper (1979) claimed that reality comprises three worlds, the world of inorganic phenomena in physics (World 1), the world of mental states in psychology (World 2), and the world of the objective content of knowledge in epistemology (World 3). In stating that *a thinker must never submit to reality*, Piaget was using this term in a different sense, at once psychological and epistemological. First, he presumably meant that there are factors at work in reality *qua* the actual world that deform truth and therefore a thinker in search of truth may in fact submit to these. The investigation of these factors is central to psychology, which sets out to chart quite precisely the empirical conditions under which human perception and understanding break down as misperception and misunderstanding. Second, he also meant that, if *ideal equilibrium* is not in fact attained, then *real disequilibria* are all that is left to the human mind. In consequence, truth is not a state of mind that is actually attained, but rather a process directed on its attainment. It is in this sense that truth (ideal equilibrium) is a limit toward which any actual equilibrium converges. Although Piaget did use a mathematical analogy in formulating this claim, in that the process of seeking truth can be viewed as an infinite series whose values approximate to without ever attaining a limit, the underlying point is epistemological, namely, that truth is a value that is not in fact attained by a human mind.

The upshot is that Piaget (1918) accepted in *Recherche* that the distinction between facts and norms is exclusive: A norm is not a fact and conversely. Even so, Piaget also proposed that norms and facts could be the joint focus of one inclusive study based on equilibrium concepts. However, there was one crucial respect in which the account in *Recherche* (and, some would say, Piaget's work generally) was incomplete. The crucial point is this: Although a commitment was made in *Recherche* to a developmental theory stated through equilibrium concepts, something more would have to be said about this developmental mechanism. This commitment would eventually run into objections in that Piaget's equilibrium concepts have been regarded as "preliminary and tentative" (Flavell, 1963, p. 244), "difficult to define" (Boden, 1979, p. 66), "obscure" (Klahr, 1999, p. 133), and "hard to test" (Bryant, 2001, p. 130). These objections are well taken. They reveal that Piaget presented neither a testable nor a formal model, but they fall short on one count: None of these objections demonstrates the incoherence of Piaget's account and this means that its intelligibility is left intact. Other developmentalists have gone further and attested that Piaget's core constructs have been persistently misrepresented (Lourenço & Machado, 1996), that they could be assigned a causal interpretation in terms of self-organizing processes in line with criteria of adequacy in the physical sciences (Molenaar & Raijjmakers, 2000), that they are directed on emergence, which is a central problem in the life sciences generally (Bickhard, chap. 5, this volume), and that they straddle empirical and normative domains and, as such, address a substantive problem in the absence of credible alternatives (Brown, 1996, 2001).

Quite so. And this is why *Recherche* merits reevaluation. A case was being made in *Recherche* for a new science with an inclusive focus on fact and value, for a unitary account in which the development of knowledge would run from "the causal to the logical" (Piaget, 1995, p. 51). This is Piaget's

(1950) developmental epistemology, his *tertium quid* as an alternative to both normative epistemology and empirical psychology. Some of the elements of this *tertium quid* will be taken up in the next section.

AEIOU EPISTEMOLOGICAL QUINTET

My interpretation of Piaget's *tertium quid* is in reference to five epistemological principles under an AEIOU mnemonic:

- Autonomy
- Entailment (modality)
- Intersubjectivity
- Objectivity
- Universality

The discussion is in two parts, one a worked example and the other a generic survey.

The example is taken from my study of reasoning by mathematical induction (Smith, in press-b). It had its origin in a marvellous design due to Inhelder and Piaget (1963). Reasoning by mathematical induction is a standard form of argument in mathematics and is widely used to advance mathematical knowledge. In their study, Inhelder and Piaget drew two conclusions. One was that such reasoning is under development during childhood, the mechanism of which was iterative action. The other was that the children's reasoning was modal, that is, the children understood the necessity of this reasoning. In my recent replication, direct evidence for the first conclusion was reported along with indirect evidence for the second. In the replication, 100 children in school Years 1 and 2 (ages 5–7 years) from NW England were interviewed twice. During each interview, they were asked to provide a response and then to give reasons for that response. The design was in line with Euclidean axioms (Heath, 1956). In the first interview, this axiom was "equals added to equals are equal," in virtue of the simultaneous addition of one counter to each of two containers that were initially empty. The second interview was similar in design, except that equal additions were made at the same time to the containers, one of which had one counter in it at the outset ("equals added to unequals are unequal").

In this second study, container *A* had a head start over the other container *B*. One of the questions concerns the addition of "a great number," no doubt an ambiguous expression the reference for which the children had to determine (or not, as the case may be). John (not this child's actual name), age 7, was asked this question and here is his reasoning:

Interviewer: How about if you put a great number in that one and a great number in that one. Would there be the same in each or more there or more there?

John: That would be right up to the cover in the sky and that would be right up to God, so then they would still have to be more.

John had reasoned by analogy. That children are capable of analogical reasoning was secured by Piaget (1992) in his account of correspondences, as well as in his empirical study of analogical reasoning (Piaget, 2000, chap. 6). The point about John's analogy was that it was a particularly good one. After the interviewer (*c'est moi*) apologized for his ignorance, John explained with a kind but telling smile: God lives up in the sky over which there is a cover. This cover is higher than God. Similarly—note John's use of *so*, which is paradigm term used in inferential reasoning—the number in A is higher (greater) than the number in B. What was also significant about this reasoning was that each member of the AEIOU quintet was exemplified. John's reasoning was:

- Autonomous: This reasoning was a free mental act with an individual characterization.
- Entailment (modal knowledge of necessity): This reasoning was modal: notice the use of *have to be*. After all, all mathematical truths are necessities and John had grasped one of these, even though it was not part of his mathematics learning at school.
- Intersubjective: This reasoning was in line with the Euclidean axiom "equals added to unequals are unequal" (Heath, 1956). This axiom is a clear case of common ground between different thinkers.
- Objective: This reasoning was justified as a response in a valid (truth-preserving) argument.
- Universal: This reasoning in this specific context amounted to a (partial) understanding of universality, namely, that this truth is always the case.

In short, five epistemological values fit John's reasoning. There is no reason to suppose that his case is unique. What follows now is a more generic characterization (cf. Smith, 1999a, 1999b, 1999d, in press-b).

Autonomy

A learner should be a free agent, but should not have free license (Piaget, 1998, pp. 213, 259). Autonomy is not anarchy, because rational thought and self-indulgent thinking are not the same thing (Piaget, 1998, p. 165). Each individual has the problem of reconciling *son moi avec la loi*, the self with normative rule (Piaget, 1995, p. 241). Reconciliation is required where "the ego's interests conflict with the norms of truth" (Piaget, 1998, p. 124). An autonomous individual has the capacity to make a commitment to laws that bind that individual's action and thought (von Wright, 1983, p. 10). At issue is which laws these are or, indeed, whether to be bound by rules at all. Autonomy excludes heteronomy, in which the values of an imperative reside in the "authority of those from whom they emanate" (Piaget, 1995, p. 304). Quite simply, normative force is not normative pressure (von Wright, 1983, p. 55). Social conformity is an act of (heteronomous) obedience in a prevailing culture where the teacher becomes "the symbol of knowledge and ready-made Truth, of intellectual authority and Ancient tradition" (Piaget, 1998, p. 162). Instead, autonomy in learning requires "obedience which is an act of reason" (Piaget, 1995, p. 60). What is required is the invidualization of knowledge, that is, autonomy in that "each individual is led to think and re-think the system of collective notions" (Piaget, 1995, p. 76). The commitment to autonomy is not to the individualism of the solitary knower (Smith, 1995, p. 6), but rather to the *invidualization of knowledge* whereby "each individual is led to think and re-think the system of collective notions" (Piaget, 1995, p. 76).

Entailment

Entailment is a paradigm case of necessity, along with equality (identity). There is an important difference between correct reasoning and modal reasoning about what is necessary, that is, understanding something as necessary (Smith, 1997, 1999c). Learning to reason modally concerns "what had to be so, and could not be otherwise" (Smith, 1993, p. 63). The importance of necessity in human understanding is a developmental problem, namely, how to make the advance from nonnecessary to necessary knowledge. As Piaget (1928) put it: "The necessity resulting from mental experiment is a necessity of fact; that which results from logical experiment is due to the implications existing between the various operations" (p. 237). Furthermore, "the problem concerns] this transition from a temporal construction to an atemporal necessity" (Piaget & Garcia, 1989, p. 15). No doubt it was for this reason that Piaget (1950, p. 23; 1967, p. 391; see Smith, 1993, p. 1; 1999c, pp. 23–24) stated this to be the principal problem in his work. Many philosophers have pointed out that necessities can be learned (Kripke, 1980; Leibniz, 1981). Piaget (1986) considered that this learning was under development during childhood, where there is an interplay between the normativity of thought and the subjectivity of thinking. According to him: "Before reasoning in the normatively right manner, the small child begins by playing with his or her thought or by using it in accordance with norms which are unique to that individual. Thus the principal task for the education of the intellect, it seems, is much more to form thought and not to furnish memory" (Piaget, 1998, p. 148). A norm lays down "what has to be." Personal modes of thinking amount to "what has to be for me." This is why the development of modal understanding is difficult, in that it requires the demarcation of normatively necessary thought from ego- and sociocentric thinking (Piaget, 1995, pp. 53, 73, 84). Necessities are not cultural norms such as the belief that " 'we adhere to our old customs for the universe to be conserved' . . . [but] from a social point of view, we are all like this primitive man" (Piaget, 1998, pp. 110–111).

Intersubjectivity

The concept of intersubjectivity is variously used to cover social interaction (Perret-Clermont, 1980) or in reference to shared culture (Cole & Wertsch, 1996). It also has a meaning in reference to self-identical thought, such as the the Pythagorean theorem (Frege, 1979). It is in this epistemological sense that intersubjectivity is important. If intersubjective knowledge is impossibe, in the sense of knowledge that is common ground between different individuals in social interaction or between the members of different cultures, then relativism prevails. Chandler (1997) pointed out that cognitive development, as traditionally understood, is incompatible with relativism. He was, of course, right, because the case against relativism is conclusive and compelling (Nagel, 1997; Searle, 1999). Relativism leads straight to George Orwell's (1983) nightmare in Room 101, where $1 + 1 \neq 2$. The intersubjectivity of knowledge was acknowledged in Piaget's claim that in logic "proof is valid for all" (Piaget, 1928, p. 24). A logical structure is the "sole instrument common to demonstration used in every science" (Piaget, 1949, p. 2). Intersubjectivity is secured by Piaget's epistemic subject, whose use of such an instrument is by means of "a general logic, both collective and individual" (Piaget, 1995, p. 94). Education should be directed on the "formation of a social attitude of reciprocity capable of being generalized in progressive steps" (Piaget, 1998, p. 260). Reciprocity in thinking is a *sine qua non* of the intersubjectivity of thought, including cases of rational disagreement.

Objectivity

Knowledge is objective just in the case where it is true. True knowledge is based on the presupposition that "there is a way that things are" (Searle, 1999, p. 34). However, it is one thing to make a response that is true and it is something else to acknowledge that the response is true. An act of judgment amounts to objective knowledge and thus requires a recognition or realization of the truth of what is known. There is a fundamental distinction between activity confined to "success or practical adaptation and verbal or conceptual thought whose function is to know and state truths" (Piaget,

1954, p. 360). Objectivity requires both knowing what is true and that it is true (Piaget, 1995, p. 184, 1998, p. 115). As noticed above, logic is the formal science of truth and from this it follows that judgments that actually have a logical justification are in line with and due to the laws of truth. It is for this fundamental reason that sound justifications, not merely correct judgments, are constitutive elements in intellectual development (Smith, 1993, sect. 13, 1999a, in press-b).

Universality

Something may be universal in two different senses: One sense concerns the transfer of knowledge across tasks and contexts (Case, 1999; Feldman, 1995; de Ribaupierre, 1993) and another concerns the universalization of thought, that is, understanding what fits all cases. Number is a case in point. It is one thing to reason correctly in different contexts such as street trading and the classroom that $35 \times 4 = 140$ (Nunes & Bryant, 1996), but it is something else again to realize in just one context that this truth is always the case. Piagetian structures bear on universalization rather than transfer. The universalization of thought is the essential task of pedagogy, which is "to lead the child from the individual to the universal [where] this ascent from the individual to the universal corresponds to the very processes of the child's intellectual and moral development" (Piaget, 1998, p. 81). Piaget's point was that local contingencies, common culture, or current experience *hic et nunc* (in the here and now) have a powerful effect on restricting the powers of the mind: They can act as constraints on the transfer of knowledge. Because all learning is shaped by such contingencies, the advance from the particular to the universal in any one context is both a difficult achievement and a liberating intellectual act. This is the breakthrough that is potentially available to any living agent through his or her use of a lively mind in action.

These five epistemological values are merely five cases that do not exhaust the class. They should be augmented with other cases with dual properties in being both factual and normative. In a developmental epistemology, it is such values that develop over time in the construction of knowledge. Because these are values, they have normative properties. Because they develop over time, they also have factual properties. In the final section of this chapter, a reconciling perspective with this joint focus is sketched.

IMPLICATIONS FOR DEVELOPMENTAL PSYCHOLOGY

There are four main implications dealing with psychology, normative facts, acts of judgement as the unit of analysis, and developmental mechanism.

Psychology

Psychology is an empirical science. The argument due to Frege (1979), discussed earlier, was that any empirical investigation of human thinking requires a psychological account. Human thinking is a mixture of logical and psychological properties. The only way in which the psychological aspects of thinking can be identified is by the use of a psychological account. This is a strict requirement that the only way to study human thinking is through empirical psychology. This conclusion may seem trivial to psychologists, but it is not. The requirement points only to the necessity of psychological investigation, not to it sufficiency, with regard to the problem of knowledge. In this respect, it is important to be mindful of the ambiguity of cognitive development that was noted at the outset. Psychologists with an interest in children and their mental development may well be content with a psychological account and only a psychological account. The argument in this paper is that this is to leave something important out of the picture, namely, knowledge and its development during childhood.

Some other account is required as well in order to identify the normative (Frege's (1979) logical) properties of human thinking. A valid inference is made *salva veritate*, that is, it is truth preserving (Frege, 1950, p. 76). To make the same point: This normative requirement in logic is that truth is conserved in valid inference. This raises all the problems of conservation during children's reasoning, in that "a self-identical premise is preserved (*conserver*) through a mental experiment" (Piaget, 1928, p. 239; amended translation).

Truth is a paradigm case of an intellectual norm and this leads to an epistemological problem: "Logic is the study of true reasoning [and so the question arises of] how the child controls the truth of these deductions, how the idea of truth is successfully gained in the first place" (Piaget, 1923, p. 57). The point that Piaget was making is twofold. First, there is an exclusive distinction between logic and psychology. Second, this distinction is not exhaustive because there is a mediator. This is effectively a commitment to nonpsychologism, as discussed above. Using Flavell et al.'s (1993) distinction between "not in," "first in," and "fully in," psychological investigation could establish that, say, transitive reasoning is optimally displayed by individuals belonging to some population under one set of experimental conditions, successfully displayed under a different set, and not displayed at all under another set. However, the manipulation of experimental variables does not guarantee normative control. A successful response with a situational aetiology is not thereby a response made in due recognition of normative criteria. These norms should also be taken into account and would be in a developmental epistemology. If there is normative control, what was its origin and how did it develop? This is an empirical question, even though it is not (exclusively) psychological.

Normative Facts

Psychology is an empirical science that sets out to explain the facts in the domain covered by psychological perspectives. For ease of reference, I refer to these as "causal facts." This is because experimentation is central to psychology as currently conceived. Its principal focus is on the control of variables under experimental conditions, with a view to the causal explanation of psychological phenomena (Bryant, 1985; Campbell & Stanley, 1963). However, causal facts are not the only facts in the reckoning. There are "normative facts" as well. Because normative facts are facts, they too are empirical. It does not follow from this, however, that causal explanation through experimentation on causal facts is similarly appropriate. Isaacs (1951, p. 123) put it this way: "The new discipline envisaged by Piaget concerns psychological logic, or psycho-logic, or the psychology of normative facts, [that is,] normative psychological facts." The point that Isaacs was making is that psycho-logic is not psychology. One way to clinch this distinction is by reference to the facts that are central to each, because these are normative facts in the former case and causal facts in the latter.

Piaget (1950) set out his stance in this way: Normative facts are "facts in experience permitting the observation that subject such-and-such considers him- or herself to be obligated by a norm, irrespective of its validity from the observer's point of view" (p. 30). This means that they are "imperative rules whose origin is in social interactions of all kinds, and which act causally, in their turn, in the context of individual interactions" (Piaget, 1995, p. 69).

A developmental epistemology has an empirical component that can be clarified in relation to the observational phenomena. When asked about an incipient conflation of facts and norms by Jacques Derrida, Piaget (1965, p. 49) replied thus: "You experience the norms in yourself; I, the observer, observe them and describe them as the facts they are. If my observations stay faithful and correct, there will never be a contradiction between your norms and my facts, since my facts will be a description, an analysis, a causal explanation of your norms."

A normative fact is the use made by an individual of a norm or value. This use is open to observation and, as such, it is empirical. However, because it is the use of a norm, it also has a normative component. There is a parallelism here, not the reduction of one to the other. An example of normative facts in the subject John's reasoning was given earlier. Faced with this example, two reactions are likely. One is to say: Let us check the causation by changing the task for a better control of causal facts. Indeed, this could be done, but only on condition that it is combined with the second reaction. Otherwise, this first reaction would revert to a parting of ways in an exclusively psychological account. The second reaction is different: Let us check this reasoning to ascertain the quality and range of its normative properties. What is left open here is a more generalized account, with a dual focus on both causal and normative facts.

Act of Judgment

An act of judgment is a unit of analysis with inclusive properties. This unit of analysis is required in Frege's (1979) epistemology: "To think is to grasp a thought. Once we have grasped a thought, we can recognize it as true (*make a judgment*) and give expression to our recognition of its truth" (p. 185; his emphasis). It is also required in Piaget's epistemology as "the search for truth" (Piaget, 1923, p. 76) and the advance from practical success to human judgment (Piaget, 1953, p. 410). Any such act always has a causal origin for investigation in empirical psychology. Any such judgment is based as well on normative criteria in virtue of which it is legitimated. Logical norms legitimate a judgment by providing good reasons that make the judgment true (or false) in accordance with logical laws. A psychological explanation has to show that the act is in accordance with psychological laws that are compatible with a specified norm. An epistemological explanation has to show that the judgment is due to the use of a norm. Aristotle (1987), long ago in his *Nichomachean Ethics*, pointed out that an action in accordance with a moral rule is not thereby an action due to that moral rule. Social conformity due to "normative pressure" is a case in point; social conscience due to normative reasoning is another matter (von Wright, 1983). This distinction equally fits the intellectual domain. It is one thing to make a correct response. It is something else again to realize that it is correct, to acknowledge its truth in some appropriate way.

One implication of this unit of analysis is that, if action has a logic, a logical model can be used in a statement of the model. This is exactly what Piaget (1949) set out to do and to redo (Piaget & Garcia, 1991). A second implication is that it fits exactly Piaget's (1970, p. 704) own position about action as the source of knowledge. At issue is what someone can do ("*ce que peut faire le sujet*," Piaget, 1967, p. 119), including which reasons can be given for a response. Reason giving is an important human capacity. A third implication is that "action-logic" and "mental logic" are not the same thing, although their difference has not yet been well brought out in accounts of deductive reasoning (Johnson-Laird, 1999). There is scope here for a deontic logic of action (von Wright, 1983), which would be empirically investigated in a developmental epistemology (Smith, in press-b).

In a developmental epistemology, "all knowledge can be considered as being relative to a given previous state of lesser knowledge and also as being capable of constituting just such a previous state in relation to some more advanced knowledge" (Piaget, 1950, p. 13). Piaget's position is distinctive in three respects. First, it includes the hierarchical commitment that an available state of knowledge can, through the processes of intellectual development, result in a more advanced (intellectually better) state of knowledge. Second, it also includes a commitment to self-regulation in that the actions and operations carried out by an agent are a contributory factor in intellectual development (Piaget, 1985). In turn, self-regulation is tied to action as initiated by an agent, that is, the intentionality of action (Piaget, 1953, p. 148). There is a "horizon of intentionality" (von Wright, 1983) through which the development of knowledge has to pass. Third, it includes relationalism or relativism in that one norm is defined as better in relation to other norms. A developmental epistemology charts the hierarchical growth of better knowledge due to self-regulation activity.

Developmental Mechanism

There is an outstanding problem in psychology with respect to developmental mechanisms (Bryant, 1985). It is well known that both nature and nurture are implicated, but no one knows how their interaction is adequately characterized (Richardson, 1998; Wachs, 2000). Piaget's (1918, 1970) argument was that neither was individually sufficient, nor taken together were they jointly sufficient, although both were necessary conditions. Once again, his argument was a *tertium quid* such that equilibration was stated to be a better third alternative in line with the discussion above (see Smith, in press-a). Right now, it is worth noticing two of its main implications. One is that, on this view, developmental advance is not entirely "in the genes" or entirely "in the culture." The other is that it is "in the reasoning."

According to this proposal, it is by reasoning, with due attention to reasons amounting to good reason, that intellectual advances are made (Moshman, 1994; Smith, 1997, p. 233). The argument is as follows. Response making and reason giving are actions. Typically, in a psychological study, a response is made without any investigation of the agent's reasons, which are inferred by the investigator through task design (Smith, 1993, sect. 13). However, this is to deprive the agent of the feedback that the dependent action of reason giving can provide. Piaget (1985, p. 16) regarded this as the regulation of one of an agent's actions by another action. It is the relationships between the agent's own actions that is a source of further reasoning by the agent. What relation was there between a particular action token of response making and one of reason giving? Which relation could it be? The general point here is not that these two questions exhaust the class. Rather, the general point is that questions such as these can arise for the agent.

Here is a specific example. In the study of mathematical induction (presented earlier), the children were interviewed in the first study about the iterative addition of the same quantity. Because they had agreed on the initial equality of the two containers, had agreed that equal additions had then been made, and had also agreed that there was still an equality, the children were asked whether this truth-functionally correct response was also modally necessary: "Does there have to be the same, then, or not?" In forming their responses, most of the children denied this. Their answer to this question was "No." As such, this amounted to a modal error in their reasoning. What was significant, however, was that they offered a sound modal reason that was consistent with this denial. Here are some examples:

- Well you can cheat them if you want.
- You could make it a secret, like no one seeing, you could get two in each.
- Because if you had them all on your desk and your mother shouted and then you just stood up and knocked them all off, some could have landed in the bin.
- It doesn't have to be, because you can do anything you want with them.

The use of the modal terms *can, could,* and *have to* is explicit in these reasons. These modal expressions were also used with flair in a forthright statement of their beliefs. This means that these children were able to use modal language in stating their beliefs. What is also evident is their modal understanding. Their reasons were in line with the standard definition of necessity, namely, that something is necessary if it could not be otherwise (Smith, 1997, 1999c). In making their responses, the children had denied a necessity. In making good this response through their reasoning, they had identified possible ways in which things could have been otherwise. As such, these reasons are a potential source of advance. By reconsidering and reevaluating these reasons in relation to their own responses, the children had at their disposal an individual way to profit from their learning. Moreover, such an advance would be due to the self-regulation of their own actions. In other words, the mechanism would be equilibration. It could be argued that the responses made by these children did not involve a modal error. My reply is that they did, to the extent that their responses were about the properties of number—a paradigm case of an abstract object— whereas their reasons were about an actual object (such as mother's shouting, which led to the counters falling to the ground). Piaget (1928) long ago identified attentional switching as a source of developmental delay (see Smith, in press-b).

The main point is not that equilibration could function independently of factors in nature and nurture. This was expressly ruled out by Piaget (1970). Rather, the main point is that this mechanism can function interdependently with the other two. Under this proposal, a developmental advance could be made on the basis of what is in the genes, what is in the culture, and what is in the reasoning.

In conclusion, there are two questions to confront:

- What are the experimental conditions of the display of such-and-such reasoning?
- How are the normative criteria of such-and-such reasoning developed by agents?

One concerns causal facts in developmental psychology. The other concerns normative facts in developmental epistemology. Flavell (1963) may have made a fair point about causal facts. Piaget (1950) had made a good point long beforehand in declaring that normative facts were his principal concern. It has been my argument that this crucial distinction has not been given due recognition in current research in developmental psychology. I have also proposed that developmental epistemology is an empirical study with a future that promises quite a lot.

AUTHOR NOTE

Leslie Smith, Department of Educational Research, Lancaster University, Lancaster LA1 4YL, Great Britain; e-mail: L.Smith@lancaster.ac.uk.
My thanks to Terry Brown for his gracious and astute comments on the first draft of this paper. The faults remaining are, of course, all mine. My thanks also to the Leverhulme Trust for providing a research grant (RF&G/ 4/9700405) that made a welcome contribution to the funding of my study, as well as Lancaster University for granting me sabbatical leave to carry it out.

REFERENCES

Aristotle (1987). *Nichomachean Ethics*. In J. Ackrill (Ed.), *A new Aristotle reader*. Oxford, England: Oxford University Press.

Bickhard, M., & Terveen, L. (1995). *Foundational issues in artificial intelligence and cognitive science*. Amsterdam: North-Holland.

Boden, M. (1979). *Piaget*. Brighton, England: Harvester Press.

Boole, G. (1958). *An investigation of the laws of thought*. New York: Dover.

Brown, T. (1996). Values, knowledge, and Piaget. In E. Reed, E. Turiel, & T. Brown (Eds.), *Values and knowledge* (pp. 137–170). Mahwah, NJ: Lawrence Erlbaum Associates.

Brown, T. (2001). Bärbel Inhelder and the fall of Valhalla. In A. Tryphon & J. Vonèche (Eds.), *Working with Piaget: Essays in honour of Bärbel Inhelder* (pp. 179–192). Hove, England: Psychology Press.

Bryant, P. (1985). Parents, children and cognitive development. In R. Hinde, A.-N. Perret-Clermont, & J. Stevenson-Hinde (Eds.), *Social relationships and cognitive development* (pp. 239–251). Oxford, England: Oxford University Press.

Bryant, P. (2001). Learning in Geneva: The contribution of Bärbel Inhelder and her colleagues. In A. Tryphon & J. Vonèche (Eds.), *Working with Piaget: Essays in honour of Bärbel Inhelder* (pp. 129–140). Hove, England: Psychology Press.

Campbell, D., & Stanley, J. (1963). *Experimental and quasi-experimental designs for research.* Chicago: Rand McNally.

Carnap, R. (1962). *Logical foundations of probability* (2nd ed.). Chicago: University of Chicago Press.

Case, R. (1999). Conceptual development in the child and in the field. In E. Scholnick, K. Nelson, S. Gelman, & P. Miller (Eds.), *Conceptual development: Piaget's legacy* (pp. 23–52). Mahwah, NJ: Lawrence Erlbaum Associates.

Chandler, M. (1997). Stumping for progress in a post-modern world. In E. Amsel & K. Renninger (Eds.), *Change and development* (pp. 1–26). Mahwah, NJ: Lawrence Erlbaum Associates.

Chapman, M. (1988). *Constructive evolution.* Cambridge, England: Cambridge University Press.

Chapman, M. (1992). Equilibration and the dialectics of organization. In H. Beilin & P. Pufall (Eds.), *Piaget's theory: Prospects and possibilities* (pp. 39–60). Hillsdale, NJ: Lawrence Erlbaum Associates.

Chisholm, R. (1977). *Theory of knowledge* (2nd ed.). Engelwood Cliffs, NJ: Prentice Hall.

Cole, M., & Wertsch, J. (1996). Beyond the individual-social antinomy in discussions of Piaget and Vygotsky. *Human Development, 39,* 250–256.

Feldman, D. (1995). Learning and development in nonuniversal theory. *Human Development, 38,* 315–321.

Flavell, J. (1963). *The developmental psychology of Jean Piaget.* New York: Van Nostrand.

Flavell, J. (1982). On cognitive development. *Child Development, 53,* 1–10.

Flavell, J., Miller, P., & Miller, S. (1993). *Cognitive development* (3rd ed.). Engelwood Cliffs, NJ: Prentice Hall.

Frege, G. (1884). *Die Grundlagen der Arithmetik.* Breslau: Verlag von Wilhelm Koebner.

Frege, G. (1950). *The foundations of arithmetic.* Oxford, England: Blackwell.

Frege, G. (1972). *Conceptual notation and related articles.* Oxford, England: Clarendon Press.

Frege, G. (1979). *Posthumous papers.* Oxford, England: Blackwell.

Goldman, A. (1986). *Epistemology and cognition.* Cambridge, MA: Harvard University Press.

Haack, S. (1978). *Philosophy of logics.* Cambridge, England: Cambridge University Press.

Hamlyn, D. (1978). *Experience and the growth of understanding.* London: Routledge & Kegan Paul.

Heath, T. (1956). *The thirteen books of Euclid's elements.* New York: Dover.

Inhelder, B., & Piaget, J. (1963). Itération et récurrence [Iteration and recurrence]. In P. Gréco, B. Inhelder, B. Matalon, & J. Piaget (Eds.), *La formation des raisonnements récurrentiels* [The formation of recurrent reasoning]. Paris: Presses Universitaires de France.

Inhelder, B., & Piaget, J. (1980). Procedures and structures. In D. Olson (Ed.), *The social foundations of language* (pp. 10–25). New York: Norton.

Isaacs, N. (1951). Critical notice: Traité de logique [Treaty on logic]. *British Journal of Psychology, 42,* 185–188.

Johnson-Laird, P. (1999). Deductive reasoning. *Annual Review of Psychology, 50,* 109–135.

Kant, I. (1933). *Critique of pure reason* (2nd ed.). London: Macmillan.

Kant, I. (1963). *Introduction to logic.* Westport, CN: Greenwood Press.

Karmiloff-Smith, A. (1994). Précis of *Beyond modularity:* Author's reponse. *Behavioral and Brain Sciences, 17,* 693–746.

Kenny, A. (1995). *Frege.* London: Penguin Books.

Kitchener, R. F. (1986). *Piaget's theory of knowledge.* New Haven, CT: Yale University Press.

Klahr, D. (1999). The conceptual habitat: In what kind of system can concepts develop? In E. Scholnick, K. Nelson, S. Gelman, & P. Miller (Eds.), *Conceptual development: Piaget's legacy* (pp. 131–162). Mahwah, NJ: Lawrence Erlbaum Associates.

Kneale, W., & Kneale, M. (1962). *The development of logic.* Oxford, England: Oxford University Press.

Kripke, S. (1980). *Naming and necessity.* Oxford, England: Blackwell.

Kusch, M. (1995). *Psychologism: A case study in the sociology of philosophical knowledge.* London: Routledge.

Lakatos, I. (1974). Falsification and the logic of scientific research programmes. In I. Lakatos & A. Musgrave (Eds.), *Criticism and the growth of knowledge* (pp. 91–196). Cambridge, England: Cambridge University Press.

Leibniz, G. (1981). *New essays on human understanding.* Cambridge, England: Cambridge University Press.

Lourenço, O., & Machado, A. (1996). In defense of Piaget's theory: A reply to 10 common criticisms. *Psychological Review, 103,* 143–164.

Macnamara, J. (1994). *The logical foundations of cognition.* New York: Oxford University Press.

Maffie, J. (1990). Recent work on naturalized epistemology. *American Philosophical Quarterly, 27,* 281–293.

Mandler, J. (1998). Babies think before they speak. *Human Development, 41,* 116–126.

Markovits, H. (1995). Conditional reasoning with false premises: fantasy, and information retrieval. In L. Smith (1996). *Critical readings on Piaget.* London, England: Routledge.

Molenaar, P., & Raijmakers, M. (2000). A causal interpretation of Piaget's theory of cognitive development: Reflections on the relationship between epigenesis and nonlinear dynamics. *New Ideas in Psychology, 18,* 41–55.

Moser, P. (1995). Epistemology. In R. Audi (Ed.), *The Cambridge dictionary of philosophy* (2nd ed., pp.). Cambridge, England: Cambridge University Press.

Moshman, D. (1994). Reason, reasons and reasoning. *Theory and Psychology, 4,* 245–260.

Müller, U., & Overton, W. (1998). How to grow a baby: A reevaluation of image-schema and Piagetian action approaches to representation. *Human Development, 41,* 71–111.

Nagel, T. (1997). *The last word.* Oxford, England: Oxford University Press.

Nunes, T., & Bryant, P. (1996). *Children doing mathematics.* Oxford, England: Blackwell.

Orwell, G. (1983). *Nineteen Eighty-Four.* London, England: Penguin Books.

Perret-Clermont, A.-N. (1980). *Social interaction and cognitive development in children.* London: Academic Press.

Piaget, J. (1918). *Recherche.* Lausanne, Switzerland: La Concorde.

Piaget, J. (1923). La psychologie des valeurs religieuses [The psychology of religious values]. *Association Chrétienne d'Etudiants de la Suisse Romande, 1922,* 38–82.

Piaget, J. (1928). *Judgment and reasoning in the child.* London: Routledge & Kegan Paul.

Piaget, J. (1949). *Traité de logique: Essai de logistique opératoire* [Treatise on logic: Essay on operational logistics]. Paris: Colin.

Piaget, J. (1950). *Introduction à l'épistémologie génétique* [Introduction to genetic epistemology] (Vols. 1–3). Paris: Presses Universitaires de France.

Piaget, J. (1953). *The origins of intelligence in children.* London: Routledge & Kegan Paul.

Piaget, J. (1954). *Construction of reality in the child.* London: Routledge & Kegan Paul.

Piaget, J. (1963). Foreword. In J. Flavell (Ed.), *The developmental psychology of Jean Piaget* (pp. vii–ix). New York: Van Nostrand.

Piaget, J. (1965). Discussion: Genèse et structure en psychologie [Discussion: Genesis and structure in psychologie]. In M. de Gandillac & L. Goldman (Eds.), *Entretiens sur les notions de genèse et de structure* (pp. 158–175). Paris: Mouton.

Piaget, J. (1967). *Logique et connaissance scientifique* [Logic and scientific knowledge]. Paris: Gallimard.

Piaget, J. (1970). Piaget's theory. In P. Mussen (Ed.), *Carmichael's handbook of child psychology* (4th ed., pp. 703–732). New York: Wiley.

Piaget, J. (1971). *Biology and knowledge.* Edinburgh, Scotland: Edinburgh University Press.

Piaget, L. (1972). *The principles of genetic epistemology.* London: Routledge & Kegan Paul.

Piaget, J. (1985). *Equilibration of cognitive structures.* Chicago: University of Chicago Press.

Piaget, J. (1986). Essay on necessity. *Human Development, 29,* 301–314.

Piaget, J. (1992). *Morphisms and categories.* Hillsdale, NJ: Lawrence Erlbaum Associates.

Piaget, J. (1995). *Sociological studies.* London: Routledge.

Piaget, J. (1998). *De la pédagogie* [On pedagogy]. Paris: Odile Jacob.

Piaget, J. (2000). *Studies in reflective abstraction*. Hove, England: Psychology Press.

Piaget, J., & Garcia, R. (1989). *Psychogenesis and the history of science*. New York: Columbia University Press.

Piaget, J., & Garcia, J. (1991). *Toward a logic of meanings*. Hillsdale, NJ: Lawrence Erlbaum Associates.

Piaget, J., & Inhelder, B. (1969). *The psychology of the child*. London: Routledge & Kegan Paul.

Popper, K. (1979). *Objective knowledge* (2nd ed.). Oxford, England: Oxford University Press.

Reichenbach, H. (1961). *Experience and prediction: An analysis of the foundations and the structure of knowledge*. Chicago: University of Chicago Press.

de Ribaupierre, A. (1993). Structural invariants and individual differences: On the difficulty of dissociating developmental and differential processes. In R. Case & W. Edelstein (Eds.), *The new structuralism in cognitive development* (pp. 88–120). Basel, Switzerland: Karger.

Richardson, K. (1998). *Models of cognitive development*. Hove, England: Psychology Press.

Russell, B. (1903). *The principles of mathematics*. London, England: George Allen & Unwin.

Sainsbury, M. (1991). *Logical forms*. Oxford, England: Blackwell.

Searle, J. (1999). *Mind, language and society*. London, England: Weidenfeld & Nicolson.

Smith, L. (1993). *Necessary knowledge*. Hove, England: Lawrence Erlbaum Associates.

Smith, L. (1995). Introduction. In J. Piaget (Ed.), *Sociological studies* (pp. 1–22). London, England: Routledge.

Smith, L. (1997). Necessary knowledge and its assessment in intellectual development. In L. Smith, J. Dockrell, & P. Tomlinson (Eds.), *Piaget, Vygotsky, and beyond* (pp. 224–241). London, England: Routledge.

Smith, L. (1999a). Eight good question for developmental epistemology and psychology. *New Ideas in Psychology, 17*, 137–147.

Smith, L. (1999b). Epistemological principles for developmental psychology in Frege and Piaget. *New Ideas in Psychology, 17*, 83–117.

Smith, L. (1999c). Necessary knowledge in number conservation. *Developmental Science, 2*, 23–27.

Smith, L. (1999d). What Piaget learned from Frege. *Developmental Review, 19*, 133–153.

Smith, L. (in press-a). Piaget's model. In U. Goswami (Ed.), *Handbook of cognitive development*. Oxford, England: Blackwell.

Smith, L. (in press-b). *Reasoning by mathematical induction in children's arithmetic*. Oxford, England: Pergamon.

Vidal, F. (1994). *Piaget before Piaget*. Cambridge, MA: Harvard University Press.

Vonèche, J. (2001). Bärbel Inhelder's contribution to psychology. In A. Tryphon & J. Vonèche (Eds.), *Working with Piaget: Essays in honour of Bärbel Inhelder* (pp. 1–12). Hove, England: Psychology Press.

Wachs, T. (2000). *Necessary but not sufficient: The respectives roles of single and multiple influences on individual development*. Washington, DC: APA.

von Wright, G. H. (1983). *Practical reason*. Oxford, England: Blackwell.

Author Index

Subject Index